D1249291

# The Metropolitan Critic

by the same author

Collections of lyrics set and sung by Pete Atkin on the RCA label
BEWARE OF THE BEAUTIFUL STRANGER
DRIVING THROUGH MYTHICAL AMERICA
A KING AT NIGHTFALL
THE ROAD OF SILK

# THE
# Metropolitan Critic

## CLIVE JAMES

FABER AND FABER
3 Queen Square
London

*First published in 1974*
*by Faber and Faber Limited*
*3 Queen Square London WC1*
*Printed in Great Britain by*
*Western Printing Services Ltd, Bristol*
*All rights reserved*

*ISBN 0 571 09998 X*

*to my mother*
*and to my father's memory*

# Foreword

The essays in this book were all written over the last five years, mostly in the normal course of reviewing. At several points within I make the large claim that literary journalism is the substance of criticism, not the shadow. With due allowance for polemical emphasis, that principle still seems to me to be true enough: anyway, it's too late now to start all over again in cloistered solitude.

There would have been less to select from, and the selection itself would have been less coherent, if it were not for the generosity and seriousness of the London literary editors. My thanks are due to the late Nicholas Tomalin, who gave me my start on the *New Statesman* and his friendship for the years he had left to live; to Karl Miller and Derwent May of the *Listener*; to Paul Barker and Richard Boston of *New Society*; to Terence Kilmartin and Miriam Gross of the *Observer*; and to Arthur Crook of the *Times Literary Supplement*. Special thanks go to Stephen Spender, who commissioned the article on D. H. Lawrence for his anthology *D. H. Lawrence: Novelist, Poet, Prophet*.

Very little in this book would ever have seen the light without the encouragement, supervision and inspiration provided by Ian Hamilton, for all this period literary editor of the *Times Literary Supplement*, editor of the *Review* and trailblazer for his generation. For his companionship and example, mere gratitude will not serve: everything I write is a way of making recompense.

Errors of fact and ill-judged phrases which have rankled since the day they were set down have at last been corrected, but otherwise – apart from a certain winnowing of recurring themes – these essays remain as they were first published. Some of them I wouldn't dream of writing that way now, but it seemed right then. Hence the appended dates. Issues arise in their own time and we can't hope to deal with them in order – only in earnest.

7

# Contents

## Part Three
### CARRY THAT WEIGHT

## Part Four
### PAST MASTERS

## Part Five
### CLERICAL TREASON

## Part Six
### FROM THE LARGEST ISLAND

# PART ONE

# Two Extramural Minds

# I

## The Metropolitan Critic

Edmund Wilson writes in the 1957 chapter of *Upstate*:

Looking out from my window on the third floor, I saw the change made here by autumn in the landscape and the atmosphere: they become distinctly more serious, Nature begins to warn us, reassuming her august authority; the luxury of summer is being withdrawn.

In context, this passage carries many times the weight of any ordinary nature-notes: the book is already half over, a splitting head of steam has been built up and the reader is by now in no doubt that the luxury of summer is being withdrawn from the writer himself, from the historical district in which he writes, from all the artists he has ever personally known and from the America which he has for so long chronicled and which he is now ceasing even to distrust – *Upstate* shivers with the portent of an advancing ice-cap. Wilson's monumental curiosity and zest of mind have not grown less, but by now they are like Montaigne's, exiled within their own country and awaiting, without real hope, a better age which will know how to value them. Self-confidence remains, but confidence in one's function ebbs; one's books do not seem to have been much use; the public weal has proved itself an illusion and private life is running out of time. 'C'est icy un livre de bonne foy, lecteur,' wrote Montaigne, dampening the reader's ardour.

Il t'advertit dez l'entree, que ie ne m'y suis proposé aulcune fin, que domestique et privee: ie n'y ay eu nulle consideration de ton service, ny de ma gloire; mes forces ne sont pas capables d'un tel dessein.

Just so long as we understand each other.

Wilson's tone is similarly self-sufficient. 'The knowledge that death is not so far away,' he writes in 1963,

that my mind and emotions and vitality will soon disappear like a puff of smoke, has the effect of making earthly affairs seem unimportant and human beings more and more ignoble. It is harder to take human life seriously, including one's own efforts and achievements and passions.

That was the year in which he was writing *The Cold War and the Income Tax* – a profound growl of dissatisfaction about owing the United States Government a swathe of back-taxes which it would only have wasted on building and dropping bombs if he had handed it over. Dealings with the revenue men were prolonged and wearying, making a general disappointment with life understandable. In 1966 things were going better, but his view of existence didn't much lighten. To go with his Kennedy Freedom Medal he was given a $1,000 award by the American Academy of Arts and Sciences and a $5,000 National Book Award, but he found himself feeling let down rather than puffed up. 'They make me feel that I am now perhaps finished, stamped with some sort of approval and filed away. . . .' He is hard on himself, and no softer on humanity as a whole. 'Reading the newspapers, and even the world's literature, I find that I more and more feel a boredom with and even scorn for the human race.' In such ways his darkening mood is overtly stated, but what gives it power – and makes *Upstate* such an elegiac and at times unmanning book – is the way in which the selectivity of his impressions presents picture after picture of decay, confusion and loss. Talcottville, NY, is presented as a last vestige of the old, hopeful America, and Wilson – not hiding or even sheltering, just waiting – takes up residence there each summer to find that the new and vengeful America has always moved a bit closer. Not that it matters much any more.

By the end of the book we're a long way from the mood in which Wilson first evoked Talcottville, in his 'The Old Stone House' essay of 1933, later collected in *The American Earthquake*. In the first place, that essay recalled the hopes of the New Englanders who had grown sick of narrowness and were all for pushing on into the realm of unlimited opportunity:

I can feel the relief myself of coming away from Boston to these first uplands of the Adirondacks, where discarding the New England religion but still speaking the language of New England, the settlers found limitless space. They were a part of the new America, now forever for a century on the move.

The thrill of the great American experiment is still there in the writing, and even though this old essay was just as disenchanted as the new book is, the disenchantment worked in reverse: Talcottville was the opposite of a refuge, representing a past that needed to be escaped from, not returned to.

Thirty years or so later, in *Upstate*, he is cricking his neck to get back to it, but it is too late. Material progress has already made its giant strides. Juvenile delinquents and uproarious bikers maraud and destroy. The John Birch Society slaps up flagrant stickers. Treasured windows on which poet friends have inscribed verses with a diamond pen are shattered in his absence. The Sunday *New York Times* is too heavy for him to carry. There is a spider in the bathtub of a motel. An old aquaintance, Albert Grubel, keeps him abreast of the ever-escalating car-crash statistics. His daughter Helena grows up and starts having car-crashes of her own. In 1963 he finds out that he has for all this time been living virtually on top of a SAC air-base, and is therefore slap in the middle of a prime target area. By the end of the book there is a distinct possibility that a four-lane highway will be constructed a few inches from his front door.

The detail is piled on relentlessly, and if there were nothing else working against it, then *Upstate* would be a dark book indeed. But several things stop it being disabling. First, there are revelations of the Wilsonian character, as when he faces the bikers and asks them why they can't ride on the highway instead of around his house, or when he argues about iambic pentameters with Nabokov (who insists that Lear's 'Never, never, never, never never' is iambic), or when he tells Mike Nichols that Thurber is not alone in lacking self-assurance and that he, Wilson, often gets up at four o'clock in the morning to read old reviews of his books. In bits and pieces like these there is enough singularity and sheer quirkiness to keep things humming.

Second, there is evidence of the Wilsonian curiosity, as when he deepens his knowledge of the county's history, or when he becomes interested in the founding and the subsequent fate of the old Oneida community. Wilson can't stop learning things, and it's worth remembering at this point that the curious information which

crops up in the book is only the topmost molecule of the outermost
tip of the iceberg. In the period covered by *Upstate* (1950–1970),
Wilson was producing exhaustively prepared books like *The Shock
of Recognition* and *Patriotic Gore*, breaking into new cultures with
books like *The Scrolls from the Dead Sea*, *Apologies to the Iroquois*
and *O Canada*, turning out important investigatory pamphlets like
*The Cold War and the Income Tax* and *The Fruits of the MLA* (a
crucially important attack on boon-doggling academicism which has
yet to be published in Britain) and editing *A Prelude* and the second
and third in his series of literary chronicles, *The Shores of Light* and
*The Bit Between My Teeth*—the first, *Classics and Commercials*,
having appeared in 1950.

Only the European panoptic scholars come near matching Wilson
for learning, and for sheer range of critical occupation there is no
modern man to match him, not even Croce. If *Upstate* tends to give
the impression that his wonted energy now only faintly flickers, the
reader needs to remind himself sharply that the mental power in
question is still of an order sufficient to illuminate the average city.
Seemingly without effort, Wilson dropped *A Piece of my Mind* (1957)
somewhere into the middle of all this hustle and bustle, and in the
chapter entitled 'The Author at Sixty' announced:

I have lately been coming to feel that, as an American, I am more or
less in the eighteenth century – or, at any rate, not much later than the
early nineteenth. . . . I do not want any more to be bothered with the
kind of contemporary conflicts that I used to go out to explore. I make
no attempt to keep up with the younger American writers; and I only
hope to have the time to get through some of the classics I have never
read. Old fogeyism is comfortably closing in.

Taking him at his word on this last point, most critics and reviewers
were relieved, which was very foolish of them.

But on the first point, about feeling himself to be an eighteenth-
century or nineteenth-century figure, Wilson was making a just
estimate, even if he meant only that he didn't drive a car and couldn't
bear to pronounce the word 'movies'. As Alfred Kazin argued in his
review of *The American Earthquake* (collected in his fine book
*Contemporaries*), the men to compare Wilson with are the literary
artists driven by historical imaginations—men like Carlyle.

The third thing which lightens the darkness of *Upstate* is the author's gradually revealed – and revealed only gradually even to himself – interest in a local young woman striving to better herself. Perhaps without really willing it, Wilson is telling a subtle story here: flashes and fragments are all we get. But by the time the book is over, we are convinced that her story is the story of the book, and that the story has gone against the mood. Kazin suggested that Wilson's secret was to gaze at America with a cold eye without being cold on America. *The American Earthquake* inexorably recorded the shattering effects of industrialism and the spiritual confusion of the New Deal, but it was not a hopeless book – it responded to the period's vitalities, even (while castigating it) the vitality of Henry Ford. *Upstate* very nearly *is* a hopeless book, and for a long while we suspect that Wilson *has* gone cold on America. But finally we see that he hasn't, quite: as the girl Mary works to establish herself in a way that her European origins would probably not have allowed, the American adventure haltingly begins all over again, at the eleventh hour and in the fifty-ninth minute.

Against the Stygian background of the book's accumulated imagery it is not much hope to offer, but it is not nothing, and Wilson was never in the consolation business anyway. Which leaves us – as we shelve *Upstate* beside *A Prelude* and prudently leave room for the books dealing with the thirty uncovered years between them – with the question of what business Wilson *has* been in.

What does Wilson's effort amount to? Is there an atom of truth in his dispirited suggestion that his books have dated? Supposing – as seems likely – that Wilson belongs with the great, copious critical minds like Saintsbury, Sainte-Beuve, Croce, Taine: is he doomed to survive like them only as an emblem of the qualities a mind can have, Saintsbury for gusto, Sainte-Beuve for diligence, Croce for rigour, Taine for drama? Wilson makes Van Wyck Brooks's output look normal, Eliot's look slim, Empson's, Trilling's and Leavis's look famished. Just how is all this avoirdupois to be moved forward? We need to decide whether critical work which has plainly done so much to influence its time vanishes with its time or continues. To continue, it must have done something beyond maintaining standards or correcting taste, important as those functions are: it must have embodied, not just recommended, a permanent literary value. And we do not have to re-read much of Wilson's criticism – although it would be a year of perfect pleasure to re-read all of it – to see that it does embody a value, and embodies it in a way and to a degree that no other corpus of twentieth-century work has approached. But this value, so easily sensed, is very difficult to define, since it must perforce reside in whatever is left after opposing high estimations of Wilson have cancelled each other out. Lionel Trilling (in 'Edmund Wilson: A Background Glance', collected in *A Gathering of Fugitives*) says that an interest in ideas is the very essence of Wilson's criticism. Alfred Kazin, on the other hand, says that ideas are things Wilson is not at home with. If both these men admire the same thing in Wilson, what is it?

The answer is that Wilson has a mental style – a mental style which reveals itself in the way he writes. He is proof by nature against metaphysics of any kind (sometimes to the damaging extent that he cannot grasp why men should bother to hold to them), and this characteristic gives his work great clarity. He never has to strive towards perspicuity, since he is never tempted even momentarily to abandon it. And in more than fifty years of activity he has put up such a consistent show of knowing what he means – and of writing it down so that it may be readily understood – that he has invited underestimation. The most difficult escape Houdini ever made was from a wet sheet, but since he was in the business of doing difficult-looking things he had to abandon this trick, because to the public it seemed easy. What Wilson was doing was never easy, but he had the good manners to make it look that way. If he could only have managed to dream up an objective correlative, or a few types of ambiguity, or if he had found it opportune to start lamenting the loss of an organic society, he would be much more fashionable now than he is. But we can search his work from end to end without finding any such conversation-piece. What we do find is a closely argued dramatic narrative in which good judgment and misjudgment both stand out plainly. The dangerous excitement of a tentatively formulated concept is absent from his work, and for most of us this is an excitement that is hard to forgo: the twentieth century has given us a palate for such pepper.

But there is another, more durable excitement which Wilson's entire body of work serves to define. There is a clue to it in *Upstate*, in the passage where Wilson discusses the different courses taken by Eliot and Van Wyck Brooks:

They were at Harvard at the same time, Brooks of the class of 1908, Eliot of 1910, and both, as was natural then, went, after college, to England. Eliot took root there, but Brooks said that, during the months he spent in England, he found himself preoccupied with American subjects. This difference marks the watershed in the early nineteen hundreds in American literary life. Eliot stays in England, which is for him still the motherland of literature in English, and becomes a European; Brooks returns to the United States and devotes himself to American writing, at the expense of what has been written in Europe. Eliot represents the growth of an American internationalism: Brooks, as a spokesman of the twenties, the beginnings of the sometimes all too conscious American literary self-glorification which is part of our American imperialism.

As it happened, Wilson was to go on to cover American subjects with all Brooks's thoroughness and more; and to parallel Eliot's internationalism while yet holding to the tacit belief that the American achievement could well be crucial in the continuity of that internationalism; and to combine these two elements with a total authority of preparation and statement. For that preparation, he had the brilliant education available in prewar Princeton to a young man ready to grasp it. For that statement, he was obliged to evolve a style which would make his comprehensive seriousness unmistakable in every line. Out of these two things came the solid achievement of judgments based on unarguable knowledge ably supplied to meet an historical demand. From the beginning, Wilson was a *necessary* writer, a chosen man. And it is this feeling of watching a man proving himself equal to an incontestably important task – explaining the world to America and explaining America to itself – which provides the constant excitement of Wilson's work.

Commanding this kind of excitement his prose needed no other. Wilson grew out of the great show-off period of American style. He could not have proceeded without the trail-blasting first performed by Mencken and Nathan, but he was fundamentally different from them in not feeling bound to over-write.

Wilson's style adopted the Mencken-Nathan toughness but eschewed the belligerence – throwing no punches, it simply put its points and waited for intelligent men to agree. It assumed that intelligence could be a uniting factor rather than a divisive one. In the following passage (from 'The Critic Who Does Not Exist', written in 1928 and later collected in *The Shores of Light*) this point is made explicitly:

What we lack, then, in the United States, is not writers or even literary parties, but simply serious literary criticism (the school of critics I have mentioned last, ie, Brooks, Mumford and Joseph Wood Krutch, though they set forth their own ideas, do not occupy themselves much with the art or ideas of the writers with whom they deal). Each of these groups does produce, to be sure, a certain amount of criticism to justify or explain what it is doing, but it may, I believe, be said in general that they do not communicate with one another; their opinions do not really circulate. It is astonishing to observe, in America, in spite of our floods of literary journalism, to what extent literary atmosphere is a non-conductor of criticism. What actually happens, in our literary world, is that each leader or group of leaders is allowed to intimidate his disciples, either ignoring all the other leaders or taking cognizance of their existence only by distant and contemptuous sneers. H. L. Mencken and T. S. Eliot present themselves, as I have said, from the critical point of view, as the most formidable figures on the scene; yet Mencken's discussion of his principle rival has, so far as my memory goes, been confined to an inclusion of the latter's works among the items of one of those lists of idiotic current crazes in which the *Mercury* usually includes also the recall of judges and paper-bag cookery. And Eliot, established in London, does not, of course, consider himself under the necessity of dealing with Mencken at all . . . Van Wyck Brooks, in spite of considerable baiting, has never been induced to defend his position (though Krutch has recently taken up some challenges). And the romantics have been belaboured by the spokesmen of several different camps without making any attempt to strike back. It, furthermore, seems unfortunate that some of our most important writers – Sherwood Anderson and Eugene O'Neill, for example – should work, as they apparently do, in almost complete intellectual isolation, receiving from the outside but little intelligent criticism and developing, in their solitary labours, little capacity for supplying it themselves.

Wilson's innovation was to treat the American intelligentsia as if it were a European one, speaking a common language. 'For there is one language', he wrote in the same essay, 'which all French writers, no matter how divergent their aims, always possess in common: the language of criticism.' That was the ideal, and by behaving as if it had already come about, he did a great deal to bring it into existence. The neutral, dignified tone of his prose was crucial here: it implied that there was no need for an overdose of personality, since writer and reader were on a level and understood one another. As Lionel Trilling has convincingly argued, Wilson's years in an editorial chair for *The New Republic* were a big help in getting this tone right – he was in action continuously (more than two-thirds of the pieces in *The Shores of Light* first appeared in *The New Republic*) before a self-defining audience of intelligent men, all of whom were capable of appreciating that opinions should circulate.

The literary chronicles, especially *The Shores of Light*, are commonly valued above Wilson's more integrated books, and although it seems likely that the people doing the valuing have not correctly judged the importance of the latter, the evaluation nevertheless seems just at first glance. As has often been pointed out, there is nothing in criticism to beat the thrill of hearing Wilson produce the first descriptions and definitions of the strong new American literature that was coming up in the 1920s – the first essays on Fitzgerald and Hemingway will always stand as the perfect objects for any literary journalist's envy and respect. But here again we must remember to avoid trying to nourish ourselves with condiments alone. What needs to be appreciated, throughout the literary chronicles, is the steady work of reporting, judging, sorting out, encouraging, reproving and re-estimating. The three literary chronicles are, among other things, shattering reminders that many of the men we distinguish with the name of critic have never judged a piece of writing in their lives – just elaborated on judgments already formed by other men.

A certain demonstration of Wilson's integrity in this regard is his ability to assess minor and ancillary literature about which no general opinion has previously been built up: *The Shock of Recognition* and *Patriotic Gore* are natural culminations of Wilson's early drive towards mining and assaying in territory nobody else had even staked out. Wilson is a memory; he never at any stage believed that the historic process by which writings are forgotten should go unexamined or be declared irreversible. Remembering is one of the many duties the literary chronicles perform: not so spectacular a duty as discovering, but equally important. For Wilson's self-posed task of circulating opinions within an intelligent community (a community whose existence depends on such a process for its whole existence), all these duties needed to be scrupulously carried out, and it is the triumph of the literary chronicles that they were carried out in so adventurous a way.

Unless all these things are held in mind, the true stature of the literary chronicles cannot be seen, even by those who value them above the rest of Wilson's work. In *The Shores of Light* it is necessary to appreciate not just 'F. Scott Fitzgerald' and 'Emergence of Ernest Hemingway' but also pieces like 'The Literary Consequences of the Crash', 'Talking United States', and 'Prize-Winning Blank Verse'. In *Classics and Commercials* we need to cherish not only the stand-out hatchet-jobs like 'Who Cares Who Killed Roger Ackroyd?' and 'Tales of the Marvellous and the Ridiculous' but also the assiduous labour of weighing up – never impatient, even when repelled – which went into essays like 'Glenway Wescott's War Work' and 'Van Wyck Brooks on the Civil War Period'. And unless we can get rid of the notion that picking winners was Wilson's only true calling in life, we will have no hope at all of reaching a true estimation of *The Bit Between My Teeth* – a book disparaged as tired and thin by reviewers who in the full vigour of youth could not have matched the solidity of the least piece in it. 'The Pre-Presidential T.R.' and 'The Holmes-Laski Correspondence' are masterly examples of what Wilson can accomplish by bringing a literary viewpoint to historical documents; and 'The Vogue of the Marquis de Sade' got the whole Sade revival into focus and incisively set the limits for its expansion.

The literary chronicles would have been more than enough by themselves to establish Wilson's pre-eminence: to a high degree they have that sense of the drama of creativity which Taine had been able to capture and exploit. If people are going to read only some of Wilson instead of all of him, then the chronicles are what they should read. But it is one thing to say this, and another to accept the assumption – distressingly widespread in recent years – that *Axel's*

*Castle* and *The Wound and the Bow* and *The Triple Thinkers* have in some way done the work they had to do and may be discarded, like used-up boosters. There is not much doubt about how such an idea gained currency, books of long essays being so much harder to read than books of short ones. But there is no reason for anyone who has actually read and understood a book like *Axel's Castle* to go along with such a slovenly notion. When, in the Yeats chapter of that book, Wilson compared the Yeats of 1931 to the Dante who was able 'to sustain a grand manner through sheer intensity without rhetorical heightening', he was writing permanent criticism, criticism which can't be superseded, certainly not by pundits who are boning up their Dante from a parallel text instead of learning it the hard way from a teacher like Christian Gauss. It is barbarism of a peculiarly academic kind to suppose that truths of this order – not insights, explications, or glosses, but truths – can be appropriated to a data-bank or dismissed as obsolete. A Dantesque 'epigrammatic bitterness' is *precisely* the quality to see in the mature Yeats, and in 1931, before the last poems were written, it was virtually prescient to be able to see it, since that quality had not yet reached its full concentration.

Wilson paid heavy penalties for being plain – or rather we paid heavy penalties for not seeing the force of his plainness. In the Eliot chapter of *Axel's Castle* he said something about Eliot that forty years of theses and learned articles have done their best to bury, something which we are only now capable of seeing as criticism rather than conversation, the intervening hubbub of academic industry having revealed itself as conversation rather than criticism:

We are always being dismayed, in our general reading, to discover that lines among those which we had believed to represent Eliot's residuum of original invention had been taken over or adapted from other writers.... One would be inclined *a priori* to assume that all this load of erudition and literature would be enough to sink any writer, and that such a production as 'The Waste Land' must be a work of second-hand inspiration. And it is true that, in reading Eliot and Pound, we are sometimes visited by uneasy recollections of Ausonius, in the fourth century, composing Greek-and-Latin macaronics and piecing together poetic mosaics out of verses from Virgil. Yet Eliot manages to be most effective precisely – in 'The Waste Land' – where he might be expected to be least original – he succeeds in conveying his meaning, in communicating his emotion, in spite of all his learned or mysterious allusions, and whether we understand them or not.

In this respect, there is a curious contrast between Eliot and Ezra Pound.

With Pound, Wilson was like Tallulah Bankhead faced with a tricksy production of Maeterlinck: he wasn't afraid to announce. 'There's less in this than meets the eye.' With Eliot, he was bold enough to say that things were simpler than they appeared at first blush. Both these judgments were backed up by a deep learning which had nothing to fear from either man, by a sense of quality which knew how to rely on itself, and by a seriousness which was not concerned with putting up a front.

There is no need to go on with this part of the argument. It's more merciful simply to state that Wilson's entire critical corpus will go on being read so long as men are prepared to read widely and well. His strategy of using magazines – first *The New Republic*, later the *New Yorker* – as shipyards in which to assemble books was triumphantly successful. He is the ideal of the metropolitan critic, who understood from the beginning that the intelligence of the metropolis is in a certain relation to the intelligence of the academy, and went on understanding this even when the intelligence of the academy ceased to understand its relation to the intelligence of the metropolis. When Wilson called the Modern Language Association to order, he performed the most important academic act of the postwar years – he reminded the scholars that their duty was to literature.

For Wilson literature has always been an international community, with a comprehensible politics of its own. He learnt languages not just out of passionate curiosity but out of quasi-political purpose, becoming acquainted with whole literatures in the same way that a man who carries an international passport proves himself a part of the main. As late as the mid-1950s Wilson was apologizing for not having done enough in this line: he has always been a trifle guilty about failing to get interested in Portuguese and Spanish. But to a chastening extent he had already made himself the universal literatus, and in the later decades of his life we find

him becoming increasingly conscious that this is his major role –
if he has any significance in the realm of action, then this is it.
Modesty has never been among Wilson's characteristics, but a
certain diffidence does creep in, of which the quietism and resigna-
tion of *Upstate* are the logical culmination. The central paradox of
Wilson remains unresolved: he has put himself above the battle,
inhabiting an Empyrean of knowledge by now fundamentally
divorced from an unworkable world. The paradox was vicious from
the beginning, becoming more and more so as modern history un-
folded in front of him. Wilson was a born internationalist in literature and a born isolationist in politics, and there is a constant tension
between the achieved serenity of his literary judgment and the
threatening complexity of his self-consciousness as an American.

A patrician individualist by nature, Wilson was automatically
debarred from running with the pack. His radicalism in the 1920s
and 1930s had a decisive qualitative difference from any Marxist
analyses currently available: it was elitist, harking back to the
informed democracy of the American past, and therefore on a
richer historical base than the hastily imported European doctrines
which bemused his contemporaries. Wilson's reports on Detroit are
as devastating as Marx on the working day, but the intensity is the
only connexion. Wilson was revolted by industrialism's depreda-
tions – if the ecological lobby ever wants to put a bible together,
there are sections of *The American Earthquake* which could go
straight into Revelations – but the revulsion was just as much on
behalf of what America had previously been as on behalf of what it
might become. Marxism is future-directed metaphysics: Wilson's
thought was bent towards the literary recovery of the estimable past.

Making no commitment to communism, Wilson was never compelled to scramble away from it, and he maintained his dignity
throughout the 1930s. By 1940 he had completed his analysis of the
revolutionary tradition in Europe and published it as *To the Finland
Station*. In the final paragraph of that book, he declared it unlikely
that the Marxist creeds would be able to bring about

a society in which the superior development of some is not paid for by
the exploitation, that is, by the deliberate degradation of others – a
society which will be homogeneous and cooperative as our commercial

society is not, and directed, to the best of their ability, by the conscious creative minds of its members.

America went to war again, and again Wilson was isolationist: as with the First World War, so with the Second, he saw no point in America becoming involved. He was still explaining such phenomena by market pressures and the devious conniving of Big Business – it was a Fabian position, never much altered since he first picked it up from Leonard Woolf.

Wilson has difficulty in understanding how irrational forces can be so potent. In *Europe without Baedeker* and *A Piece of my Mind* he came close to holding the Europeans collectively responsible for pulling their own houses down in ruins about their heads. It was the high point of his isolationism, further reinforced by a commitment to the American past amounting to visionary fervour. In his admiration for Lincoln we find Wilson getting very near the mysticism he spent a lifetime scrupulously avoiding. Finally he found an historical base solid-seeming enough to justify the relieved rediscovery of a Platonic Guardian class. 'To simplify', he wrote in *A Piece of my Mind* (1957),

one can say that, on the one hand, you find in the United States the people who are constantly aware ... that, beyond their opportunities for money-making, they have a stake in the success of our system, that they share the responsibility to carry on its institutions, to find expression for its new point of view, to give it dignity, to make it work; and, on the other hand, the people who are merely concerned with making a living or a fortune, with practising some profession or mastering some technical skill, as they would in any other country, and who lack, or do not possess to quite the same degree the sense of America's role.

That was as far as he got: the Republic he loved began to be overwhelmed by the Democracy he had never been sure about, and in the new reality of the 1960s he found himself taxed but unrepresented.

In *Upstate* Wilson is faced with the ruins of the American Dream, and appears to be forgetting what we are bound to remember: that the fragments can be built with and that this fact is in some measure due to him. The intellectual community which is now fighting for the Republic against its own debilitating tumours was to a considerable extent his personal creation. That Americans of good will, in the midst of wearying political confusion, can yet be so confident of their nation's creativity is again in a large part due to him. As Christian Gauss was to Wilson – master to pupil – Wilson is to nobody: nobody he can see. He now doubts the continuity he helped to define. But, beyond the range of vision now limiting itself to Cape Cod and Talcottville, there will always be young men coming up who will find his achievement a clear light. He is one of the great men of letters in our century.

(1972)

# 2

# Big Medicine

As a media event, A. Alvarez's *The Savage God* has turned out to have a lot in common with the all-star expedition to Everest, which to a great extent was insured against failure through being heavily pre-sold. Bits of the book have been trailed in *Partisan Review*, *New American Review*, the *Atlantic Monthly*, the *Listener* and finally the *Observer*, where heavy static was kicked up by the intervention of an interested party and by the editor's inexplicable desire to print the author's photograph at an even greater angle of tilt than puzzled the world on the front cover of *Beyond All This Fiddle*: at this rate the lay reader might soon get the idea that Alvarez has adopted the supine position as a matter of course. And just as it is doubtful whether the majority of mankind really knows whether the polyglot assemblage of climbers got all the way up there or not, it is doubtful whether the intelligentsia really knows about *The Savage God* or not – the publicity and free samples probably used up most of the available response, and the task of reading a dozen polite reviews perhaps exhausted what was left. To rub the point home, Weidenfeld have made the book only slightly less expensive than a Ferrari Dino, thereby ensuring that the smooth curve of its commercial success shan't be dented by too many poor clucks actually trying to get hold of it and read it.

Some eager beaver at Weidenfeld must have turned out a pilot study on *The Intellectual as Product* and fingered Alvarez as the fall guy. I hate to break up the party, but feel bound to announce that quite apart from its hit-parade status *The Savage God* is an important contribution to recent criticism. Alvarez has been one of the key literary intellectuals of the last decade and in this new book certain components of his thought have been pushed to their limits. In my view this mainly serves to demonstrate the contradictions which have at all previous stages obtained between them, but that doesn't mean that the book lacks the excitement (the real excitement, not the media excitement) and the *gravitas* which we associate with an intellectual venture. And the best way to pay tribute to these qualities is to trace within Alvarez's total argument those subsidiary lines of argument which have hit an impasse: to locate and examine the points at which discourse has ceased and forceful assertion (and there isn't much assertion more forceful than his) has taken over. There will then be a chance for discourse to begin again – and it needs to do that. In *The Savage God* Alvarez's critical effort has finally revealed its false emphasis in full clarity, but this only means that his critical effort has now reached the point where it can be valued exactly and so retained. There is no question of sweeping over the path he has taken and forgetting about it. To put it briefly, Alvarez since the late fifties has been occupied with the central question about the relationship of poetry to contemporary reality. I think it can now clearly be seen that he has got the wrong answer: but he has also helped clarify the question.

As many will by now have heard, the book takes the form of an anti-sandwich: a hunk of bread between two slices of meat, the bread being a long study of suicide through the ages and the two slices of meat being accounts of suicide attempts by Sylvia Plath and the author, the first unhappily successful, the second fortunately a misfire. These two sections on Plath and himself are the stretches of Alvarez's writing most likely to be widely remembered: they have the muscular narrative drive of the 'Shiprock' essay in *Beyond All This Fiddle* – which is to say, they draw you forward into regions where it seems at least plausible, if not natural, for a man to pit himself against extreme conditions as a necessary part of some kind

of mental exploration. I for one am never going to understand why
Alvarez should want to cling by his fingernails to a vast slab of
naked geology while vultures stagger past with one wing folded over
their eyes, but I can't deny that such experience gives his narrative
writing a certain edge: he seems to go about with his nervous system
worn externally, and I suppose it is true that if you conduct your
life in this way you will face and resolve problems that most people
shirk, and restrict the range of their sensibilities by so shirking.
But I can suppose this without supposing that it is *better* to push
things to the limit: in fact it seems clear to me by now, having lasted
this long, that limits are dangerous things which a wise man best
avoids, since he is more likely to lose than find himself when he gets
near them – and very likely to lose his wisdom.

But obviously for Alvarez it is not like this. Basic to both the Plath
chapter and the chapter on himself is the assumption that something
was being found out, and such is the seductiveness of the writing
that the assumption gains great weight. Without, however, being
clarified. If Alvarez is right about Plath's suicide not being meant as
a real attempt, then plainly it is nonsensical to suppose that her
last writings are tangible products of the supposedly special mental
territory opened up by deciding not to live. And from his own
attempt, Alvarez apparently gained no special insight beyond a
definite experience of whatever it is that pulses and throws off rays
in the fiery centre of a king-sized hangover. That, and this:

... when death let me down, I gradually saw that I had been using the
wrong language; I had translated things into Americanese. Too many
movies, too many novels, too many trips to the States had switched my
understanding into a hopeful, alien tongue. I no longer thought of
myself as unhappy; instead, I had 'problems'. Which is an optimistic
way of putting it, since problems imply solutions, whereas unhappiness
is merely a condition of life which you must live with, like the weather.
Once I had accepted that there weren't ever going to be any answers,
even in death, I found to my surprise that I didn't much care whether I
was happy or unhappy; 'problems' and 'the problem of problems' no
longer existed. And that in itself is already the beginning of happiness.

I don't think it is, but it's certainly the end of adolescence. Here at
the finale of his book, as with Plath at the beginning and with all

the historical data in the middle, Alvarez is commendably scrupulous about attaching the suicidal impulse to events in the exterior world of the suicide: eventually, he seems to suggest, suicide is a question of what formative conditions obtain in the irreducible self, and must always retreat beyond simply sociological understanding. Whole races have suicided under the threat of oppression, but others have not; people who had 'everything to live for' have chosen to die; people who had every reason to die have striven to live. If there is already an inclination to suicide, circumstances might bring it out: if there is not already an inclination to suicide, circumstances tend not to put it in.

Alvarez has been more scientifically minded – more objective, more resistant to easy mental patterning – than suits him as a critic. For his own major critical assumption is still there, but now looks shakier than ever in the face of his own arguments. He is saying that the casualty rate among modern artists has been, and has had to be, unusually high, but one of the salient conclusions of his historical investigation is that the 'rate' must be dependent on statistics and the statistics dependent on the deed being declared for what it is – on his own terms, he has not satisfactorily established the previous casualty rate among artists as being low. He is saying (as he has always said) that contemporary evils take unique forms and that the pertinent artistic reaction to them, since it must be extreme, will look suicidal and in a disturbing number of cases may end suicidally: but he is also saying that a correspondence of the suicidal impulse to a perceived deterioration in the external world is problematical and tends to retreat beyond investigation.

As an 'extremist' Alvarez has made the disarming tactical mistake of being too reasonable. It would have been too much to ask that he should go on to demolish his own critical base – but that is the way his arguments tend, and a reviewer with any sense of the high comedy of intellectual affairs ought to evince, momentarily at any rate, a proper delight at being presented with a treatise so honestly done that it contains within itself all the material necessary for its own correction.

If Alvarez had not pinned his 'casualty rate' to suicide, his famous death-roll in the title chapter could have been a lot longer. As it is, the death-roll has already been subject to fluctuations within the chapter's own short life-time, and might well be altered again before the book comes out in paper-back – Berryman is now fully eligible and Mishima needs at least a mention. On its first appearance (as 'The Art of Suicide' in *Partisan Review*) Albert Camus was numbered among the missing: 'Camus died absurdly in a car crash.' It must have crossed the author's mind that either everybody who dies in a car crash dies absurdly or else nobody does. Anyway, Camus is now out and Joe Orton is in, and the point this time is that although Orton was murdered, his *murderer* suicided, so it qualifies as a pretty suicidal scene. Alvarez still clings to his list of painters: Modigliani, Arshile Gorki, Mark Gertler, Jackson Pollock and Mark Rothko. It's hard to see how Gertler qualifies at that level of achievement (if he does, then Carrington ought to as well) but it's all too easy to see that at some point Alvarez was unimpressed with his own casualty list and felt compelled to pad it out a bit. He has widened his preoccupation from suicide to extreme self-neglect, and beyond that to ordinary carelessness, shading finally into the area where people just happen to be standing around when a hunk of twentieth-century technology goes haywire. If he had widened his definition of 'artist' to include the jazz-men, he could legitimately have pushed his casualty rate up to something staggering: the fatal car-crashes began with Bessie Smith and included Clifford Brown, who conceivably might have been a more important trumpeter than Dizzy Gillespie and Fats Navarro combined. The drug casualties have included Navarro, Bud Powell and pre-eminently Charlie Parker, whom I would put without hesitation among the two dozen most important twentieth-century artists in any medium. It's been a massacre, and of necessity a peculiarly modern one. But for the jazz casualty-list you would be compelled *ab initio* to take account of the informing sociological conditions – Jim Crow, insecurity, and the constant, tired travelling from job to job by road.

Having left jazz out of account, it's not surprising that Alvarez ignores rock music too, although it has already supplied several exemplary figures who would fit well into his sad gallery. If ever three young artists had 'everything to live for' they were Joplin,

Hendrix and Jim Morrison – quite apart from the fact that on the material plane they were among the richest artists the world has ever known. If Alvarez doesn't want to cover this shady part of the waterfront he's well within his rights, but the point is that in jazz and rock, precisely because their connection with the grand flow of modern events has no wide intellectual acceptance, it can more easily be seen that the casualty rate has something intimately to do with the way the life is lived. Taking the received 'high' art as his field, Alvarez finds it all too easy to connect the casualty rate with the 'collapse of values' which in his more thoughtful moments he is careful to present as a stimulus to creation rather than as an invitation to end it. Prematurely and fatally, he subsumes and denatures a multiplicity of sociological changes within a notion of total historical change – the one thing historical change can never be.

But a simple point emerges: before the twentieth century it is possible to discuss cases individually, since the artists who killed themselves or were even seriously suicidal were rare exceptions. In the twentieth century the balance suddenly shifts: the better the artist the more vulnerable he seems to be. Obviously, this is in no way a firm rule. The Grand Old Men of literature have been both numerous and very grand: Eliot, Joyce, Valéry, Pound, Mann, Forster, Frost, Stevens, Ungaretti, Montale, Marianne Moore. Even so, the casualty rate among the gifted seems out of all proportion, as though the nature of the artistic undertaking itself and the demands it makes had altered radically.

There are several objections that can be to this crucial passage. First, Alvarez hasn't been able to assemble an overwhelmingly impressive list of twentieth-century artists who 'killed themselves or were even seriously suicidal' – certainly there aren't enough of them mentioned to convince us that they are any less the rare exception now than they were then. Second, a galaxy might produce smooth and homogeneous light as you look back through it from its perimeter, but it is still made of individual stars, and properly examined is seen to be very violent. If Dylan Thomas is on the modern list because he drank too much, Mozart ought to be on the older list because he ate too little. Nobody knows what happened to Masaccio, and we only know a little more than nothing about Giorgione: what we can be sure of is that their loss was cataclysmic at the time. Masaccio may very well have been the most talented painter ever born – but the point is that history absorbed the shock and continued. The shocks in all these cases were tremendous, but history absorbed them and continued. That is one of the things that makes history look different from now – it contains these explosions and continues. Nor does history very well remember lost promise.

As Alfred Einstein suggested, *frühvollendet* – 'too early completed' – is a misleading term for the musicians who died young. In retrospect we see them whole and tend to forget that their premature deaths were crushing deprivations. Mozart, Weber, Purcell, Pergolesi, Mendelssohn, Chopin, Vincenzo Bellini, Schubert – nearly all of them died within a single half-century. Or consider the Elizabethan age in poetry: Marlowe never saw thirty, Greene, Peele, Nash and Kyd all died before they were forty, and Shakespeare only just made it past fifty. They drank to die in those days – Dylan Thomas would have looked like a piker. (Exercise: think of an artistic era free of visitations from the Savage God.)

Third, Alvarez's qualifying list of Grand Old Men might well have been extended – the one thing the modern era *has* got that previous centuries were short of is creative longevity. Masaccio never reached thirty, Raphael never reached forty, and in their day they were not exceptional: it was Leonardo, Michelangelo, Giovanni Bellini and Titian who were exceptional. In literature alone (Alvarez's chosen field in this passage, although elsewhere he sweeps outward without warning to take in such other arts as suit his book) the last two centuries are stiff with senescent masters, a Tolstoy and a Wordsworth paired off against every Keats, just as there is a Monet and a Renoir paired off against every Seurat. But none of this means that Alvarez has got things backwards and that history has taken the opposite turn from what he thinks. It means that history has taken no turn at all. All wars and revolutions aside, what it means is that medically speaking these are far safer times to be alive. Unless you happen to be dwelling in the vicinity when a political crisis bursts, there are incomparably fewer effective forces operating to nail you. It is one strand of history, not history itself; but it is an important strand, and Alvarez is forced into some elegant high-stepping in order to avoid it. If he had been content to stick with the genuine disaster areas of modern history his casualty lists would have retained real weight. But by spreading his field of argument to the whole literate world he forces himself towards mysticism: he vaguely puts it about that there is something dangerous in all this safety. The liberal-humanist tradition can't cope with modern events. It takes extremism to do that. And extremism is especially required when modern events, with their ineluctable cunning, have carefully contrived to leave one sitting safely on one's duff in England or America instead of getting boiled down for soap or freezing to death above the Arctic Circle.

Eventually Alvarez's whole argument depends on the twin assumptions that modern evils are unique and that, being so, they require a unique artistic response. Not only are these assumptions separately questionable, their connection is questionable too. The first assumption is, I think, entirely without useful meaning. The second, however, has the advantage of not being so vulnerable as the first: since its connections with it were tenuous in the first place, to some extent it can break free, and in fact Alvarez's formidable critical value is dependent on the paradox that though largely wrong about what has happened he is to some extent right about what art should do about it. But to begin with the first assumption.

If anyone contends that there was nothing which happened in the concentration camps which did not happen in the Thirty Years War, he is likely to be informed that he cannot imagine what a concentration camp was like. It's a failure of imagination, but not necessarily on the contender's side: it's far more likely that the informant has failed to imagine what the Thirty Years War was like. History has been one long holocaust. Most arguments for the uniqueness of our own age in this department are based on the way in which technology has inflated the scale of operations while reducing the blood-heat of the people conducting them. Certainly there is a lot to this, but there is no reason to think that pre-twentieth-century life was any more readily intelligible, or tolerable, for the victim just because he was able to look his executioner in the eye – then, as now, the innocent were likely to be chosen as the very people to be slaughtered first. The true change from previous centuries to our own has been not in the way evil manifests itself, but in the way we react to it. For large-scale crimes to look so shockingly unnatural in our own century, it first had to be widely assumed that history had grown out of them – and this, broadly, was what the nineteenth century strove to assume. The nub of the matter is that the nineteenth-century enlightened mind – the mind that had studied history in a way that history had never previously studied itself – was simply not expecting these things to happen. The twentieth century began with a very widely diffused belief in progress. The heritage of Hegelianism was Great Expectations, and they were greatly disappointed. The systematic, developmental philosophies (the philosophies which governed the study of history and, by extension, of literature too) were optimistic. Either they turned to pessimism in the face of the new twentieth-century events, or else lived on as virulent dogma.

The intellectual consequences of enforced pessimism may be seen at their most poignant in the culminating works of the European panoptic scholars – Huizinga, Curtius, Auerbach. Eventually the notion of cultural break-up was everywhere, and in one form or another its concomitant was too: if unity had been shattered, unity must once have existed, somewhere back when Christendom was still integrated, sensibility had not dissociated, society was still organic. Pessimism is the driving force of most of the finest scholarly work in our century, which means the finest there has ever been. But pessimism is no better than optimism at being realistic about history. A view of history is either pluralist or it is unreal, and on a pluralist view of history civilization and evil were never so mutually exclusive that the first could give way to the second in so complete a way. Prisoners were worked to death in the Spanish galleys while Titian painted at court; his pictures didn't make their suffering less horrible, their suffering didn't make his pictures less beautiful; the unity was never there, it was always conflict. For anyone with the imagination to sense what life has always been like, and always will be like, it must seem almost miraculous that civilization can be so tenacious – that values do *not* collapse, and that even when a whole race is driven to the wall there are forces left which unite to condemn the crime.

Alvarez doubts the capacity of the liberal-humanist intellectual tradition to act in the face of modern events, but I doubt if it is obliged to act. (I should note that Alvarez in fact uses the term 'liberal-humanist' mainly to describe what came about in New York after the intellectual defeat of Marxism in the thirties. This is to debase the term and I feel entitled to snatch it back again.) It is obliged merely to give an account of what takes place. To the extent that it got itself attached to the optimistic philosophies, it was taken for a ride: but then, it was the liberal-humanist tradition which eventually mounted the decisive critique against the optimistic philosophies. Evil, barbarism, illiberalism and inhumanity have done such a precise job of defining themselves in this century that the liberal-humanist tradition was never better placed to do its part (the intellectual part, which is not the only one) in preserving and further-ing civilization. That it withdrew from compromising positions – positions it was tempted into by the promise of extra-intellectual action – ought to redound to its credit. But Alvarez is a man of action all the way to the roots, and for him it was a logical progression to ask of art what intellect had failed to do – act in the world as a strategically contending power.

It's from this desire that Alvarez's second basic assumption springs: a unique artistic response to the unique contemporary evils. The desire itself is part of a feeling for history that gets history wrong – art is certainly in conflict with other forces but is not compelled to allow for the way those forces move, and might well choose to ignore them. The assumption is wrong to the extent that it is governed by the desire. But it is right to the extent that while art might choose to ignore other forces it cannot presume to be unaware of them. Alvarez was incorrect about contemporary evils being unique but was correct about them being *there*, and his critical requirement that the artistic intelligence should take account of what had been going on was the key critical requirement as the fifties shaded into the sixties. The 'end of ideology' had given the artists a dangerous opportunity to relax into insularity, withdrawing their work not just as a contending power but as any kind of force at all.

Unfortunately Alvarez phrased his warning as an invitation to get out there and fight – not just to take account of modern events, but to incorporate them, holding the mirror up to the A-blast and the torture cell. If his powerlessness in the face of modern events had driven the artist to desperation, that desperation was what he ought to express; was what the best artists were already expressing. It followed that anyone who kept a contemplative equilibrium was somehow suspect. And it was never questioned that extremist expression would have (when properly controlled) an ameliorative effect. Alvarez was far too experienced to place any value on possible therapeutic effects for the artist, but like all theorists of art as a contending power, he was obliged merely to assert, without demonstrating, the probability of a beneficial effect on the recipient. Finally it all came down to the assurance that Lowell, Berryman, Plath and Hughes were good for you.

If the realization of what has happened in modern history forces a sensitive man towards breakdown, then a poet who does not transmit such turmoil has to be fibbing. That, crudely, was the big idea. It started as a footnote to a few sentences on Lowell in the 'Art and Isolation' essay which closed *The Shaping Spirit* in 1958. The footnote didn't go in until the 1961 edition: Alvarez had been reviewing recent poetry regularly for the *Observer* in the interim, and during that time *Life Studies* had come out – at which point his criticism crossed the Rubicon with a mighty clashing of shields.

Not all these poems are successful. There is a certain air of poetic therapy about them which encourages looseness and make some seem almost prattling. But apparently they produced the necessary results: by writing them Lowell seems to have set his house in order and so assured himself of a firm, known base from which his work could start afresh. So in the poems which end *Life Studies* and in those which have followed it – particularly his superlative version of Villon's *Testament* – Lowell handles themes quite as personal and exacerbated as those of his earlier work, but now he does so with a control and clarity which greatly add to their power. In the process, he has also opened up a fresh area of verse – the dispassionate artistic use of material salvaged from the edge of breakdown – which several talented young writers, such as Anne Sexton, have begun to develop. He has given poetry a new impetus.

The emphasis on 'personal' poetry had been there since *The School of Donne*, most of which had been written in 1958. But to salvage material from the edge of breakdown – this was a new

requirement, and gradually through the sixties it became a requirement which divided the good from the bad in modern poetry as
decisively as Metaphysical poetry was divided from the Renais-
sance. In 1962 Berryman and Lowell were placed at the head of the
pugnacious Penguin anthology *The New Poetry*, for which Alvarez
wrote an introduction that committed him firmly to a rejection of
the gentility principle. As well as giving an account of what was
happening, it is quite possible that his editing of this anthology
helped shape what happened later – at any rate here was intellect in
action and no mistake. In 1965 Alvarez placed it on record, in *Under
Pressure*, that he had seen at least one of the dangers a personal
poetry of breakdown might conceivably run into.

But when artists begin to internalize everything – nature and society,
art and life, intimacy and response – they have to face a simple but
overbearing difficulty: beyond a certain point, the self is also boring. . . .
Extremism in the arts – the cultivation of breakdown and all the diverse
facets of schizophrenia – ends not so much in anarchy as in a kind of
internal fascism by which the artist, to relieve his own boredom, becomes
both torturer and tortured.

This essay ('America and Extremist Art', the final chapter of
*Under Pressure*) was his last chance to get out of his own aesthetic
before it trapped him. But faint heart never won fair copy, and it
must have seemed more interesting just to push on up the tunnel
and see where it led. Finally it led him to those four figures – Lowell,
Berryman, Hughes and Plath – and a formulation of Extremism (in
the title essay of *Beyond all this Fiddle*, 1968) calculated to neutralize
the objections he himself had already thought of.

Perhaps the basic misunderstanding encouraged by Extremist art is that
the artist's experience on the outer edge of whatever is tolerable is somehow a substitute for creativity. In fact, the opposite is true; in order to
make art out of deprivation and despair the artist needs proportionately
rich internal resources. Contrary to current belief, there is no short cut
to creative ability, not even through the psychiatric ward of the most
progressive mental hospital. However rigidly his experience is internal-
ized, the genuine artist does not simply project his own nervous system
as a pattern for reality. He is what he is because his inner world is more
substantial, variable and self-renewing than that of ordinary people, so

that even in his deepest isolation he is left with something more sustaining than mere narcissism. In this, of course, the modern artist is like every other creative figure in history: he knows what he knows, he has his own vision steady within him, and every new work is an attempt to reveal a little more of it. What sets the contemporary artist apart from his predecessors is his lack of external standards by which to judge his reality. He not only has to launch his craft and control it, he also has to make his own compass.

So there has to be a steadiness inside the turmoil, and all the control necessary to control the uncontrollable. ('It is an art like that of a racing driver drifting a car' he said of Plath in the same essay: 'the art of keeping precise control over something which, to the outsider, seems utterly beyond all control.') By this time Alvarez had got his Extremist aesthetic into shape, with all the loopholes plugged: the result was that it was critically inapplicable. As Lowell, Berryman, Hughes and Plath became elevated uniformly to exemplary status, it became increasingly difficult to criticize their work in any way beyond the simple assertion of inner resources (deduced from the outer resources, i.e. the poems) and control. It's almost a Leavisite fix. The Leavisite fix runs something like this: 'This is great writing and the reason it's great writing is you can *see* it's great writing and if you can't see it's great writing you're not a fit reader.' The Alvarez fix runs something like this: 'This poem manifests control through not looking quite uncontrolled enough to be out of control and somehow implies inner resources sufficiently complex to justify the presence of the material being presented as salvaged from the edge of breakdown.' At this rate criticism was bound to become a matter of trusting a favoured poet to go on being serious. Alvarez was up to his neck in a revised version of the intentional fallacy, continually referring the work back to the mind supposedly behind it and referring the mind supposedly behind it sideways to the supposed state of the world. His initial response to the quality of the language on the page was still operating, but it had precious little room to move. The trouble can be traced to the primal requirement of incorporating extreme experience. Despite the disclaimers he steadily built into his aesthetic over the ten years or so it took him to develop it, this requirement remained fundamental. It wasn't enough merely to mention an H-bomb or a concentration camp, they had to be *in* there somewhere: somehow the contemporary violence had to be reflected.

When a writer tries to hitch a ride from these themes, he usually ends only by exposing the triviality of his responses. What is needed is that extreme tension and concentration which creates a kind of silence of shock and calm around the images:

> I have done it again.
> One year in every ten
> I manage it –
>
> A sort of walking miracle, my skin
> Bright as a Nazi lampshade,
> My right foot
>
> A paperweight,
> My face a featureless, fine
> Jew linen.

Consider how the penultimate line-ending is cannily used to create a pause before the epithet 'Jew'. The effect is twofold: first shock, then an odd detachment. The image is unspeakable, yet the poet's use of it is calm, almost elegant. And this, perhaps, is the only way of handling such despair: objectively, accurately, and with a certain contempt. (*Beyond all this Fiddle*, title essay.)

    I have never been able to accept unquestioned the rightness of Sylvia Plath assimilating such infinities of torture to her own problems. I admire her late work but not this aspect of it, and would argue that it was her *distance* from these events that made her so appallingly free with them, and that this propensity for absorbing history into the self (and being under the impression that it *fits*) is the biggest and best of the very good reasons for not going to the limit. The shock around those images is the shock of sentimental excess, as the poet tries to embody what boozy old Saroyan used to call the Whole Voyald. I don't mean that there is material which poetry can't by its nature encompass – only that there is material which the poet can't by the material's nature render personal. It just can't survive the scaling down. Where such stuff works at all in Plath, it works because of the pathos of the attempt.

    Trapped in his intentional fallacy, Alvarez is betting everything on the artist's sincerity: even if the artist hasn't actually been scarified by the perception of some external event, he will possess, it is hoped, the internal equipment to justify the pretence that he has. But pretend or not, the material presented needs to be judged with some view towards the external world and away from its creator's supposed mental condition. It's possible to gesture too blithely, whatever the motivation. Here, for example, is Lowell, in a recent sonnet about Sylvia Plath. The immediate occasion for this poem seems to have been an article on Lowell in *the Review* 24 by John Bayley, who favoured Plath with an epithet Lowell found objectionable.

> *A miniature mad talent?* Sylvia Plath,
> who'll wipe off the spit of your integrity,
> rising in the saddle to slash at Auschwitz,
> life tearing this and that, *I am a woman?*

Hannah Arendt once said that finally these matters can be understood only by the poets, but when you scan a piece of journey-work like this you start wondering if she was right. A lot of rhetoric had to go over the dam before all the concentration camps in the Reich and the occupied territories got whittled down to that one word 'Auschwitz' – hundreds of journalists and television anchor-men had to do their stuff. And at last, after the whole infinitely ramified nightmare had been trimmed to that one stub and the stub itself had been crushed to powder, it was time for Lowell to come along and toss off a line suggesting that in Sylvia Plath the *Endlösung* finally met its implacable opponent. Carrying a sword. Riding a horse.

In such moments of rarefied bathos from his key poet Alvarez is confronted with the limitations of his critical position: what apparently escapes him in *Crow* ought to seize him by the throat here. Lowell's internal condition presumably being one of routine agony, the material has undoubtedly surfaced with all the correct credentials. Nor does the technical control seem much lower than average. What is wrong is the sheer, shrieking inadequacy of the event as cited to the event as it happened. For anyone who has an inkling of what the Third Reich was like, these lines will look pitiful. For anyone who has no inkling, the notion might take flower that some German character called Auschwitz finally got pinned to the mat by Sylvia Plath. Either way, small reward. These lines are part of a closed circuit, and I might add as a conjecture that they seem to me to adumbrate a wholly new kind of complacency which Alvarez has unintentionally done his share of bringing into the world: full-frontal solemnity.

Thinking of the work and the mind as a complete circuit, Alvarez is hindered from seeing what ought to be plain on the page – the actual interior weaknesses that his four front-runners are fighting, as all men must fight their own psyches at some point. He is good on Plath's problems but light on the fact that her poems are a problem too: even at their powerful best they do violence to stretches of vanished time which have had so much violence done to them already the extra flourish is simply an irrelevance, like flying a Frisbee in the Colosseum. In Berryman the magnificent multiplicity of personality – the pluralism of the mind, all out there on the paper – is continually invaded and falsified by a consciously 'creative', All-American ego making its belligerent claims. In Lowell there is the determination, growing ever more obvious, to write major poetry or nothing: there is so much significance going on you can hardly hear yourself think, and the steady clangour is split by the squeal of straining verbs. As for Hughes, it's as though the Nazis killed everybody and only the animals were left. It's part of the business of criticism to run a constant check on the intellectual component of an artist's work and help keep it from calcifying. There are large penalties to be paid if we accept without question schematic interpretations of reality which vitiate what is best in an artist's work and say nothing of interest about reality.

One absence bulks large in *The Savage God* – Solzhenitsyn. Experience doesn't come more extreme than that, and it's a token of the retrogressive nature of Soviet history that if he hadn't been a mathematician he would never have even got onto a casualty list of the young cut down in their gifted prime – he would simply have been blotted out. As it was, he lived, and wrote novels in which life lived right to the dizzy limit is contemplated and re-ordered by a mind detached, cool, balanced, integrated and classical. It would be interesting to see what vocabulary Alvarez would employ in dealing with his achievement. It's a safe bet that he'd have to dismantle his own aesthetic before starting work, or at least loosen it to the point where the flexibility of response in *Under Pressure* (where it wasn't required of an artist who had actually had extreme experience imposed upon him that he should imitate the action of Ted Hughes) could quietly be regained.

By turning against Movement poetry and developing his Extremist aesthetic Alvarez brought the relationship of art to reality into closer question than it had been subject to for a long time. It was the right move at the right moment, since the emergence of a right little, tight little, know-nothing English poetry was a clear and present danger. But for Alvarez as a critic the move had damaging consequences, not the least of which was a permanent ability to undervalue Larkin, who had never been 'immortalizing the securities and complacencies of life in the suburbs' (in *The Savage God* Alvarez is still saying that the Movement poets were doing that) but had been projecting a personal despair which fulfilled every one of Alvarez's requirements except for an adequate supply of globally apocalyptic referents. A life ending in boredom, fear and age might not seem much in comparison with the larger instances of modern frightfulness, but it's the way that most of us will get ours, when it comes. (And to that one point at least in *The Savage God* Alvarez incongruously seems to agree.) Larkin's treatment of death-in-ordinary will go on being frightening – extreme, if you like – when the slain millions have gone back into time with all the other millions, out of range of the casually significant evocation. In the teeth of all the evidence, Larkin has apparently decided that he might as well live. It's hard to see this as a drawback. The suicidal frame of mind isn't adequate to the understanding of history: it is under the delusion that its own destruction might be an appropriate response to events.

Alvarez is far too ready to assess the spirit of the age. Probably the last thing he would want is to be pigeon-holed with George Steiner, but there are times when he is not too many pigeon-holes away, particularly with his picture of civilization getting into a terminal crisis and art flailing around in search of new means to do

its duty. My closing quotation takes us back a decade or so nearer
to one of the main events, World War II. It is from Pieter Geyl – a
paragraph from one of his replies to Toynbee collected in *Encounters
in History*.

In any case I know full well, as do all who live sincerely by our tradition,
that the ideal of Western civilization we try to serve has not made angels
of us. It is an aspiration, hallowed by the labours of many generations,
even though they, too, have frequently gone off the track. It is an
aspiration which has always been and is still exposed to reactions from
inside. If these at times seem menacing, this must only incite us to be
prepared and to persevere. At the time of the national-socialist aberration
there were too many in my own country as well – I mention only
Huizinga – who treated us to gloomy admonitions as if the evil was in
fact the culmination of a process of decay of which they imagined to
detect the symptoms all around them. Toynbee now admits, in one of
those apologetic concessions which drop from his pen so frequently in
his new volume [*A Study of History*, vol. XII – C.J.], that since he cried
alarm (not against Hitler, but against ourselves) the menace had been
warded off, and yet even now it suits him to dub 'the cold-bloodedness
and highpowered organization' of the totalitarian movements 'typically
modern-Western'.

A. J. P. Taylor named Geyl as the modern historian he venerated
most. Certainly Geyl deserved a medal for self-effacement. While
arguing this point with Toynbee it apparently didn't strike him as
relevant that it was he, and not Toynbee, who had been in Buchen-
wald. One more the Savage God missed.

(1972)

PART TWO

# Some of the Poets

# 3

## When the Gloves are Off

In 1962 a brace of small but influential Penguins waddled into prominence: *Contemporary American Poetry*, selected and edited by Donald Hall, and *The New Poetry*, selected and edited by A. Alvarez. Hall picked on two immediately post-war books as marking the culmination of 'past poetries' and the beginning of a new poetry: these were Lowell's *Lord Weary's Castle* and Richard Wilbur's *The Beautiful Changes*. For tremendous power under tremendous pressure, Lowell was your only man. For skilful elegance – but not for passion – Wilbur was likewise nonpareil. As Hall went on to point out, it was Wilbur who had the most plausible imitators, and the typical duff poem of the fifties was the *poème bien fait* that was not *bien fait* – The Wilbur poem not written by Wilbur. By 1962, Wilbur, in addition to *The Beautiful Changes*, had published *Ceremony* (1950), *Things of this World* (1956) and had brought out a large selection in England, *Poems 1943–1956*. *Advice to a Prophet* (1961) was also out here by 1962, having been brought straight across by Faber with a haste well-nigh unseemly. Wilbur's stock was high on both sides of the pond.

Turning to *The New Poetry* though, we see that the two American poets Alvarez put forward as exemplary were not Lowell and Wilbur but Lowell and Berryman. Hanging by one well-muscled arm from an ice-axe lodged firmly in the north face of the Future, Alvarez wasn't interested in grace under pressure so much as in the registration of pressure itself. For the New Seriousness, 'gentility, decency and all the other social totems' were not in themselves sufficient for the task of responding to the unique contemporary evils: if skill got in the road or urgency, then skill was out. Not much room for Wilbur there.

Getting on for ten years later, Wilbur has in fact faded right out: it's doubtful if he is now thought of, on either side of the water, as any kind of force at all. Earlier this year a further volume came out, *Walking to Sleep*. A disproportionate amount of it consists of translations and although the original poems retain his customary technical perfection they hold no surprises beyond the usual polite sparkle of his aerated language – it's the same old *acqua minerale* and either it or our liver has lost tone. The book was greeted with muted satisfaction by the squarer critics but otherwise it was correctly thought to be a bit tired.

As it happens, I saw Wilbur in action at the American Embassy in that very Year of the Penguins, 1962. His reading was prefaced by a short expository routine from John Wain, who, while preparing us for Wilbur's qualities, unaccountably chose to impersonate one of his own characters, Charles Froulish from *Hurry On Down*. (I think particularly of the moment when the rumpled and wildly gesticulating Froulish, getting set to read his magnum opus aloud, rips off his tie and throws it in the fire.) Into the pocket of high pressure created by this performance strode Wilbur, the epitome of cool. It was all there: the Ivy League hair-cut, the candy-stripe jacket, the full burnished image of the Amherst phi bete. Riding his audience like the Silver Surfer, he took European Culture out of his pocket and laid it right on us. We were stoned. It was the Kennedy era and somehow it seemed plausible that the traditional high culture of Europe should be represented in a super-refined form by an American who looked like a jet-jockey and that the State Department should pay the hotel bills. As the world well knows, the dream couldn't last. It got ambushed in Dallas the following year. But it's sometimes difficult to remember now just how solid-sounding a civilized front the U.S. was putting up in that period: it all clicked and it was all official. The internationalism of a mind like Wilbur's, its seemingly relaxed roaming in the European tradition, fitted the picture perfectly.

Of that picture there is now nothing left, not even fragments, and looking back on it with what benefits accrue to a blighted hindsight we see that it was always false in the main – arrogant, insidious and self-serving. Better Johnson's or Nixon's instincts than Kennedy's pretensions. Yet within the Kennedy era's delusive atmosphere of distinction, Wilbur's own distinction was real. He could not, in the ensuing years, respond to his country's altered situation in the way that Lowell did, but I would be surprised if this meagreness of reactive energy turned out to be determined by complacency; up to 1956 at any rate, there is plenty in his poetry to show that he was deeply troubled by the huge dislocations that Alvarez saw as a characteristic, even exclusive, twentieth-century evil. But the point, I think, is that Wilbur's intricately coherent art is suited to the long allaying of an old mental wound, and not to the sudden coping with a new one. The evidence of his work is that he was able to employ the decade or so after the war as a time of tranquility in which his experience of war-time Europe could be assimilated and in a way *given back*: his images of order, his virtuosities of symmetry, are particularly orderly and symmetrical when he is dealing with Italy and France, the two countries in which he served. In a sentimentalized but still powerful form, we can see the same spirit at work in the J. D. Salinger story *For Esmé, With Love and Squalor*, and with the same emphasis on fluent, formal speech as the instrument of recuperation. In the strict senses of both parts of the word, it is recollection: the healing wisdom comes after the event. Wilbur's comparative silence in the face of the new (and this time American-inspired) disintegration of the world-picture is less likely to be a failure of response than a need for time. There is no doubt, incidentally, about what he thinks of it all – in 1967 he wrote a shattering occasional poem against Johnson's philistinism, comparing him with Jefferson 'Who would have wept to see small nations dread the imposition of our cattle-brand'. But otherwise in this decade he has mainly written mechanically in his own manner, giving the impression that an early challenge to his equilibrium had long been met and that a new one has not yet been faced. For the time being, at any rate, his poetry has lost its relevance. What I want to do now is to indicate what that relevance was when his poetry still had it.

*The Beautiful Changes* set the level for Wilbur's technical bravura and he has never since dropped very far below it: if the recent products look ordinary, it's worth remembering that they are ordinary in a way that Wilbur himself established. If there were no more going on in his early poems than the dextrous flourishes of the dab hand that put them together, they would still be of permanent interest. Suggestions that Wilbur is fundamentally a punster in his diction are misleading. He is fundamentally a precisionist – he will make a word divert to a parallel, or revert to an antecedent, etymological stage, not to pun with it but to refurbish it.

> Easy as cove-water rustles its pebbles and shells
> In the slosh, spread, seethe, and the backsliding
> Wallop and tuck of the wave . . .

The restoration of 'backsliding' to pristine condition is characteristic of his handling of language, and the enforced transfer of the reader's eye-line back and down to the next starting-point ('backsliding' – pause – 'Wallop and tuck') is an elementary example of his mastery of mimesis. These lines are actually from a poem in *Ceremony*: I choose them because they contain instances of his two main technical preoccupations handily demonstrated in the one spot. But each trick was already everywhere employed in *The Beautiful Changes* and working to perfection. This, for example, is from 'Cicadas':

> You know those windless summer evenings, swollen to stasis
> by too-substantial melodies, rich as a
> running-down record, ground round
> to full quiet.

Sound thickens when a disc slows down. Wilbur has noticed the too-muchness of the noise and neatly picked the word 'rich' as appropriate: the connotations, partly established by the preceding use of 'swollen' and 'too-substantial', are of a superabundance of nutrition rather than of pelf. As for the kinetic copy-catting, it's so neatly done he makes it look easy: the two-ton spondee 'ground round' slows the line to a crawl and the enforced pause of the enjambement kills the action stone dead. Sheer class. This point-for-point matching of form to action reached one kind of excellence (I say one kind because I think that elsewhere there is another) in 'My Father Paints the Summer':

> They talk by the lobby fire but no one hears
> For the thrum of the rain. In the dim and sounding halls,
> Din at the ears,
> Dark at the eyes well in the head, and the ping-pong balls
> Scatter their hollow knocks
> Like crazy clocks.

Just how it goes: ping/pong; SKAT! (could be a backhand smash); k/k/kk/k. Less easily noticed, but still contributory, is the preceding Din/Dark, a duller pair of consonants. What we are given is a kind of Doppler effect as the writer leaves the hotel lobby and walks towards the source of the noises. Copy-cat equivalence has here reached one kind of limit (not that Wilbur didn't go on exploiting it in later volumes) but in his superb poem 'Grace' it reached another kind – immediately more fruitful and eventually more troublesome. In these two stanzas from the poem, the first shows the first kind, the second the second:

> One is tickled, again, by the dining-car waiter's absurd
> Acrobacy – tipfingered tray like a wind-besting bird
> Plumblines his swinging shoes, the sole things sure
> In the shaken train, but this is all done for food,
> Is habitude, if not pure
>
> Hebetude. It is a graph of a theme that flings
> The dancer kneeling on nothing into the wings,
> And Nijinsky hadn't the words to make the laws
> For learning to loiter in air; he merely said,
> 'I merely leap and pause'.

The first stanza is Wilbur's customary five or so under par for the course, and one surfaces from the dictionary convinced that the transition from stanza to stanza by way of those two near-homophones is neat and just. What 'a graph of a theme' is I don't quite grasp, and can only deduce that it is the opposite of whatever motivates a dining-car waiter. But 'The dancer kneeling on nothing into the wings' is a genuinely amazing stroke, probably the best early instance in Wilbur of the mighty, or killer-diller, line. Here the mechanical principles of the mimetic effect are not fully open to inspection as they are in the earlier examples: the feeling, the 'art-emotion' that Eliot said could be created out of ordinary emotions, is not reducible to technicalities. Unprogrammed instead of programmed, perhaps even irrational instead of rational, the effect has been snatched out of the air by Wilbur during a temporary holiday from his usual punishing round of meticulous fidelity. When he showed he was capable of effects like this, he showed that the bulk of his poetry – his craftsmanship – was slightly stiff by his own best standards. As a rule of thumb, it can be said that the really glaring moments of falsity throughout Wilbur's poetry are brought about when, in pursuit of such an effect, he snatches and misses. An early example is the last couplet of 'The Peace of Cities', which like a good many of his poems has the form of a two-part contention. Cities in peace-time are characterized first, and found to be more dreadful, because more inconsequential, than cities in war-time, which are characterized thus:

> . . . there was a louder and deeper

> Peace in those other cities, when silver fear
> Drove the people to fields, and there they heard

> The Luftwaffe waft what let the sunshine in
> And blew the bolt from everybody's door.

This clinching couplet sounds transcendentally silly, like some polished and perfumed banality dropped by Oscar Wilde on an off night. But the reasons for its emptiness go beyond a mere lapse of taste: they follow from what Wilbur is trying to do with his subject matter. He is trying to absorb the war's evil into a continuous, self-regulating process – a process in which a subdued Manichaean principle is balanced against an aesthetic Grace. The material resists that absorption. The war is a mental hot-spot Wilbur tries to cool out, make sense of, reduce to order: trying to do that, he tends to devalue the experience, and his wealth of language becomes merely expensive-looking. All his poems on war-time subjects are flawed in their handling of language – his best gift goes against him. To take another example from *The Beautiful Changes*, 'First Snow in Alsace' holds a delicate balance for most of its length as the snowfall softens the deadly starkness:

> The ration stacks are milky domes;
> Across the ammunition pile
> The snow has climbed in sparkling combs.

> You think: beyond this town a mile
> Or two, this snowfall fills the eyes
> Of soldiers dead a little while.

But he rounds the poem out with an orgy of consolation, providing the exact verbal equivalent of a Norman Rockwell cover-painting:

> The night guard coming from his post,
> Ten first-snows back in thought, walks slow
> And warms him with a boyish boast:
>
> He was the first to see the snow.

With the possible exception of 'Mined Country' (and even that one is rounded out with a tough-tender metaphysical bromide) the poems in *The Beautiful Changes* that treat the war theme directly are failures in total form as well as local detail. But they cast light on the poems that treat the war indirectly or leave it out altogether – they demonstrate what kind of pressure it is that makes the successful poems such convincing examples of formal order attained with technical assurance but against great spiritual stress. 'Lightness', the best poem in the book and one of the finest things Wilbur ever wrote, is a two-part contention – and equation – about a falling bird's-nest and a dying old American lady. It ends like this ('he' being her husband):

> He called her 'Birdie', which was good for him.
> And he and the others, the strong, the involved, in-the-swim,
> Seeing her there in the garden, in her grey shroud
>     As vague and as self-possessed as a cloud,
>     Requiring nothing of them any more,
> And one hand lightly laid on a fatal door,
> Thought of the health of the sick, and, what mocked their sighing,
>     Of the strange intactness of the gladly dying.

Aware of the countless European people whom death had found by no means intact and the reverse of glad, Wilbur picked his words here with an authority that has nothing to do with glibness. Strange, now, to think of a time when America could mean peace.

In all the elements I have so far dealt with, Wilbur's first volume set the course for the subsequent ones – except that the overt treatment of war was for the most part dropped, and any concern for current, well-defined political crises was dropped along with it. He subsumed such things in a general concept of disorderly force, operative throughout history: they were the subjects his poem would redeem, rather than deal with. Each poem was to be a model of limpidity and no disturbance would be admitted which could not be deftly counterbalanced in the quest for equipoise. From *Ceremony* onwards, successes and failures accumulated in about equal number; but what *guaranteed* failure was when the disturbing force, the element of awkwardness, was smoothly denatured before being introduced as a component. It sometimes seemed possible that Wilbur was working in a dream-factory. Here is the second half of 'A Plain Song for Comrade', from *Things of this World*:

> It is seventeen years
> Come tomorrow
> That Bruna Sandoval has kept the church
> Of San Ysidro, sweeping
> And scrubbing the aisles, keeping
> The candlesticks and the plaster faces bright,
> And seen no visions but the thing done right
> From the clay porch
>
> To the white altar. For love and in all weathers
> That is what she has done.
> Sometimes the early sun
> Shines as she flings the scrubwater out, with a crash
> Of grimy rainbows, and the stained suds flash
> Like angel-feathers.

In poems like this the images of order came too easily: out-of-the-way hamlets were stiff with peasants who knew their place, and every bucket of slops could be depended upon to house an angel's ailerons. But the successes, when they happened, were of high quality. 'A Baroque Wall-Fountain in the Villa Sciarra' is the stand-out poem in *Things of This World*. Again a two-part contention, it compares an elaborate fountain with a simple one, and without the slightest sense of strain draws a subtle conclusion that doubles back through its own argument. In describing the plain fountains in front of St. Peter's Wilbur took his copy-catting to dizzy new heights:

> Are we not
> More intricately expressed
> In the plain fountains that Maderna set
> Before St. Peter's – the main jet
> Struggling aloft until it seems at rest

In the act of rising, until
The very wish of water is reversed,
   That heaviness borne up to burst
In a clear, high, cavorting head, to fill

   With blaze, and then in gauze
Delays, in a gnatlike shimmering, in a fine
   Illuminated version of itself, decline,
And patter on the stones its own applause?

Virtuose almost beyond belief, this is *perizia* taken to the limit.
The way the vocabulary deflates as the water collapses, the way
'patter' and 'applause', already connected in the common speech,
are separated and exploited mimetically – well, it'll do till something
cleverer comes along.

Of the killer-diller line there were a few instances, most notably
in 'Loves of the Puppets' from *Advice to a Prophet*. It's symptomatic,
although not necessarily sad, that the lovers in Wilbur's finest love
poem should be made of papier mâché. The desperation of the last
stanza, and the plangency of the tremendous final line, are prepared
for not only by the rest of the poem but by our knowledge of
Wilbur's whole attitude: to ensure order in the real world, the disorder of unbridled passion must be transferred to Toy-land.

   Then maladroitly they embraced once more,
   And hollow rang to hollow with a sound
   That tuned the brooks more sweetly than before,
   And made the birds explode for miles around.

But not many attempts at the art-thrill were as startling as that one.
As Wilbur solidified his position, the general run of his poetry
slipped past limpidity and got close to torpor. By the time of *Advice
to a Prophet* self-parody was creeping in.

   In a dry world more huge than rhyme or dreaming
   We hear the sentences of straws and stones,
   Stand in the wind and, bowing to this time,
   Practise the candour of our bones.

Here the pendulum has stopped oscillating or even shivering: it's
just a softly glowing, static blob.

   Ten years have gone by since *Advice to a Prophet* and for most of that time the major American poets have been sweatily engaged in doing all the things Wilbur was intent on avoiding. Instead of ordering disorder, they have revealed the disorder in order; instead of cherishing a personal equilibrium they have explored their own disintegration; where he clammed up or elegantly hinted, they have clamorously confessed. To be doubtful about the course American poetry (and a lot of British poetry along with it) has taken, you do not have to be in entire agreement with Hannah Arendt's warning that those men are making a mistake who identify their own personalities with the battlefield of history. You need only to be suspicious about artists playing an apocalyptic role. Nevertheless it is true that there is something sadly hermetic about Wilbur's recent work.

> Though, high above the shore
> On someone's porch, spread wings of newsprint flap
> The tidings of some dirty war,
> It is a perfect day:

Here Wilbur seems to be trying to get at something specific, but once again he can only generalize – which is not the same as being specific in an oblique way. Apart from the powerful but localized hit at Johnson mentioned earlier, the serenity of previous volumes continues untroubled by any hint of altered circumstances. A solitary war poem, 'The Agent', consists entirely of formula situations sketched in flat language: the hardware is World War II surplus and the setting is a back-lot assemblage of instant Europe. It reads like a worn-out answer to a new challenge. The opening lines of the long title poem guilelessly reveal the strain of a metaphysical essay being flogged into existence:

> As a queen sits down, knowing that a chair will be there,
> Or a general raises his hand and is given the field-glasses,
> Step off assuredly into the blank of your mind.
> Something will come to you.

Something does – nearly two hundred lines of wheezing exhortation. ('Avoid the pleasant room/Where someone, smiling to herself, has placed/A bowl of yellow freesias.') Wilbur's judicious retreat from raw experience has turned into mere insularity. It's a relief to get to the collection of translations at the back of the book, and the back goes more than a third of the way towards the front.

Yet with all this taken into account, there is still no reason to think that Wilbur will not eventually come up with something. At present he is off balance, a condition he is constitutionally unfitted to exploit. While he was on balance, though, he wrote a good number of poised, civilized and very beautiful poems. They'll be worth remembering when some of the rough, tough, gloves-off stuff we're lately supposed to admire starts looking thin. The beautiful changes – nobody denies that – but it doesn't change that much. I don't think it changes into *Crow*.

                                                                    (1971)

# 4

## Everything's Rainbow

Reviewers of Elizabeth Bishop's work have small trouble in demonstrating its perfection: she is an easy poet to quote from, and it rarely occurs to them that this very fact might indicate limitations to that perfection. The cisatlantic notices for *The Complete Poems* almost all singled out as exemplary her eyeball-to-eyeball encounter with a big fish.

> I looked into his eyes
> which were far larger than mine
> but shallower, and yellowed,
> the irises backed and packed
> with tarnished tinfoil
> seen through the lenses
> of old scratched isinglass.

You would have to catch a big fish of your own to check up on any of this, and it would have to be old and sick like the fish in the poem ('He didn't fight./He hadn't fought at all,') if it was going to lie still enough to allow the faculty of observation full play. But the point of such writing is that it is not only precise – I will accept that she is precise here, as she is so demonstrably precise elsewhere – but it makes a point of its precision, and creates emotion in making that point. As moments like these accumulate, the build-up in authority becomes more and more convincing, to the stage where the reader simply hands over control: even if he stops long enough to admit that he finds tarnished tinfoil hard to imagine, tacitly he will insist that it can still be imagined.

An appreciation of Bishop's work travels from point to point along a line of such observational intensities, and that is the unity of her poetry – intense moments accumulating. Since there are half a dozen such instances packing out even the smaller of her poems, the tendency is to ascribe unity to the poems as well. And after all, I suppose it could be argued that any poem, no matter what shape it is in otherwise, has established its reason for being if it contains even one observation like this:

> Below, the tracks slither between
> lines of head-to-tail parked cars.
>
> (The tin hides have the iridescence
> of dying, flaccid toy balloons.)

This idea comes from 'Going to the Bakery', a poem set in Rio de Janeiro. Now it happens to be a fact that a toy balloon has to be inflated and allowed to die down before its colour will take on the pastel glow that Bishop here equates with an iridescent Detroit paint-job: I can assert this with such boldness solely because a tired balloon left over from our baby daughter's party reminded me, on the day before I first read this poem, of the opalescent finishes supplied as an option on the Oldsmobiles assembled in Australia in the late fifties. A not-yet-inflated balloon would scarcely have worked the trick: it's something to do with the stretching and relaxation of the rubber. So to this image I bring a certain capacity of verification; and someone else who had never made that particular mental connection might see that it was nevertheless likely to be true; and one way or another we are both involved.

All well and good, and it could be said that this is involvement enough, that there are not many poets who will make the faculty of sight a public issue. The vision is personal only in its power. Otherwise, it is as community-minded as you like. We and the writer are united in identifying truths which, like scientific truths, are finally tautologies: this does not deprive them of interest, but it does deprive them of animus, and the ultimate effect is one of consolation in a universe where everything has been stripped of unpredictability through being defined in terms of something else.

Obviously this line of argument would quickly collapse if it could be shown that the moments of observation in Bishop's work are as incidental as they are powerful, and really go to serve a further purpose, that of being combined into a poem which supplies them with a transfiguring energy as well as drawing from them a store of tangibility. 'One is first struck by the magnificent surfaces of her poems,' the blurb quotes Martin Dodsworth, and indeed one is; 'later one sees that the point is to feel something else underlying the descriptions and lending them an air of dream, despite (and perhaps because of) their clarity.'

I think that Dodsworth here has intuitively recognized, without raising the problem to the plane of intellect, that 'to feel something else underlying the descriptions' is an activity that needs to be *recommended* and won't come naturally to a mind discriminating enough to be impressed by her faculty of observation in the first place. In fact there is a frequently ruinous dualism at work in Bishop's poetry. A poem is likely to be critically demolished by its own best moments. The self-contained quality of the intense observations amounts to inertia, and the argumentative lines joining them together, far from being lines of force, are factitious even at their best and at worst degenerate into whimsy. Here the opening stanza and a half of 'Going to the Bakery', leading up to the lines I last quoted, are sufficiently illustrative:

> Instead of gazing at the sea
> the way she does on other nights,
> the moon looks down the Avenida
> Copacabana at the sights,
>
> new to her but ordinary.
> She leans on the slack trolley wires.

Sheer marmalade. It would take a more unsophisticated poet than
Bishop to indulge in anthropomorphism with a show of technical
conviction: trying it, she lapses instantly into the trained poet's
equivalent of automatic writing. In another poem, 'Seascape', she
goes all free-verse in an attempt to give the device some muscle,
but there is no cure for it.

> But a skeletal lighthouse standing there
> in black and white clerical dress,
> who lives on his nerves, thinks he knows better.
> He thinks that hell rages below his iron feet,
> that that is why the shallow water is so warm,
> and he knows that heaven is not like this.
> Heaven is not like flying or swimming,
> but has something to do with blackness and a strong glare
> and when it gets dark he will remember something
> strongly worded to say on the subject.

The observation about the lighthouse's clerical paint-work is not
enough to offset the speculative rigmarole that follows. Additionally
it can be conjectured that in trying to get *above* the equation of the
lighthouse and the clerical garb, in trying to make something more
out of the automatic and inertial device of establishing those two
entities in terms of each other, she admitted her first limitation by
running slap into the second. The observation tends to precede the
poem, and by preceding it precludes it. Fancy takes over from the
stymied imagination.

Bishop's faculty of observation works mainly in the sense of
sight and there are strict rules governing it which are occasionally
made explicit, as in these lines from 'The Bight':

> Absorbing, rather than being absorbed,
> the water in the bight doesn't wet anything,
> the color of the gas flame turned as low as possible.
> One can smell it turning to gas; if one were Baudelaire
> one could probably hear it turning to marimba music.

Tempted with the boundless opportunities offered by synaesthesia,
she takes refuge on the far side of a semi-colon and rejects the
temptation by diverting it to Baudelaire. Little dramas of scrupulousness like this one are constantly fought out. They are triumphs

of minor tactics. Perhaps it is an obsession with these tiny battles that allows far larger ones to rage ungoverned. Getting back to 'The Fish', for example, we have more than seventy lines of meticulous observation before the speaker makes her decisive move. The local brilliance of the writing is unquestionable:

> While his gills were breathing in
> the terrible oxygen
> – the frightening gills,
> fresh and crisp with blood,
> that can cut so badly –
> I thought of the coarse white flesh
> packed in like feathers,
> the big bones and the little bones,
> the dramatic reds and blacks
> of his shiny entrails,
> and the pink swim-bladder
> like a big peony.

Now this really does go like a dream, and precisely because of its clarity: the observation (the 'feathers'), the presentation (that concrete use of the abstract 'dramatic') and the technique (the folded in and snapped out p-b/b-p sequence in the last two lines) are absolutely in accord. But what the poet never realizes is that seventy lines of this painstaking stuff are taking *time*: in the reader's mind the fish is croaking while she runs the micrometer over it, making nonsense of the poem's punch-line.

> I stared and stared
> and victory filled up
> the little rented boat,
> from the pool of bilge
> where oil had spread a rainbow
> around the rusted engine
> to the bailer rusted orange,
> the sun-cracked thwarts,
> the oarlocks on their strings,
> the gunnels – until everything
> was rainbow, rainbow, rainbow!
> And I let the fish go.

Whereupon, muttering 'Thanks for nothing, lady' with its dying gasp, it undoubtedly sank like a plummet. It's not so much the tone failing here, as the tactics. When tactics and tone fail together, the results can stagger towards the gruesome, as in her 'Invitation to Marianne Moore', where her fellow poetess is made to share the attributes of Mary Poppins.

> From Brooklyn, over the Brooklyn Bridge, on this fine morning,
>     please come flying.
> In a cloud of fiery pale chemicals,
>     please come flying,
> to the rapid rolling of thousands of small blue drums
> descending out of the mackerel sky
> over the glittering grandstand of harbor-water,
>     please come flying.

But it would be misleading to suggest that there are many Bishop poems dismissible on grounds of tweeness. The tone at its lowest is usually comfortably above that, at a level where the prosaic and intellectually platitudinous are twisted towards poeticized quiddities by professionally executed changes of direction. These closing lines from 'Quai d'Orléans', which cap a series of brilliantly exploited observations on water-lights and leaves, illustrate the point.

> We stand as still as stones to watch
>     the leaves and ripples
> while light and nervous water hold
>     their interview.
> 'If what we see could forget us half as easily,'
>     I want to tell you,
> 'as it does itself – but for life we'll not be rid
>     of the leaves' fossils.'

Thus with a gasp and a quick flurry of soul-searching does the poem haul itself onto the metaphysical plateau, making the exterior interior at the price of abandoning the judicious – and genuinely suggestive – language that places 'nervous' just so as to concentrate the effects of trembling the poem has already established, and places 'interview' to clinch the consistently employed vocabulary of seeing.

It's instructive that when Richard Wilbur gets a poem wrong, this is exactly the way he gets it wrong: the tag falls so perfectly pat that it reads like a bromide. But Wilbur's sense of tactics, perhaps in the light of her example, has always been more highly developed than Bishop's, showing itself as an acute sense of sustained argument. So similar in many ways, the two poets differ in their approach to form. Rather than plug a gap with prose, Wilbur will tighten the argument a notch and let the sequence of thought become a riddle. Bishop, eager to be clear and unwilling to perpetrate asymmetries, will interpose something that contributes to the total sonic unity but which fails to measure up to the standards that the fully felt sections of the poem have already set. The prosaic half of the dualism feels a duty to the poetic half: it feels bound to get in there and comment, compose a motto, ask a rhetorical question, round things out. And it seems to me that she comes closest to striking a balance when she realizes that a dualism exists and makes a link out of the gap's unbridgeability, as in her classic poem 'Cirque d'Hiver', whose marvellously observed toy horse has so little to say to her.

> His mane and tail are straight from Chirico.
> He has a formal, melancholy soul.
> He feels her pink toes dangle towards his back
> along the little pole
> that pierces both her body and her soul
>
> and goes through his, and reappears below,
> under his belly, as a big tin key.
> He canters three steps, then he makes a bow,
> canters again, bows on one knee,
> canters, then clicks and stops, and looks at me.
>
> The dancer, by this time, has turned her back.
> He is the more intelligent by far.
> Facing each other rather desperately –
> his eye is like a star –
> we stare and say, 'Well, we have come this far.'

It is probably too neat to say, but I will risk saying it, that such a poem dramatizes her own poetic situation to perfection. The whole force of her talent is to establish the thingness of things; which being done, the things have nothing much to add. It is as if a composer were to be frustrated in his symphonic ambitions by an irrepressible gift of producing short and self-sufficient melodies: he would be disabled by an excess of talent.

I don't want to suggest that this book is a record of failure. On the contrary I believe it contains more than its fair share of excellent poems, and where the poems are not excellent, their component parts are frequently enthralling. Elizabeth Bishop is an important modern poet if anybody is. But I think that the very terms in which her work is praised serve to indicate that hers is a poetry of a particular emphasis, and that it has not yet been sufficiently questioned whether this emphasis might be damaging to the aims implicit in her forms and themes. She aims beyond precision. If 'precision' is the cardinal word in our aesthetic vocabulary, we will be praising her for the very thing that she has striven (correctly, in my view, although not often successfully) to transcend.

(1971)

# 5

## Settling for Dust

*The Last of England* is the fourth Peter Porter collection to appear, and the first to be published by Oxford, who have issued it in paperback at fifteen shillings, which is steep but in his case the market will probably stand it. Porter's first collection, *Once Bitten, Twice Bitten* (1961) was published by Scorpion, who were also responsible for its two successors, *Poems Ancient & Modern* in 1964, and *A Porter Folio* in 1969. Added up and rounded out, the four books represent about ten years in the creative life of an Australian expatriate settled in England – the seventh decade of the century and the fourth decade of the poet's age.

Before the age of thirty, Porter simply drops off the map: by British standards he's almost completely untraceable, whether to school, university or class. When he does get on to the map, he can be only approximately identified, as the man from nowhere who talks with a slight Movement accent in Group company. In 1962 he was a Modern Penguin, provoking a deathless question from Stephen Spender ('Who is Peter Porter?') and slicing straight through to a new public which was eventually to render categorical labels less important – on the practical level, at any rate – for everybody. His own practical reasons for pursuing the Group association notwithstanding, the tacky label slowly worked loose of its own accord, and by now Porter is solidly established as an individual voice. But since even individuality must have its tag, he lately finds himself regarded as the social poet who sees English life all the more clearly, all the more remorselessly, for having come to it as an outsider – a wrong-way D.P., or a 'reffo' on the rebound. There is certainly this element in his work. But there is also something more, something deep-seated and permanently disturbing: a referential scope which enables him, perhaps even forces him, to deal with cultural breakdown on a European scale.

The eschatological thread in Porter's work would seem obsessive if it were pinned – as criticism tends to pin it – to an exclusively personal concern with his own certain doom. Equally it would seem tiresomely provincial if it were pinned to the declining quality of life in a supposedly debilitated England. The fearlessly reported ordinariness of one's own mortality, and the progress of English life towards characterlessness – these are the two main thematic areas which have not only served the best of recent poetry in this country but have made all save the very best of it predictable, spiritually constricted, emotionally insufficient. Porter certainly deals in both these areas: in his more mechanical poems he deals in nothing else. But below them, bubbling fiercely and waiting to be drawn upon, there is this deeper and more important referential area, which when tapped gives him the imaginative power to bring his own past (including his Australian past) into the service of interpreting his English present, and simultaneously to bring the European past (particularly the cultural past) into the service of interpreting the disintegrated European present.

Ideally (I mean as an aesthetic ideal: it could be nobody's personal ideal) these two interpretations combine to provide the unsettling spectacle of an individual history and a cultural history arriving at the finish line locked together. The eschatological boast of Porter's work is consequently on a far grander scale than is commonly appreciated. Similarly the poetry is of a rather higher order than is commonly appreciated. It has flaws, flaws which are lately becoming more glaring: density now verges on incomprehensibility, as the poet gathers in and fuses the historical details – the Last Things – which he alone will contemplate, in the last act of conscious remembrance before the whole show folds up. But apart from these considerations, the thing works: it convinces. In fact Porter's poetry convinces me without my much liking it. Faced with work of this order, I recognize the necessity to expand my aesthetic vocabulary beyond the like/dislike dichotomy and find measures to deal with a poetry which doesn't seem to *care* about being liked, or even care about neatening itself up and sweetening its tone the better to face posterity. Most of the things I look for in recent poetry are emphatically absent from Porter's work. But a few of the things I never look for – because I know I won't find them – happen to be present.

And it's because these qualities can now, after four books, be more clearly seen to be present, that his more mechanical writing – usually involving slap-dash technique and agglutinative assemblages of journalistic *frasi preparate* – can now be more easily explained. Statements like 'Love goes as the M.G. goes' (from 'John Marston Advises Anger', one of the best poems in *Once Bitten, Twice Bitten*) once looked to me to be decisive grounds for divorce: you didn't want to know about a poet who was sowing squibs like that under the impression they were powerful mines. After ten years he is still capable of effects equally cheap. But it is now more apparent that this carelessness of phrasing, this copy-writer's notion of verbal encapsulation, is contributory to his main qualities: his is a technical, as well as a spiritual participation in cultural collapse, and whether he is conscious of this or not doesn't really matter much, since the larger justifying context has been thoroughly established. The vulgarity of language is part of the show: the fine classical instrument of speech reveals its own injuries as part of its task of conveying the general injury. It would be too neat to contend that technique is therefore unified with content, content with intellectual preoccupation, and so forth: things are never that simple, and anyway the discovery of 'unity' is the point where critical response stops and the American tragedy of modern scholasticism begins.

But I *would* like to contend that it is a serious mistake to get the criticism of an effort like Porter's buttoned up on an elementary level before you have looked into what it has to offer on a more ambitious level. Criticism needs negative capability, too.

If the emphasis I have tried to make thus far is held in mind, the short poem 'The Civil War', which is placed early in the new volume, can usefully be regarded as something more penetrating than its recognizably neophobic content might at first suggest.

> Calm lie the plains of golden races,
> Dark the forest where Europe died:
> The Counter Reformation takes a bride
> The Container Revolution is a war –
> No man's hand may be held against his neighbour,
> Same against same is what the same is for
> The hire of death is worthy of the labour.

Regarded as a straightforward exercise in neophobia and mandarin nostalgia, such a piece would be open to objection line by line. I, for one, am all for the Counter Reformation taking a bride, if that means what I think it means – that priests want to get married. Similarly I am all for Container Revolutions in preference to Thirty Years Wars, even at the price of a cheapening of language. Likewise I am all for bags of sameness, if by that is meant egalitarian rights and opportunities and a smashing-up of all the dreary old swindles. As for the last line, it seems to me to be characteristically tricksy. But over and above all this, the poem has its limpidity: regarded as a whole it has a sweep of vision which supervenes its component prejudices – the message reads that history is losing shape, *like it or not*. Porter's central boldness is to make the statements that his sensitivity to language ought theoretically to inhibit him from making, since they have been made too often, by too many predictable voices. But in breaking through to say the unsayable, he builds up a convincing context for his own dislocation – a context for the poetic voice which steadily reveals itself as geographically, historically, occupationally and temperamentally homeless.

The picture comes over only fragmentarily in individual poems: it is a picture that builds up in the aggregate of work, which is why it has taken so long to emerge. Made overt, stated prosaically, it tends to come out distorted, as in this couplet from 'A Meredithian Treatment' –

> The past is dead, the future dead, the now
> Is here, an apotheosis of girls begins

– which could easily be taken as a Movement reflex, along the lines of history being bunk and sensory satisfaction being the only kind of experience safe from the rationalizing mechanisms of the middle-class mind. But a wide reading in Porter's work puts such a glancing stroke in a more interesting perspective. For Porter, the loss of historical continuity is not to be seen as a means of disowning the past and sharpening one's focus on the present: it *destroys* the present. The apotheosis of girls is a grim joke. On a larger and eventually a more disturbing scale than in the Dai Evans poems of Kingsley Amis, the Sex Man in Porter is the Lost Man. Seen in this context, the sex poems in his earlier books gain in weight: it is clear now that the 'flesh-packed jeans' would have led to nothing even if access had been gained, and that the desperate randiness of the excellent 'Conventions of Death' (in *Once Bitten, Twice Bitten*) is susceptible of an explanation beyond the implied deficiencies in personal charm, absence of luck, lack of courage – all the self-lacerating admissions that represented emotional courage for the Movement, their wet strength. Against the seemingly ordinary whinge and whine of the poem's minor argument –

> What I want is a particular body,
> The further particulars being obscene
> By definition. The obscenity is really me,
> Mad, wanting possession: what else can mad mean?

– can be set the extraordinary, bleakly disinherited percipience of its ending:

> So give up thinking, work hard, buy a car,
> Get married, keep a garden, bring up kids –
> Answers to all the problems that there are,
> Except the love that kills, the death that lives.

As an early expression of Porter's conviction that the disjointed times have injected a death principle into love itself, 'Conventions of Death' should properly be grouped with two other ambitious poems in *Once Bitten, Twice Bitten*: 'Metamorphosis' and 'Beast and the Beauty', which last poem would have been class-shy even at its inception (no matter how frankly expressed) if written by an Englishman, but coming from Porter turned out to be simply an early, and ideal, expression of his total disinheritance. Throughout Porter's 'love' poetry, it is essential not to let the Condé-Nast slickness of the beloved's glamour throw you: the meretriciousness is the message. Representing values which are no longer desirable, the poet is no longer desired; attempting to embody the values which *are* desirable, he corrupts himself in the market-place; the distorted longing finding no response in its distorted object, the poet is finally driven back into his own drama, and ends up satirising himself. Porter's main difference from his Latin satirical models is that his poetic effort is almost completely interiorized. The privilege which the poet has traditionally enjoyed – that of confidently occupying a place in a cumulative continuity even when the whole world is ranged against him – is no longer operative. He fights himself, perhaps to a standstill.

In the closing section of the poem 'The Worker', the apotheosis of girls finds a remarkable expression, even for Porter. The girl Valerie, through being located in Continental Europe and bombarded with the imagery of centuries, is not only defined historically, she *defines herself* historically; but only on the understanding that the tumult of recent ages took place to lead up to her – that is, to nothing.

> she has a vision
> that all the rest are in the mines
> where the D Major is dug,
> the perruked miners,
> workers at the star-hot centre
> filling the hoppers with life
> and she and her lover at the end
> of the beautiful cables, fed and balanced
> and warmed, thinning down, rarefied
> and soon to have wings –
> the libraries and the switches and the slurry
> are programmed for this,

> her delicacy and radiant quickness,
> her crystalline migraine which they like ants
> are the distant and decent makers of

So the poem drops out of sight without even a full stop, like an idea too big to be grasped. I find Porter in this vein extremely disturbing, unquestionably important, and increasingly hard to follow. From a too literal practical interpretation of his own poetic stance, he seems to feel justified in not explaining himself – nobody is listening properly anyway. This would not matter so much if it were not for the magnitude of the culture he is deploying. The tendency to botch together a multitude of arty fragments can result in chastening examples of the Higher Nonsense – a tendency already well established in his first volume, where poems like 'Euphoria Dies' boiled the wax in the gullible reader's ears. But when the thing works (and in 'The Workers' it undoubtedly does) the opacity is somehow functional – it helps with the distancing, sets things appropriately adrift. It should be mentioned, however, that Porter's acknowledged master, Auden, the most abundantly cultivated of all the twentieth-century English poets, employs an unrivalled range of cultural reference without ever driving the reader to distraction: it is mainly a matter of tact in setting the effects up, of making sure they are structurally intelligible even in those instances where the reader lacks the necessary preparation. Incidentally, Auden's direct influence is not so obvious in this volume as it was in the three previous ones, and especially in *A Porter Folio* – the Fit City and the Adversary have this time been frozen out, for which relief much thanks.

In Porter's minor, least cluttered and immediately most effective manner, poems like 'Christenings', 'Consumer Report' and 'Applause For Death' keep up the good work. They represent the kind of exteriorized satirical attack for which Porter is most often praised, and which I have tried to suggest is not his whole secret. In these poems, as in the more ambitious ones, the social reportage has the up-to-the-minute selective accuracy found flattering by sage and trend-hound alike: as I argued earlier, this is a neutral attribute, and can't be regarded as a virtue except when the poet treats his own interest in such stuff as a component in the total

intellectual drama of his major work. After all, the ability to notice
a Led Zeppelin poster on a wall (and then disguise it in the poem so
that only those who know what a Led Zeppelin poster looks like
will know what you're on about) 'fixes' nothing except your ability
to notice such things. A mere mention is not in itself transfigurative
and loosely mounted ephemera can make a functional show only in
poetry that is determined to die, which Porter's is obviously not –
except in his imaginative universe, where, of course, everything is
due to die at about noon next Wednesday. One's objection here is
to flashy opportunism: items dragged in for the sake of it, dis-
figuring work which is at its best much more rigorously considered.

In this volume the fruitful occupation with the Latin satirists
continues. The up-dated Martial versions are vividly successful,
the temporal transpositions working to perfection.

> receive these seven modest
> books, with the author's latest
> emendations (these alone
> will enable your heirs to sell them
> to a North African University) –

Spot on, especially since Porter's own activities in the MS-flogging
field are by now well known. 'Nine Points of the Law' and the five-
part 'How To Get A Girl Friend', both bright moments in *Poems
Ancient & Modern*, are matched in this volume by the diverting
'Stroking The Chin': Porter really shines in these multiple minia-
tures:

> If I centre my thumb
> in the almost non-existent
> dimple of my chin and touch
> my four reachable moles
> with my four fingers
>     that brunette
> will leave her publisher
> and cross the tiled floor
> of the restaurant to invite
> me back to Montagu Square
> for the afternoon.

It's noteworthy that even in a miniature, randy sport like this one,
his urge to specify is well in evidence. Why does Montagu Square

matter? Does it matter that Porter lets it matter? Probably it does: even in his slightest verses, Porter is trying to connect with society, to find a fixed point. And because there is no stability in a flux, his points of reference must be continually relocated, or else updated and refurbished. The coffee bars of his early Kings Road all have new names. The Jensens have moved on. The beach-buggies have moved in. Led Zeppelin has arrived. Not being able to help *caring* about this kind of crap is part of the fix he is in. And the fix is part of the subject.

The Australian background is not so much in evidence in this volume, although it might well return, since he has proved already that it can provide a usefully unexpected mental setting for the European situation. 'Requiem For Mrs. Hammelswang' (in *Poems Ancient & Modern*) was the first full-blown European elegy of his grand manner, even though set in Australia; and 'Homage to Gaetano Donizetti', in the same volume, had nifty Audenesque couplets like this –

> Teutons still come south to add a little
> Cantilena to their klangschönheit

– flying around some Australian al fresco caravanserai called the Everest Milk Bar. In the present volume such tactics are mainly confined to 'On This Day I Complete My Fortieth Year', with its revealing air of regret for having been so late to board the European apocalyptic bus.

> to have a weatherboard house and a white
> paling fence and poinsettias and palm nuts
> instead of Newstead Abbey and owls and graves
>     and not even a club foot;
>
> above all to miss the European gloom
> in the endless eleven o'clock heat among
> the lightweight suits and warped verandahs,
>     an apprenticeship, not a pilgrimage –

Those are a couple of goodish moments in a poem that doesn't add up to much. His vocational dilemmas, situational uncertainties, emotional imbalances – these are things that it is the business of his whole poetry to transmit by complex implication, and a straight-forward account of them rings hollow. His truly personal note is in the uncanny, doomed triumph of the volume's central work, 'Europe, An Ode', which ends like this:

> There for the fallen Gothic Museums glow,
>     Enthusiastic doubt like sun motes
>         Turns to dandruff on old shoulders:
>         At the start of the world, the beholders
>
> Find the permanent kingdom and this
>     Peninsula, its rational Europe
>         Where the blood has dried to Classic
>         Or Gothic, cinema names in aspic.
>
> But the giant iron is ours, too:
>     It flies, it sings, it is carried to god –
>         We come from it, the Father, maker and healer,
>         And from Oviraptor, the egg-stealer,
>
> Launched in the wake of our stormy mother
>     To end up on a tideless shore
>         Which this is the dream of, a place
>         Of skulls, looking history in the face.

It has been said that the beautiful form Leopardi gave his nihilism negated the validity of nihilism. I would say that even though cultural dissolution is Porter's main subject, the quality of his treatment of it demonstrates that the moment of cultural dissolution is not yet.

(1970)

# 6

## Two Essays on John Berryman

### (1) On the *Dream Songs*

If the contention is accepted that an excess of clarity is the only kind of difficulty a work of art should offer, John Berryman's *Dream Songs* (it is surely permissible by now to call the complete work by that name) have been offering several kinds of unacceptable difficulty since they first began to appear. It was confusedly apparent in the first volume of the work, *77 Dream Songs*, that several different personalities within the poet's single personality (one doesn't suggest his 'real' personality, or at any rate one didn't suggest it at that stage) had been set talking to and of each other. These personalities, or let them be called characters, were given tones of voice, even separate voices with peculiar idioms. The interplays of voice and attitude were not easy to puzzle out, and many reviewers, according to Mr. Berryman and their own subsequent and sometimes abject admissions, made howlers. With this new volume of 308 more dream songs comes a rather impatient corrective from the author pointing out how simple it all is.

Well, the first book was not simple. It was difficult. In fact it was garbled, and the reviewers who said so and later took it back are foolish. *His Toy*, *His Dream*, *His Rest*, this new and longer book, is simpler, with many of the severally-voiced conversational devices abandoned. Its difficulties are more of texture than of structure: the plan is less schematic but the indulgences are proportionately greater, eccentricity proliferating as the original intellectualized, constructional gimmicks fold up under the pressure of released expression. There are passages that are opaque and likely to remain so. Some of the language is contorted in a way designed to disguise the platitudinous as a toughly guarded verity. The range of reference is very wide (the *Dream Songs*, like dreams in sleep, draw freely and solidly on the cultural memory) but there are some references which go well beyond the legitimately omnivorous curiosity of the poetic intelligence and achieve impenetrable privacy through not being, like most of the rest, explained by their general context.

This last, the general context, is the true structure of Berryman's complete book of 385 individual, but not isolated, lyrics. It is not wise to contend that the ambitions of structure (with a capital S) can go hang, the individual lyrics being all that matters. In fact, the lyrics mostly explain each other's difficulties – sometimes across long distances – by tilting themes to a different angle, revisiting a location, repeating a cadence or redefining a point. It was Yeats's way and for that matter it was Petrarch's – the long poem as an arrangement of small ones. One proof that this is the operative structure in the *Dream Songs* is that the work feels more comfortable to read as one gets further into it. But if it is not wise to say that the structure is nothing and the individual lyric everything, it is still less wise to say that the work is unintelligible without a perception of its grand design. It is unlikely that a clear account of such a grand design will ever be forthcoming, although the chances of several bright young academic things building a career on the attempt are unfortunately 100 per cent. It will probably not be possible to chart the work's structure in the way that the *Divine Comedy*, for example, can be charted out in its themes, zones and stylistic areas. The development of the *Dream Songs* is much more a development by accretion: Ezra Pound and William Carlos Williams are the two obvious models. An indication of this is the already mentioned fact that the multi-voiced interplay of 77 *Dream Songs* is in these later ones not so much in evidence: as a device it has yielded to ideas more productive, especially to the unabashed elegiac strain, sonorous as lamenting bagpipes, which in many ways makes this new book a convocation of the literary ghosts. One feels at the end of this new volume that there is no reason, except for the necessary eventual loss of inspiration, why the work shouldn't go on literally for ever – just as the *Cantos*, whose material is *un*digested information (Berryman digests his) could obviously go on to fill a library. The work has no pre-set, confining shape to round it out, and one doesn't see why the 385th song need absolutely be the last one; not in the way one sees that the last line of the *Divine Comedy*, for many previously established reasons, must bring the poem to an end.

In brief, with the *Dream Songs* Berryman has found a way of pouring in everything he knows while still being able to tackle his themes one, or a few, at a time. Attacking its own preliminary planning and reducing it to material, the progressive structure advances to fill the space available for it – a space whose extent the author cannot in the beginning accurately guess at but must continue with the poem in order to discern.

The *Dream Songs* are thus a modern work, a work in which it is possible for the reader to dislike poem after poem and idea after idea without imagining that what he likes could have come into existence without what he dislikes. It is particularly worth remembering this point when one comes across gross moments which make one feel like kicking the book around the room. And it is particularly worth making this general point about the *Dream Songs* having the title to a work (rather than just a trendily labelled grab-bag) in view of the virtual certainty that the weirdball academic studies will soon be upon us, bringing with them the inevitable reaction into an extreme commonsensicality which would deny the existence of a long poem rather than have it 'studied' in brainless terms.

It was a masterfully asserted, overwhelmingly persuasive version of commonsensicality which enabled Croce to liberate the *Divine Comedy* (the case is again relevant) from an inhumanly attentive *wissenschaft* and release the poetry within it to immediate appreciation. But of course the Crocean case was over-asserted. The poem *does* possess an informing structure, a structure which the reader must know in detail, though better later than sooner and better never than in the first instance. Berryman's *Dream Songs*, on their much smaller, less noble scale, likewise have a structure, and will continue to have it even when the scholars say they do. That is the thing to remember, that and the fact that the structure is inside rather than overall. Especially when a long poem is such a present to the academics as this one is, the humane student is engaged in a fight for possession from the very outset: he needs to remember that to be simplistic is to lose the fight. He must admit complication: certainly here, for the *Dream Songs* are extremely complicated, having almost the complexity of memory itself. They depend on the perception that the mind is not a unity but a plurality, and by keeping the talk going between these mental components, by never (or not often) lapsing into a self-censoring monologue, they convey their special sense of form. It's even possible to say that the poorest sections of the work are the sections where the poet's sense of himself is projected into it as a pose – where an attitude is struck and remains unquestioned in a work of art whose unique quality is to question all attitudes through the critical recollection of their history and a sensitive awareness of all the clichés attendant on the concept of the creative personality. And the personality in play is, all along, the creative one: the central motive of the *Dream Songs* can be defined as an attempt by a poet to examine himself without lapsing into self-regard. 'The poem then', Berryman writes in his prefatory Note.

whatever its wide cast of characters, is essentially about an imaginary character (not the poet, not me) named Henry, a white American in early middle age sometimes in blackface, who has suffered an irreversible loss and talks about himself sometimes in the first person, sometimes in the third, sometimes even in the second; he has a friend, never named, who addresses him as Mr. Bones and variants thereof.

Not the poet and not me. But obviously, in what is mainly the story of a poet who is currently writing a poem which sounds remarkably like the one the reader is reading, the poet *is* the hero, a fact readily ascertainable from the amount of autobiographical material being used, some of which would be embarrassing if not rendered neutral by the poem's universalizing mechanisms, and some of which is not rendered neutral and consequently *is* embarrassing. The question is always being turned up, as the reader ploughs on, of whether the author *knows* that every so often a certain insensitivity, a certain easily recognizable 'creative' belligerence, is getting through unqualified to the page. Here and only here is the central character 'me' in the raw sense: in the refined sense the 'me' is representative of all artists and hence of all men in their authentically productive moments. The embarrassments are probably best accepted as a contributory quality, a few turns of the stomach consequent upon the many thrills. The poem's devices of voicing are not meant to distance personality but to reveal it: the doubts begin when we suspect that attitudes are reaching us which the poet has not analysed, that he does not realize he is being revealing in a crude sense. But really there are bound to be these. The important thing to say here is that the personality in the poem, manifold, multiform and self-examining in an obsessive way, keeps all one's attention. The language never settles into anything less than readability, and even when the restlessness becomes a shaken glamour in which one can see little, it is evident that something is being worried at: we are not just being dazzled with an attempt to churn meaning into existence. There is not much fake significance, though quite a lot of blurred.

Thematically, these new songs are first of all a disorderly, desperate and besotted funeral for Berryman's literary heroes, who might be called, following the author's own terminology, the 'lovely men'. Of these, Delmore Schwartz is easily the star. His decline is convincingly (one hopes fairly) illustrated. There are sketches towards blaming this writer's collapse on society at large, but there is also a more powerful evocation of a sheer inability to cope. 'Admiration for the masters of his craft' was one of the emotions Edmund Wilson picked out as characterizing *77 Dream Songs*. In the new book the simple admiration for the masters continues, but in Schwartz's case (and to a lesser extent in Randall Jarrell's) it goes a long way beyond admiration, and a good deal deeper than craft, into a disturbed exploration of the artist's way of life in America now – and this concern again, through the internalizing way the poem has, is referred back to the condition of the poet-narrator, a condition of physical crack-up and a fearful but no longer postponable facing of the unpalatable truths. Some of the evocation of Schwartz's life seem a trifle cheap, like all those Greenwich Village memoirs conjuring up the less than compelling figure of Little Joe Gould: here as in the sporadic scenes of Irish pubbing and loosely buried claims to a hairily abrupt way with the ladies, the underlying ideas of bohemianism sound a touch conventional, the reactions provincially American as opposed to the acutely modern, prolix Western intelligence of the work's usual tone.

Exemplified by the poet's cacophonous admiration of Shirley Jones, the supposedly 'genuine' identification with the straightforward and simple reads as hick gullibility and sheer bad taste. Another thumping example of bad taste is the unsufferably patronizing farewell for Louis MacNeice. A lack of 'good taste' is one of Berryman's strengths, in the sense that he can range anywhere for images without a notion of fitness barring his way. But positive *bad* taste is one of his weaknesses. His tough, anti-intellectual line on the American virtues can bore you in an instant by the insensitivity of delivery alone. There are moments when Berryman writing sounds a bit like John Wayne talking. For all his absorptive capacity for the fine details of life, Berryman's conception of America and of civilization itself seems cornily limited, and even the book's elegiac strain, its congested keening for the gifted dead, edges perilously close to an elementary romanticism whose informing assumption is the withdrawal of support by the gods. Waiting for the end, boys. But at its best the *Dream Songs* is a voice near your ear that you listen to, turn towards, and find that you must turn again; a voice all around you, unpinnable to a specific body; your own voice, if you had lived as long and could write in so condensed a way; a voice not prepossessing, but vivid and somehow revivifying. A solitary quotation makes an appropriate finale:

... I can't read any more of this Rich Critical Prose,/he growled, broke wind, and scratched himself & left/that fragrant area.

(1969)

## (2) On *Love & Fame*

Berryman's self-inflicted extinction has probably already lent *Love & Fame* the status of a portentous technical collapse, but in the short interval between its publication and his death it looked more like a sport – an amiable, shambling bout of touch football before once again donning full armour and tucking his tail down on the grid-iron. Admittedly some of the poems set in the present or near-present employ material even more doom-laden than the average run of hospital poems in the *Dream Songs*, but there are few in-built guarantees against our assuming that he isn't just piling up effects as of old: the drawback of high-intensity accumulation is that it cries Wolf.

> Nights of witches: I dreamt a headless child.
> Sobbings, a scream, a slam.
> Will day glow again to these tossers, and to me?
> I am staying days.

There is a lot of that, principally and intelligibly about himself, secondarily and tendentiously about death-bound fellow inmates barely out of their teens who are glibly paraded as being natural communicants in a holy sacrament of hopelessness.

Heroin & the cops were Tyson's bit
I don't know just what Jo's was, ah but it
was more self-destructive still.
She tried to tear a window & screen out.

One doesn't doubt the fact of this; one merely worries at the neatness
with which the fact suits Berryman's book. Expert beyond experience, these fearsome children are granted the transcendental
nimbus of Seymour Glass – and never a qualification expressed.

The charismatic quality of these charming & sensitive girls
smiled thro' their vices; all were fond of them
& wished them well.
They sneered: 'We prefer Hell.'

What will their fates be? Put their heads together,
in their present mental weather,
no power can prevent their dying. That is so.
Only, Jo & Tyson, Tyson & Jo,

take up, outside your blocked selves, some small thing
that is moving
& wants to keep on moving
& needs therefore, Tyson, Jo, your loving.

With *Love & Fame* the tortured flux of the *Dream Songs* breaks
out into clear country, spreading shallow and perspicuous: in the
elementary sense it's his most readable volume by a mile, and makes
very obvious his place in the modern tradition of poets who worked
by accretion. Unguarded by tangled nets of Dream Song syntax, a
strophe like the following demonstrates his reliance on the hallowed
Poundian conviction that all the object needs is presentation: with
the explanatory held to a minimum, the sententious should emerge
at its maximum – but unfortunately the unargued claim to significance turns out to be an extension of rhetoric by other means.

And Bertrand Russell's little improbable son
said to his teacher, a friend of ours at Princeton,
when they came to 'two plus two equals four'
piped up 'My *father* isn't sure of that'.

In the *Dream Songs* the story of this wee weisenheimer would have
been told with greater compression and the gesture towards revela-

tion would have seemed less automatic. Here, forced into Berryman's line-up of teenage suicides, the boy radiates symbolic significance on the open band. He's like those embarrassing moments in the *Cantos* when Pound quotes some gnarled old salt's salty old saying and ticks it with that Chinese ideograph that's supposed to mean 'precision'. No argument given or received.

The first half of the book, before the suicide-laden poems and the exhausted addresses to the Lord, is a portrait of the artist as a young man at school, Columbia and Cambridge. It bears a startling resemblance to Norman Podhoretz's *Making It*, not just in its itinerary (Phi Beta Kappa, Clare New Court) but in its psychological outline. The relish for the literary horse-race is exactly the same, except that Berryman raises it from relish to positive mania. Throughout his work since the early *Dream Songs*, Berryman's ambitions for major status have been nakedly confessed and played off against his equally intense ambitions to be the poet *maudit*, like Ginsberg or (more relevantly) like Tristan Corbière, to whose memory *Love & Fame* is dedicated. Corbière has been called *une chienlit permanente* and Berryman for a long time sought the same title. But even in the *Dream Songs*, where the interplay of these two ambitions is at its most successfully complex, the determination to spill the beans about the dark side of his nature was compromised by an unjustified readiness to forgive himself in the name of art. In this way his ambitions served each other to produce a self-serving poetry: he would complicate the account of his drive towards artistic greatness by revealing himself as a slob, and take the edge off that revelation by justifying his behaviour as the experience necessary to artistic greatness. Berryman was a highly introspective poet, alive to many things going on in his own mind, but he was never aware of just how consistently he worked this trick. It is the reason why the *Dream Songs*, which at their best offer a convincing poetic recreation of the mind's plurality, lapse finally from dialogue into monologue – the pride at the mind's centre heaps humiliation on itself but remains obstinately intact.

In all the looseness and plainness of *Love & Fame* there is not much successful intensity, but the anecdotes and reminiscences draw you forward at a great clip, keen to see how it all comes out. Well, now we know: and reading this book after his death we can even convince ourselves that we saw it coming.

(1972)

# 7

## Two Essays on Theodore Roethke

### (1) On his *Collected Poems*

When Theodore Roethke died five years ago his obituaries, very sympathetically written, tended to reveal by implication that the men who wrote them had doubts about the purity and weight of his achievement in poetry. Now that his collected poems have come out, the reviews, on this side of the water at least, strike the attentive reader as the same obituaries rewritten. Roethke was one of those men for whom poetic significance is claimed not only on the level of creativity but also on the level of being: if it is objected that the poems do not seem very individual, the objection can be headed off by saying that the man was a poet apart from his poems, embodying all the problems of writing poetry 'in our time'. It is a shaky way to argue, and praise degenerates quickly to a kind of complicity when what is being praised is really only a man's ability to hold up against the pressures of his career. Criticism is not about careers.

From the small amount of information which has been let out publicly, and the large amount which circulates privately, it seems probable that Roethke had a difficult life, the difficulties being mainly of a psychic kind that intellectuals find it easy to identify with and perhaps understand too quickly. Roethke earned his bread by teaching in colleges and was rarely without a job in one. It is true that combining the creative and the academic lives sets up pressures, but really these pressures have been exaggerated, to the point where one would think that teaching a course in freshman English is as perilous to the creative faculties as sucking up to titled nobodies, running errands for Roman governors, cutting purses, grinding lenses, or getting shot at. If Roethke was in mental trouble, this should be either brought out into the open and diagnosed as well as it can be or else abandoned as a point: it is impermissible to murmur vaguely about the problems of being a poet in our time. Being a poet has always been a problem. If the point is kept up, the uninformed, unprejudiced reader will begin to wonder if perhaps Roethke lacked steel. The widening scope and increasing hospitality of academic life in this century, particularly in the United States, has lured many people into creativity who really have small business with it, since they need too much recognition and too many meals. Plainly Roethke was several cuts above this, but the words now being written in his praise are doing much to reduce him to it.

This collection is an important document in showing that originality is not a requirement in good poetry – merely a description of it. All the longer poems in the volume and most of the short ones are ruined by Roethke's inability to disguise his influences. In the few short poems where he succeeded in shutting them out, he achieved a firm, though blurred, originality of utterance: the real Roethke collection, when it appears, will be a ruthlessly chosen and quite slim volume some two hundred pages shorter than the one we now have, but it will stand a good chance of lasting, since its voice will be unique. In this respect, history is very kind: the poet may write only a few good poems in a thousand negligible ones, but those few poems, if they are picked out and properly stored, will be remembered as characteristic. The essential scholarly task with Roethke is to make this selection and defend it. It will need to be done by a first-rate man capable of seeing that the real Roethke wrote very seldom.

Of his first book *Open House* (1941) a few poems which are not too much reminiscent of Frost will perhaps last. Poems like *Lull* (marked 'November, 1939') have little chance.

> Intricate phobias grow
> From each malignant wish
> To spoil collective life.

It is not assimilating tradition to so take over the rhythms of poetry recently written by another man. It is not even constructive plagiarism, just helpless mimicry. To a greater or lesser degree, from one model to the next, Auden, Dylan Thomas, Yeats and Eliot, Roethke displayed throughout his creative life a desperate unsureness of his own gift. In his second book *The Lost Son*, published in 1948, the influence of Eliot, an influence which dogged him to the end, shows its first signs with savage clarity.

> Where's the eye?
> The eye's in the sty.
> The ear's not here
> Beneath the hair.

There are no eyes here, in this valley of dying stars. In his five-part poem *The Shape of the Fire* he shows that he has been reading *Four Quartets*, giving the game away by his trick – again characteristic – of reproducing his subject poet's most marked syntactical effects.

> To see cyclamen veins become clearer in early sunlight,
> And mist lifting out of the brown cat-tails;
> To stare into the after-light, the glitter left on the lake's surface,
> When the sun has fallen behind a wooded island;
> To follow the drops sliding from a lifted oar,
> Held up, while the rower breathes, and the small boat drifts quietly
>     shoreward;

The content of this passage shows the pin-point specificity of the references to nature which are everywhere in Roethke's poetry. But in nearly all cases it amounts to nature for the sake of nature: the general context meant to give all this detail spiritual force usually has an air of being thought up, and is too often just borrowed. In the volume *Praise to the End!*, which came out in 1951, a certain curly-haired Welsh voice rings loud and clear. It is easy to smile at this, but it should be remembered that a poet who can lapse into such mimicry is in the very worst kind of trouble.

> Once I fished from the banks, leaf-light and happy:
> On the rocks south of quiet, in the close regions of kissing,
> I romped, lithe as a child, down the summery streets of my veins.

In the next volume, *The Waking* (1953), his drive towards introspective significance – and a drive towards is not necessarily the same thing as possessing – tempts him into borrowing those effects of Eliot's which would be close to self-parody if it were not for the solidly intricate structuring of their context.

> I have listened close
> For the thin sound in the windy chimney,
> The fall of the last ash
> From the dying ember.

There it stands, like a stolen car hastily resprayed and dangerously retaining its original numberplates. His fascination with Yeats begins in this volume –

> Though everything's astonishment at last,

– and it, too, continues to the end. But whereas with Yeats his borrowings were mainly confined to syntactical sequences, with Eliot he took the disastrous step of appropriating major symbolism, symbolism which Eliot had himself appropriated from other centuries, other languages and other cultures. The results are distressingly weak, assertively unconvincing, and would serve by themselves to demonstrate that a talent which has not learnt how to forget is bound to fragment.

> I remember a stone breaking the edifying current,
> Neither white nor red, in the dead middle way,
> Where impulse no longer dictates, nor the darkening shadow,
> A vulnerable place,
> Surrounded by sand, broken shells, the wreckage of water.

Roethke's good poems are mostly love poems, and of those, most are to be found in the two volumes of 1958 and 1964, *Words for the Wind* and *The Far Field*. Some of his children's poems from *I Am! Says the Lamb* are also included, and there is a section of previously uncollected poems at the very end of the book including a healthy thunderbolt of loathing aimed at critics. Roethke achieved recognition late but when it came the critics treated him pretty well. Now that his troubled life is over, it is essential that critics who care for what is good in his work should condemn the rest before the whole lot disappears under an avalanche of kindly meant, but effectively cruel, interpretative scholarship.

(1968)

## (2) On his *Selected Letters*

Ralph J. Mills, Jr., has done a good, solid, scholarly job of selecting and editing Roethke's letters. He has picked the ones that 'illustrate particularly his career as a poet': not a bad brief for an editor to give himself at this stage. When a biography appears we should get the rest of the picture, including a straight account of Roethke's psychic upsets – an account which would be welcome, after all these years of innuendo, if it were not that having it available will almost certainly complete the work of elevating Roethke to emblematic status as a casualty of the age.

If this sounds rough, perhaps it is best to get the gloves off early. I don't like much of Roethke's poetry, and the little of it I do like I don't like intensely. I like this book of letters scarcely at all. A biography that spills all the beans could well tip the balance towards active loathing. Very little of such a negative tropism would be solely Roethke's fault – when we react against a reputation, it is rarely the fault of the reputed – but likewise very little of it would be unfounded. It would be a justifiable contempt directed against a reputation in which the man has got mixed up with the work. For at the centre of Roethke's reputation is the idea that the man has an artistic status away from his poems; that the weaknesses of the poems are to be attributed to the psychic damage inflicted on him as a consequence of practising his art in a hostile society; that these weaknesses, having such symbolic value, are perhaps strengths. Even if Roethke's poetry itself were very strong there would be good reasons for attacking such a line of thought, because really it is not a line of thought at all: it is a chain of error.

As it is, Roethke's poetry is quite weak even at its best – though I do not mean to say that it didn't cost him great effort, and perhaps his sanity, and perhaps even his life. But what you have here in this amalgam of Roethke the poet and Roethke the Sick Man is an art-surrogate: what is under consideration, indeed adulation, is a Career.

It is evident from these letters that Roethke himself was prone to think in careerist terms, but that much is an accident: it's probable that Mailer and Lowell and other important Americans do too, and go much further in regarding themselves as children of their time, victims of a culture and that kind of thing. The case would not be altered if Roethke had had no such idea in his head. What matters is the critical view taken. And it should be obvious by now that the general critical view of Roethke has not a great deal to do with poetry, and everything to do with his efforts (heroic efforts, considering what he went through: but heroism is a term of accentuation, not necessarily of approval) to get established as a poet, to Make It.

Roethke proved, like the visitor to Brigadoon who wished the village into existence on a day it was not scheduled to appear, that if you want something deeply enough anything is possible. What he wanted to be was a great artist, and by the end of his career there were one or two really great artists (certainly Auden) willing to concede that Roethke was of their company. But just as often as they are right in such judgements, real artists are wrong. Like anybody else, they tend to admire sincerity, dedication, industry, openness, intellectual generosity, a sense of fun – and like anybody else they have trouble, once they know him, in getting the man who possesses these attributes separated from his work. Which is as far as I want to pontificate along this particular line, except to say that it seems probable that in Roethke's case the general critical view has followed the lead of his fellow poets, who simply liked him, just as much as it has followed the lead of industrious scholarship, which finds his work such a luxuriant paradise of exfoliating symbols. In both cases what is now needed is some healthy scepticism, even at the cost of seeming harsh. The sceptical mind can not long be totally impressed by opinions current within the freemasonry of poets: such opinions are often things of comfort. Still less can it be impressed by the academic discovery and canonization of a perfectly representative modernist: here a sharp nose ought to smell pastiche.

A straight read through Roethke's *Collected Poems* should convince even the moderately informed reader that Roethke's incipient individuality as a voice was successively broken down by a series of strong influences – from the close of the thirties these were, roughly in order: Auden, Eliot, Dylan Thomas, Yeats and Eliot again. Estimations of Roethke's poetry which do not confront this problem can't really be of much use, since the question of originality, if it arises at all, can never be peripheral: originality is more than a requirement in good poetry, it is a description of it. Most critics dealing with Roethke are ready to admit the question but seem to believe that his tendencies towards pastiche were momentary weaknesses, instantly corrected when a true subject came up. The more perceptive among them might go on to admit that even Roethke's most admired poems, the ones felt to be uniquely his, are stained at the edges with the tinctures of other men's gifts. Very few, however, would admit that Roethke is *saturated* with these tinctures – that a 'major' Roethke poem like *The Shape of the Fire*, for example, is soaked right through with the cadences, and therefore with the sensibility, of *Four Quartets*. From *Open House* (1941) through to *The Waking* (1953) it is almost as though he responded to each new challenge as it came up – or rather that he shadow-boxed in the style of each new champion. In *Open House* it was Auden. In *The Lost Son* it was Eliot. In *Praise to the End!* it was Dylan Thomas. In *The Waking* it was Yeats (arriving late) and Eliot (who had never been away). In the last two volumes, *Words for the Wind* and *The Far Field*, though the influences of Yeats and Eliot never wholly died, he hit a nice line of regret and wrote his best love poems. But all in all it's a sad story, and one that Mr. Mills (perhaps unintentionally) makes clearer by including a few unpublished poems along with the letters. One of these, 'Suburban Lament', enclosed with a letter to Stanley Kunitz in June 1940, tells you all you need to know about how hard Roethke was hit by Auden.

> Even the simple and insentient are unhappy:
> Horn-honkers find their neighbours unresponsive;
> Mechanical sheep stop bleating at the curbstone:
> Hands yank the shade before an unlighted window;
> A child bursts into tears before the hard-kneed stranger,
> The pure in heart cherish obscene ambition ...

> Not enough feet have passed in this country,
> Stones are still stones, and the eye keeps nothing,
> The usurious pay in full with the coin of the gentle,
> Follies return on the heads of innocent children,
> The evil and silly remain too long in tenure,
> And the young, mimetic, fall into the old confusion.

And the not-so-young, too: when he wrote this Roethke was thirty-two years old, which is a bit late to get knocked sideways by another voice. A year later (the editor says 'probably') he enclosed another sub-Auden effort in a letter to Dorothy Gordon.

> Though the geography of despair had no limits,
> To each was allotted some corner of comfort
> Where, secure as a seed, he could sit out confusion.
> But this is another regime: the preposterous bailiff
> Beats on the door with his impossible summons
> And the mad mayor holds nightly sessions of error.

In 1939 he had written to Louise Bogan: 'Oh, why am I not smart like Auden?' Too much of his first volume, *Open House*, revealed his success in getting smart *exactly* like Auden. In being able to add these unpublished poems to the Auden-influenced poems in *Open House*, what we have is not an improved case – the case must be made on the evidence of the published volume alone – but a broadened field of study in which to observe something strange and rather terrible going on: something more intimately bound in with Roethke's neuroses, I suspect, than has yet been realized. Admiration, emulation and, always, aspiration, as the perpetual *doppelgänger* tries to catch up with the *zeitgeist*. A career conceived of as staying level with the leaders.

Evidently the Dylan Thomas influence was in the wind as early as 1947, although it shows to full effect only in the volume *Praise to the End!* which came out in 1951. Writing to John Sargent, his editor at Doubleday, Roethke made a few suggestions about how to flog a batch of poems to *Harper's Bazaar*.

As you say, these people are very name-conscious. If Aswell (of *Harper's Bazaar*. C.J.) got the idea that Auden, Bogan, Burke, Martha Graham, W. C. Williams, Shapiro, etc., think these are fresh and exciting, she would jump at the scheme, I think. Auden, for instance, liked this last one best; read it over four or five times, kept saying 'This is extremely good,' etc. The last part, – the euphoric section, – made him think of Traherne, as I remember: no 'influence' but the same kind of heightened tone, I think he meant. I mention this because Aswell is currently on a Dylan Thomas jag: sees that Welshman in everything. If she trots out his name, give her the admirable Bogan's dictum. Said that eminent poet and critic: 'You do what Thomas thinks he does.'

This letter is crucial in several ways. First of all it shows that Roethke was aware, and wary, that an accusation of Thomas-influence might be made. Second it shows that Roethke was beginning to develop defence mechanisms; in this case the *common ancestor*, the pre-modern poet who perhaps influenced both him and the man he could be accused of copying. A month later he was writing to John Crowe Ransom: 'But I am nobody's Dylan: I never went to school to him. If there's an ancestor, it's Traherne (the prose).'

By 1948 the Thomas-Traherne connection is firmly installed as a mental tic, and he writes to Babette Deutsch:

An eminent lady poet said, 'You do what Thomas thinks he does.' The remark seems unnecessary: I do what I do; Thomas does what he does. My real ancestors, such as they are, are the bible, Mother Goose, and Traherne.

Unnecessary as it may have been to the field of critical judgement, Bogan's remark was obviously vitally necessary to Roethke's estimation of himself. In the letters at least there is no further sign of the common ancestor until 1959, when a letter from Mr. Mills proposing a book on Roethke incidentally triggers off the whole notion again. Mr. Mills regrettably does not include his own letter but says in a footnote that he had mentioned to Roethke that 'certain parts of "Meditations of an Old Woman" seemed to contain parodies of Eliot; however, I did not mean to be understood as thinking the individual poems or the group of them constituted mere parodies.' Mr. Mills's footnote reads with the beautiful sincerity of a collector writing to Van Meegeren and mentioning that certain sections of the Vermeer seem to be reacting strangely to X-rays, but let that pass. What counts is Roethke's reply.

(I'm oversimplifying: what I want to say is that *early*, when it really matters, I read, and really read, Emerson (prose mostly), Thoreau, Whitman, Blake, and Wordsworth; Vaughan and real slugs of dramatic literature – Jacobeans, Congreve, & W.S., of course.) My point is this: I came to some of Eliot's and Yeats's ancestors long before I came to them; in fact, for a long time, I rejected both of them. . . . So what in the looser line may seem in the first old lady poem to be close to Eliot may actually be out of Whitman, who influenced Eliot *plenty*, technically (See S. Musgrove, T. S. Eliot and Walt Whitman, U. of New Zealand Press – again not the whole truth, but a sensible book.) – and Eliot, as far as I know, has never acknowledged this – oh no, he's always chi-chi as hell: only Dante, the French, the Jacobeans, etc. My point: for all his great gifts, particularly of the ear, Eliot is not honest, in final terms, even about purely technical matters. It's here I guess your point about the *parody* element comes in – though I hate to call such beautiful (to my mind) poems mere parodies.

To get this interchange between novice and guru down to ground level, all we have to do is look at 'Meditations of an Old Woman' (*Words for the Wind*, 1958). Here are some sample fragments, easily flaked off:

> All journeys, I think, are the same:
> The movement is forward, after a few wavers . . .

> As when silt drifts and sifts down through muddy pond-water
> Settling in small beads around weeds and sunken branches,
> And one crab, tentative, hunches himself before moving along the
> bottom,
> Grotesque, awkward, his extended eyes looking at nothing in
> particular . . .

> There are no pursuing forms, faces on walls:
> Only the motes of dust in the immaculate hallways,
> The darkness of falling hair, the warnings from lint and spiders,
> The vines graying to a fine powder . . .

Roethke's subject matter is nominally different from Eliot's, but the forms are the same, with the result that he is using somebody else's poetry to write with. It's in this sense that Roethke is a representative modernist – he can write in all the modern styles that matter, at the price of writing very little that matters. To be a fan of Roethke's it is necessary to have read nothing else. In the same letter to Mr. Mills Roethke goes on to say:

> I can take this god damned high style of W.B.Y. or this Whitmanesque meditative thing of T.S.E. and use it for other ends, use it as well or better. Sure, a tough assignment. But while Yeats' historical lyrics seem beyond me at the moment, I'm damned if I haven't outdone him in the more personal or love lyric. Why Snodgrass is a damned earless ass when he sees Yeats in those love-poems. . . . Teckla Bianchini, one of

W. H. Auden's closest friends and a woman of unimpeachable verity, told me on the beach at Ischia that Wystan had said that at one point he was worried that I was getting too close to Yeats, but now he no longer did because I had outdone him, surpassed him, gone beyond him. Well, let's say *this* is too much, in its way . . .

Somewhere between the 'god damned high style' and 'the Whitmanesque meditative thing' most of Roethke's later poetry got lost.

Roethke's difficult life was full of worries about his tenure at each and every one of his many universities, forcing him to seek and circulate testimonials to his teaching abilities: there are enough of these in the book to convince anyone that he must have been a remarkable teacher. Against this must be put his applications (which Mr. Mills unwisely includes) for Guggenheims, Fulbrights, and sojourns under the wing of the Corporation of Yaddo. They make destructive reading. Roethke waited a long time to be accepted as a poet, and when he had been could never accept that it had happened: he was always waiting for the final reassurance – a common trait in people who are uncertain of their work. No amount of Pulitzers, or even Nobels, can satisfy a need like that. In a way the critics who see him as a casualty of the age are right – it's only the context that they've got wrong. He was a casualty of the American age of the Career in the Arts, an age which has even managed to industrialize the traditional rhetoric of the practising artist and so decorate in eternal terms what is really a vulgar struggle for preferment.

(1970)

# 8

## An Instrument to Measure Spring With

The plush Harcourt Brace volume of Cummings's verse (*Poems 1923–1954*) carries a line of caps on its dustcover immediately above the Marion Morehouse closeup of her husband's head: FIRST

COMPLETE EDITION. These two volumes MacGibbon and Kee are now putting out in this country constitute the second complete edition, which so far as the poetry is concerned will probably remain the essential compilation of the master's work. It adds *95 Poems* (1958) and *73 Poems* (1963) to what appeared in *Poems 1923–1954*, which ended with the last poem of *XAIPE*. The layout is an improvement: much more open, so that any poem, no matter how small, gets its own page. The typesetting is modelled directly on the old standard forms worked out by Cummings with his personal typesetter at Harcourt Brace and in fact the new face is so close to the original that it looks for a while like a laterally squeezed and longitudinally stretched photograph of it until you compare the fine detail of the serifs. Poem 44 of *No Thanks* is still blank after more than thirty years: it is still asterisked as being available 'in holograph edition only'. I have never seen this poem. I imagine it was originally knocked out of *No Thanks* as being too sexy (the original edition of *No Thanks* was dedicated to the fourteen different publishing houses who turned it down, Harcourt Brace being among them), but how it could still be considered so in this day and age is beyond me. The copyright of the whole body of poetry remains in the possession of Marion Morehouse, which, on the assumption that only the beautiful deserve the brave, is just as it should be. Doubtless more poems will be unearthed in time, and strictly there are whole stretches of Cummings's prose (especially in *Eimi*) which are poetry in all but name, but for the nonce this is it: the poetry collection of the year and for that matter the decade.

There is no reliable public picture of Cummings and it is doubtful if there will ever be one now. The only full-length study which existed up until the time I stopped following the secondary literature was desperately naïve, wide-eyed in worship, and as a PhD subject he is too 'easy': ideas-wise, he can be wrapped up in a couple of thousand words. He exists 'only' as a poetic personality, in the sense that the small amount of information available concerning his life fails to enrich (i.e. contradict) the picture you get from the attitudes he strikes in his work. As a figure eating ordinary food and breathing the air of this green earth, he can be reliably caught only in age-old sketches by Edmund Wilson and a few lesser figures, sketches in which he makes momentary appearances to talk faster and more brilliantly than anyone else before abruptly departing. No argument for the essential unity of art and intellect, the compatibility of the intuitive and the considered statement, and the schematic goal-achievement of an extended creative act, is complete without a consideration of Cummings's ability to resist any such notions. His relevance to formal intellect was the relevance of a high-speed tap-dancer or a totally committed whore, both of whom he could admire and celebrate, with each of whom he was temperamentally at one.

As ideas, Cummings's themes lead to immobility when they don't lead to Broadway. He pushes a concept of individuality which would render civilization impossible to carry on, and his formulae for sexual spontaneity attained their apotheosis with Carol Lynley reading aloud from *Puella Mea* to her straight-arrow boyfriend in the movie version of *Under the Yum-Yum Tree*. But of course the ideas were never meant to be ideas. Like Lawrence, Cummings was extremely insistent, and often tedious, on the opposition of sexual expression and abstract thought but, unlike Lawrence's, Cummings's statements on the subject can't be picked off the page without going off in your hand. They are present in this life only as art, and rarely try to stop being art: where they do, as in his blurbs for his own books and the burlesques he once contributed to *Vanity Fair*, the hyperbole is monotonous and the conflated language tiresome.

As a poet Cummings is not open to the accusation that he neglected to bar the way to people who might get him wrong, but it is certainly a pity that the emphasis of his work makes it easy for the superficial critical mind to line him up with the genuinely irrational writers in our time. Cummings never proposed that intellect should be swept from the world. His retort to such a statement would have been 'What world?' and his response to a further elaboration: 'You call *this* a world?' As far as Cummings was concerned, the artist's responsibility to the world cannot be discussed, since it cannot even be proposed. Cummings presumed to test and report the quality of life directly, without reference to ideology of any kind. The results were not necessarily naïve. His purely artistic, wholesale rejection of the Soviet Union in the early thirties proved in the end to be personally less damaging than the piecemeal intellectual withdrawal of his contemporaries. *Eimi* is at least the equal of *Retour de l' U.R.S.S.* for prescience based on the creative instinct, and contains by implication everything that Cummings valued in the America he was to needle for the rest of his life. Anyone still rocking with disgusted amusement after Mr. Muggeridge's extraordinary *Observer* review of the re-issue of *The Enormous Room* might like to compare *Eimi* with Mr. Muggeridge's own achievements of that period and decide whether dandies are ever right, even when they are not wrong. The two men reached the same conclusions, but look at the generosity of Cummings's book, the sweep of its pity, the prophetic urgency of its demand for the poetic in the affairs of everyday – you need to have kept your innocence to write like that.

What little we do know about Cummings's life ties in tightly with his work, and he is like Camus or Pavese in that you think of work and life together. Where they expressed doubts, he expressed certainties, but he is like them in suggesting that the writer's life must shape itself to his art or else crack open. The important thing, when your art makes claims of this kind, is that in your private life you do nothing to contradict them. And in fact Cummings never did sell himself or align himself with any dogma, was kind, was proud, was individual. That anyone should find this unity of life and work difficult to accept reveals two things, one intellectual, one temperamental, about the age in which we live. Intellectually, the fundamental modern aesthetic concept divorcing the artist's 'actual' and creative personalities has been successful to the point where the academic mind has difficulty in speaking at all when faced with an individual case in which the two personalities in fact match: a two-faced, vicious phoney like Verlaine not only seems more fruitfully complicated than a man like Cummings, but also more *artistic*. Temperamentally, the age is scared stiff of being taken for a sucker: deafened by the crash of fallen idols, it scans unblinkingly for the tell-tale signs of a splitting image. Believing that faults make men human, it eventually finds corruption admirable.

Cummings wrote little confessional poetry and it's permissible to assume that this was because he had little to confess. He had seen in advance the temptations his era would offer the artist and had

armoured himself against them. One tends to ascribe this in-
vulnerability to an innate primitivism – the lucky fool – but it is
probably more correct to say that it was the result of a conscious
act of dedication and courage, of highly developed mentality. It
isn't easy nowadays, to accept the suggestion that the man of honour
is not the man who exquisitely analyses his capitulation, but the
man who never surrenders at all. Far easier to write Cummings into
a secondary category of inspiration in which his heated simplicities
can be appreciated as a kind of inspired foolishness. (Some of
Cummings's love poetry looks pretty naïve, of course, beside
Lowell's: Cummings has few doubts, few fears, spills few beans and
doesn't seem to suffer much. What century did he think he was
living in, for Christ's sake?) These elementary themes of Cummings
might have begun as a pose, but with some men the attitudes begun
as a pose are confirmed by practice into a constitution of the mentality. Not necessarily a meretricious process: the brave men whose
braveness counts usually have to talk themselves into being brave.
From eccentricity to individuality, from self-assertion to a massive
vocational presence, Cummings simplified and hardened his attitude
to life until it supported him all by itself: he could stand up in it like
a steel suit.

Cummings's poetry splits up into two main lots: poetry cele-
brating love, and poetry defining, satirizing and discrediting the
forces trying to attack it. In the first lot, the love itself ranges
from the crystal-clear concentration of a child roller-skating
on a sidewalk all the way across to the titanic image of his
father,

> so naked for immortal work
> his shoulders marched against the dark

a picture of honour directly comparable with the figure of Farinata.
But the bulk of this side of his work is taken up with poetry about the
love between men and women, and this is the poetry most intelligent
people think of when they think of Cummings. It, too, splits up:
into the frankly randy and the close to holy. Almost everybody is
acquainted with at least one Cummings poem of each kind. But
Cummings is no nearer being two-faced here than he is anywhere

else. He has no Victorian component to his mind and doesn't suffer from a pulsating pornographic vision continually bursting through to sully the serene adoration of the beloved. Nor is there any post-Victorian component: no compulsory freedom, no screwing to prove a point. It is all as unstudied, yet fully as entranced with itself, as the little girl roller-skating over the expansion strips between the slabs of cement. He simply thinks (or simply writes, if you prefer to believe he is fibbing) of a continuum between the lady lusted after as pure gash and the lady contemplated as a divine revelation: the same lady, and, in some of his really remarkable poems, at the same moment. And it seems to me that he is very successful at this, that his raunchy poems are as cleanly good as Herrick's, that his sacred ones have an affinity with the *dolce stil novo* in its most highly refined form, and that he succeeded during his long creative life in joining something up which before his advent had seemed irreparably broken. In the best of the latter-day love sequences in English – Meredith's and Hardy's, to take two outstanding examples – you are given the lady on the human scale, and on the whole human scale, and are glad for the boldness. But Cummings managed something different and more difficult. Whether deeply versed in, or merely acquainted with, the sacred tradition in the love-song (I suspect deeply versed: he was well-read in several of the modern languages as well as both the classical) he succeeded in duplicating its singing voice of dedication, and produced love poems of which the greatest are comparable, even in divinity, with Dante and Petrarch. It is well known by now that Cummings's randier poems are in constant use on campuses across the English-speaking world for seducing girls. But there is a possibility, too, that his sacred poems might first seduce the seducer, making him realize that what breathes beneath him has a soul. Cummings was powerfully influenced by the figure of Beatrice and disguised as a child, a dancer or a disintegrating old slag she is in his poems often: camouflaged but not secularized. When, in 'She being Brand' he describes a deflowering in the terminology of a test-drive in a Rolls, you are immediately in roaring company with the Herrick who dreamed of his own metamorphosis into a laurel and woke to find himself the proud owner of an erection and the copious results of a wet dream. But when he writes, in 'it may not always be so, and i say',

> Then shall i turn my face, and hear one bird
> sing terribly afar in the lost lands.

you are not far from the Dante who had pushed the thematic frontier of the *stil novo* all the way to the staggering moment when Beatrice turns her silent smile from the poet to the Godhead. Whether Cummings in real life did or did not experience this continuity of feminine matter and universal spirit I have no means of knowing (Mr. Muggeridge uniquely suggests that Cummings might have been a queer), but in the best of his love poetry his implacable creative drive towards establishing exactly that continuity ignites a cluster of stellar points numerous and radiant enough to form a Milky Way of divine good will. Like Yeats, he learned a good deal from Dowson about how to write majestically: majesty means pomp and pomp needs drill. Sonnett III of 'Sonnets – Unrealities' in *Tulips and Chimneys* is a concentration of every effect in Dowson's technical book and it can be recommended as an example of how one great poet masters another's mechanics in order to be with him in spirit. Cummings turned Dowson's tone of voice away from doom towards exaltation and from frustration to fulfilment. Also he like *big* girls. But the sense of dedication is the same.

As an example of toughly articulated benevolence, the pagan love-song elevated to sublimity through tenderness, there is hardly anything in this century which will bear comparison with Cummings's love poetry except the very best products of Tin Pan Alley. And as his successes are Tin Pan Alley's successes – simplicity, self-definition, formal drive, the phrase pointed to revivify the words within it – so his failures are Tin Pan Alley's failures – sentimentality, self parody, the limpidity that gels too soon. Reading Cummings through now, I skip about 60 per cent of his love poems, since they are adequately covered by the other forty. It's a failure-rate considerably smaller than that with which any song writer is content to live: eventual repetitiveness is the inevitable penalty for being plain from the beginning. In his love poetry alone he wrote himself at least seven tickets to immortality: 'when thou hast taken thy last applause, and when'; 'it may not always be so, and I say'; 'this is the garden: colours come and go'; 'who's most afraid of death? thou art of him'; somewhere I have never travelled, gladly beyond'; 'you shall above all things be glad and young' and 'hate blows a bubble of despair into'. Scores more of his poems parallel, and scores more again merely parody, these few, but that doesn't make the few vulnerable or the many extraneous. A slim selection of the best wouldn't be much help, since you need to be acquainted with a couple of hundred of the lesser poems to sort out the language difficulties in the thirty or so (counting in the satires) which are really tremendous. In short, Cummings needs real study – not the fake kind, but the kind with generosity built in. It's not enough to be able to trace Cummings's debts to Baudelaire, Flecker and *Krazy Kat*, although that helps.

Cummings's other poetry is mainly a defence of the thematic unity I have just described. Eliot once defined humour as the weapon with which intelligence defends itself: a profound statement in that it described the dynamics of the business, by suggesting that humour moves always from a base. Cummings's humour (and his satire is usually funny enough to be dignified by this categorically superior word) moves from a base in his fertile territory of love, and by gruesomely specifying the enemy forces helps convince the reader that the home base is not Cloud Cuckoo land but the only viable actuality: you must live in love or else nowhere.

> take it from me kiddo
> believe me
> my country, 'tis of
>
> you, land of the Cluett
> Shirt Boston Garter and Spearmint
> Girl With The Wrigley Eyes (of you
> land of the Arrow Ide
> and Earl &
> Wilson
> Collars) of you i
> sing

And so on in a thousand details, all of them aimed at establishing the 'real' as the false: politics, the army, the police, the academy, the science whose microscopes 'deify one razor blade into a mountain range'. None of this is literary news now, of course, but Cummings paved the way and nobody since has done the job better. The real objection to the bulk of the work of Ginsberg, Ferlinghetti and the rest is that the man who started it all could squeeze their scattered effects into a form and make the whole thing travel like a skilfully aimed custard pie. The technical difference mirrors the difference in mental make-up, not to say mental intensity: Cummings isn't kidding. He really loathes what they are half in love with. His field of observation is broad enough and deep enough to get the detail right, but the detail is not *loving* detail: a concentration of Menckenese at its very best, his invective is a roar of pain. And again like Mencken's, Cummings's pain is founded on a knowledge of the past, of what has always been valuable. Cummings was superbly educated, he had his measures of excellence and he was not at sea. He knew exactly what he did not want. There is no element, in his condemnation, of complicity in what he condemns. Unlike his successors, he is deeply rational and it is only through complete trust in his own rationality that he is able to condemn intellect. There is not an atom of mysticism in him: he proposes no dualisms, but simply asserts the divine as the sole level of reality and perpetual revelation as the only mode of vision. Cummings, as well as bringing a tradition into being, was winding one up: a New England tradition, and hence a European tradition, and hence a tradition of civilization in the West. He is far closer to Catullus than he is to a man like Ginsberg. The old way was all *perizia*, and Cummings takes that to pretty near the limit. The new way is all *dummheit*: a new start, a new rate of speaking for a world growing to look like Los Angeles – a speech clumsily spectacular, semi-constructed, half articulate, a bit thick. In this world the intensity, and above all the *velocity*, of an intelligence like Cummings's will be close to incomprehensible.

Cummings's love poetry is beautiful on the one hand, and his attacking poetry explosive on the other, because of a sense of form trained up high and punishingly maintained. He rewrote the sonnet-form as a jazz solo in which the tag phrase jolts what you have been hearing into rhythmic intelligibility. Treating the whole sonnet as a rhythmic unit and using its traditional inner partitions only to lean against for a quick intake of breath, he avoided the usual caboose effect of squeaky couplets, quatrains or sestets tugged along behind. His sonnets finish so strongly that it is a fair guess to say he wrote them from the bottom up: certainly he hardly ever let the formal requirements trap him into a forced thought. Working for him always, in this and in any other form, was a strictly sensational capacity to propel a line: the special feature of Cummings's technique is not typography but kinetics.

> when every thrush may sing no new moon in
> if all screech-owls have not okayed his voice
> – and any wave signs on the dotted line
> or else an ocean is compelled to close

The packed stresses at the end of the first line are the knuckles of the hand which unrolls the second like a bolt of cloth. Cummings's diction was often self-indulgent (as Edmund Wilson pointed out at the beginning, Cummings overworked the long 'i'), his super-precise looking adverbs were often only padding, but the impetus of his line remained a miracle from first to last. Except for some largish poems early on, he never used a form bigger than he could control in a single rhythmic breath, but the alterations of pace within that rhythmic unit were, in the jazz-man's sense of the word, ridiculous. In a sense he was *too* good. Able to move anything at any pace, he was tempted to move hunks of nothing like a rocket, and you come across fast-travelling assemblages which have velocity but no momentum.

Cummings's true technical triumphs were all sonic. Except where they freed him into new areas of audio effect, his typographical tricks – the Apollinaire-raids – were an irrelevance. They gave courage to a generation of bad poetry, they give courage to bad poetry still, but they came from the graphic, merely talented side of his mind and were very limited in their poetic usefulness. The 'concrete' effects can always be related to the theme, but only mechanically. 'Moon' is just as suggestive a way as 'mOOn' of writing moon. Cummings was dedicated to typographical innovation all his life and set great store by meticulously indirect layout. He will be remembered for little of this: he can no more be credited with it as an invention than held responsible for the damage it has since caused. Several of Cummings's pages of alphabet soup (now seen in this country for the first time, since Faber & Faber, who handled his work here in previous years, never took them on) are really exploded sonnets. Put them back together and you quickly find they are not as good as the sonnets he was careful to leave in one piece.

A more troublesome technical point concerns his syntactical effects, which are numerous enough to constitute a private language and render his poetry virtually untranslatable. One of Quasimodo's translations illustrates this point well. Cummings has written

> the great advantage of being alive
> (instead of undying)

and Quasimodo renders this as

> il grande privilegio di essere vivo
> (anzi che immortale)

exactly reversing the sense, since by 'undying' Cummings doesn't mean 'immortal' at all, but means the ordinary existence which everybody except his chosen people lead and (mistakenly in his view) dignify with the name 'life'. *Questa voce . . . potremmo paragonare a un canto a bocca chiusa o a un canto lontano di cui non si percepiscano le parole* writes Quasimodo hopefully. In fact Cummings is quite clear and quite consistent in his untiring use of such effects, which are misleading only if you attempt to do a prac. crit. on single poems and neglect to read him entire. The real trouble with his syntax starts when whole poems are made up of nothing but negatively or tangentially defined concepts hemming in a falsely thrilling platitude. This poem is one of the neater examples:

> when god decided to invent
> everything he took one
> breath bigger than a circus tent
> and everything began

when man determined to destroy
himself he picked the was
of shall and finding only why
smashed it into because

The circus-tent saves the day for the first stanza, but it takes more
than a passing acquaintance with Cummings's work to make sense
of the second, and by the time you have acquired a certain familiarity
you are well aware that this is the side of Cummings which needs to
be left alone to die off by itself. Probably it will be pummelled to
death in brainless articles for PMLA circa 1990. But this is an extreme example and with steady reading his use of such devices
becomes perfectly clear. As it becomes clear, it tends to become
tedious. Like his typography, this component in Cummings's use
of language did its work by making him feel special as he slogged on.
Now that he is dead its importance should very much lessen.
Young poets who admire him will always betray themselves by
echoing this sort of thing, but really it is a mannerism and can't be
followed. Caught up in his commitment to the unique, Cummings
was often a mannerist – but at least it was his own manner.

Cummings's satirical poems, with their crazy-quilt diapering of
billboard slogans, campaign buttons and patriotic clichés now long
forgotten, have a receptivity to the emergent American idiom which
reminds us that his vital development was contemporaneous with
the gradual appearance of that great repository of informal poetry,
Mencken's *American Language*. As Valéry once suggested, the
language itself is the real poem. As a contributor to this poem any
bus-conductor with an authentic gift for swearing has the edge on
the darling of the literary society. Cummings measured himself
against the anonymous contributors to the language, to joy, to the
traditions of skill: balloon men, good-time girls, strippers on the
ramp, whores, acrobats who climb on ladders of swords, dancing
elephants. Of the small amount of his poetry which is perfect we
can say that it is good enough for its author's name to be forgotten
in safety. Of the large amount which is less so, we can say that it
needs understanding in the light of its author's manifest intentions,
and that these intentions were life-giving, basically sane, lyrically
inspired, and good. He also measured himself against the finest

poets of the near and far past, prepared himself to join them, and is with them now.

(1969)

# 9

## Keyes and Douglas

Keith Douglas and Sidney Keyes go together, or rather went together, like Owen and Rosenberg – they were the World War II version of the pair of utterly different young poets yoked by death. Keyes died in North Africa in 1943, before he had turned twenty-one. Douglas also served in North Africa but had to wait until the Normandy invasion before getting killed: it happened after he had been in France three days. He was twenty-four. Soon it will be thirty years since they were brushed from the board.

There's no question that Douglas is the easier poet to admire. First of all he had more raw talent. In the business which Yeats called 'articulating sweet sounds together' Douglas left Keyes nowhere. On top of this, he was completely unhindered by abstract imagination. An abstract imagination takes a long time to form into anything resembling coherence. A concrete imagination, like Douglas's, is usually coherent from the beginning, and from then on may expand steadily by accretion; whereas an abstract imagination, like Keyes's, is usually over-expanded at the start and shows only a fitful development as it hunts about for something to focus on. Douglas was only nineteen when he wrote

> The stars still marching in extended order
> Move out of nowhere into nowhere. Look, they are halted
> On a vast field tonight . . .

Douglas could do that at will when Keyes just had to grope. As an extended metaphor this poem ('Stars') is more than just an exercise, yet somehow less than serious. It illustrates – or perhaps exhibits – his military preoccupation, 1940 keen to be 1942, and most of the romanticism it displays is boyish. But beyond that, there is a superb cleanliness to the way the idea has been registered. He isn't saying that the stars are marching tonight: he is saying that they marched today, and will march again tomorrow. Tonight they are encamped. So we get the sense of a huge stillness dotted with innumerable camp-fires, and the fixed spaces between those fires. From the way the verse is handled we can tell the exact dimension of the events. 'Move out of nowhere into nowhere' gives the sense of majestic arrival, and 'vast field' is an expansive, totally relaxing thing to say, almost like a yawn. When such an idea is handled with such an easy-seeming neutrality of language, we are obviously in the presence of a prodigious gift. More profoundly than a direct allusion, such a piece of writing demonstrates the solidity of the young poet's background in Classics – he has extracted the essence of Virgilian presentation in the same way Dante did. Almost from the start, and certainly from his first few minutes in Oxford, Douglas was able to produce a sumptuous resonance from plain statement. Here is more of it:

> The long curtained French windows conceal
> the company at dinner by candlelight.
> I am the solitary person on the lawn,
> dressed up silver by the moon . . .

Effortlessly suggestive. A certain effect of wordiness can also be noticed, which Douglas was never to get rid of entirely. Determined to avoid the iambic thump, he packed out his major stresses with minor stresses and rhythmically pleonastic syllables, giving a conversational movement which exactly suited a poetry designed to argue, rather than accumulate effects. But the reader often stumbles, not knowing quite where to tread. 'Canoe' was probably his first perfectly realized poem, but an extra and unlooked-for tension is produced in the reader by the fact that it hovers on the brink of technical disaster: that last/part/art/aghast progression in the first stanza is like ski-ing on one ski, and rather overdoes its part in the job of setting up the powerful recurrence of the same sound in the beautiful third line of the second.

> Well, I am thinking this may be my last
> summer, but cannot lose even a part
> of pleasure in the old-fashioned art of
> idleness. I cannot stand aghast
>
> at whatever doom hovers in the background;
> while grass and buildings and the somnolent river
> who know they are allowed to last for ever
> exchange between them the whole subdued sound
>
> of this hot time . . .

But the poem's force of argument is unquenchable, and from that point the story is closed out with confident authority. In the second line of the last stanza he has avoided a regular plod only to verge on a mumble, and so nearly ruins that line's relationship with the calculated – and wholly successful – sublimity of the one that grows out of it, but it scarcely matters.

> . . . . What sudden fearful fate
> can deter my shade wandering next year
> from a return? Whistle and I will hear
> and come another evening, when this boat
>
> travels with you alone towards Iffley:
> as you lie looking up for thunder again,
> this cool touch does not betoken rain;
> it is my spirit that kisses your mouth lightly.

Plenty of young men have written love poems announcing their imminent demise, but not many of them ever wrote one like that. For a moment, until you come to your senses, it almost makes you glad he was killed – an aberration helped along by that brilliantly functional (and again classical) affectation of fearing not death but the Fate which might stop his ghost returning. Even before he had left Oxford, Douglas commanded the poetic resources to make a *Liebestod* convincing. Though a decorated, not a stripped, vision, it's a massively strong one, capable of presenting the most heavily adorned intimations of doom without sacrificing credibility: 'but till the jewelled heart is dust and the gold head/disintegrates, I shall never hear the tread/of the visitor at whom I cannot guess,/ the beautiful stranger, the princess.'

When he got to the desert his concrete imagination was faced with a vastly expanded field of reference, and technically the chief fascination of his 'later' (i.e. least early) poetry lies in the way in which his powers of argument accommodated themselves to it, or failed to. The diet was rich. He gagged on it, producing only a few poems equalling the fully worked-out integrity of the Oxford ones. Everyone knows 'Vergissmeinicht', and there are two or three more as good, but in general the later work – locally piercing though it is – is fragmentary by his own standards. Not even a maturity as precocious as Douglas's could grow up at that rate without becoming distorted, and in too many cases we find him being twisted aside from the steady progress of his discursive cogency and trying for an overcrowded, aridly mimetic equivalent of what he had been forced to look upon. Given time to ponder it all, there is no telling what he might have achieved. Critics are right to say that his best War poetry is in the same league with Alun Lewis's, but wrong to suggest that he was writing at the top of his talent. Artistically, the real tragedy of Douglas's death was that it occurred in a second formative period – it caught him when he was being born again.

Turning to Keyes, we see little of the maturity Douglas bore like a divine attribute. More correctly, we see none of it: he is altogether otherwise both in personality and mind – the type of the swot where Douglas was the type of the demigod – and immature even beyond his years. You have only to look at their war-time photographs to see the differences: Douglas the very image of the lean-lidded fighter, Keyes the large-lipped fish out of water. It's easy to imagine them on patrol together, Keyes mooning along with his head up and Douglas shouting at him to get it down. Incoherence was practically Keyes' medium. It wasn't so much that his ear was tin, as that it simply wasn't listening.

> I am the columbarium of winged
> Souls, full of wind and windblown prayer.

Temporarily chuffed with 'columbarium', he perhaps thought that 'full of wind' would go unremarked, but it's more likely that he simply didn't notice: his mind was too full of the dove-like lovers in *Inferno V*. He seems to have believed that a word can die its own length, and so leave room for another that interferes with its sense.

> He noted singing birds that raked the sky
> With pointed rods of sound like surgeons' knives.

Those rods not only rake, they're like knives. And then we are given comparisons so dead they're practically coming out the other side and gaining eternal life as parody.

> Fear of the enormous mountain leaning
> Across thought's lake, where blinded fishes move
> as cold and intricate as love: . . .

As cold and intricate as that. Keyes's Symbolist/Romanticist aesthetic was an intellectual lash-up with a disturbing resemblance to Surrealism, and his more flagrantly surrealistic excursions provide us with all we need to know about the forties at their dreariest.

> Night's work is momentary, and dividing
> The coloured shapes of passion which it spawned,
> Night strikes through the membrane to the gristled socket
> And tumbles like a pebble through the skull.

Appropriate to Keyes's abstract imagination was his habit of using literature as subject matter. Michael Meyer's notes to the 1945 edition of the *Collected Poems* trace the crushing debt of the long poem 'The Foreign Gate' to Rilke, but he's missed out on the hefty borrowings from Dante.

> '. . . . Künersdorf
> Fought in the shallow sand was my relief.'
> 'I rode to Naseby' . . . 'And the barren land
> Of Tannenberg drank me.'
> . . . . 'At Dunkirk I
> Rolled in the shallows, and the living trod
> Across me for a bridge . . .'

For some of this he is copying Eliot copying *Purgatorio V*, and for the last part he has independently picked up on the Buonconte da Montefeltro episode in the same canto. In other poems you will find lines like 'The shadows of gulls run spiderlike through Carthage', which seems to be a scrambled echo of Rilke's idea about bat-tracks running like cracks in a tea-cup. It is all about as un-assimilated as it can be, but it is an impressive token of how high Keyes was setting his sights. We need to remember that a wide and too-readily regurgitated reading is characteristic of this kind of imagination, whose beginnings are necessarily chaotic: the chaos being compounded, in this instance, by the fact that Keyes really *was* sensitive and intelligent, and wanted desperately to say something large about life. Scattered here and there throughout his work are moments of sudden intensity which show that his aspiring supra-logical mind could actually make the leaps he believed a poetic intelligence needed to be capable of.

> My mind is a stone with grief going over it
> Like white brook-water in the early year.

The only thing wrong with that striking first line is that the line after it kills it off, the word 'early' being a certain sign of Keyes's Symbolist kit of parts getting dumped into the poem. Characteristic locutions were: early year, early month, earlier. The lovers' (any-thing); love's (anything); the (anything) (anything) of love. The brain (as in 'The doubtful season of the brain's black weather'). The eyeball. It's impossible in Keyes to find a single passage in which limp language does not queer the act, but there is still a dignity in some of his writing which could have led on to important things. The promise of comprehensive imagination which Keyes held out to his contemporaries is hard for us to recapture now, but in a stanza like the following we can find a hint of it.

> Guarded from love and wreck and turbulence
> The sad explorer finds security
> From all distraction but the thin lament
> Of broken shells remembering the sea.

Keyes, as Philip Larkin put it, 'could talk to history as some people talk to porters'. For a boy of twenty it was a considerable achieve-ment even to give the impression of doing this. There is a literary ambition in Keyes that is worth respecting, even though – especially because – it largely remained an ambition. Of Douglas's talent we can be in no doubt. Of Keyes's talent we ought to do the decent thing and remain in doubt. He shouldn't be written off: there was too much to him. He died young in a way Douglas didn't, before his special type of mind had had a chance to prove itself. Criticism, I think, must take account of potential as well as actuality. Keyes needed time. Douglas didn't. They both ran out of it. The sharpest difference between them as poets is that Douglas requires no sympathy. Keyes requires plenty, and the best way to supply some is to picture a brilliant, sensitive young man – drunk with too much literature, struggling distractedly with irreconcilable pretensions united only in being beyond his technique – who is buttoned into an ill-fitting battledress and shunted off to get killed. Wars rob young poets of achievement and leave only promise. Younger poets they rob even of that. My generation, I have been trying to remind myself, has been given the opportunity to grow from boys to men, but our cherished critical rigour will mean nothing – will be merely dismissive – if we forget that some of the men we place and judge were only boys.

(1972)

# 10

# Sniper-Style

A poet in a country where anything can be turned in for a new one, W. D. Snodgrass stays loyal to his unpoetic surname, and the essential claim his poetry makes is that it is necessary to write beautifully in spite of circumstances. Reading his list of acknowledgements in *After Experience* (they have already been quoted by British reviewers, to whom names like the Corporation of Yaddo will always sound as if a homeward-bound Dickens is contemptuously pronouncing them) and remembering earlier awards and fellowships from the Ingram Merrill Foundation and the *Hudson Review*, the reader is more than mildly put off, as by the abstractly unimpressive multiple rows of fruit salad on the chests of American generals.

But the crucial point is that all this information is available: Snodgrass does not cover up. It is nowadays very difficult for an American
poet of manifest talent to be put out of business by want or by neglect.
Snodgrass does not pretend otherwise. Hemmed in by endpapers
and wrappers proclaiming his jobs, honours and awards (naturally
the Foundation will bear your expenses), his poetry steers clear of
the poet's condition, which is obviously in A1 shape, and concen-
trates on the personal condition, which seems to be in a fruitful
state of permanent confusion.

If 'confessional' poetry exists at all (and if it does, Snodgrass and
Lowell are still the two best Americans writing it), its basic assumption is that the time-honoured separation of the private man and
the public artist can now be closed: the pose is over, and all the
masks can be put away. The trick is worked, when it works, not by
lowering the universal to the level of personality, but by elevating
the vicissitudes of private life to the level of the universal. Insofar
as the poet succeeds in convincing the reader that his personal
suffering has an impersonal resonance his work will chime: insofar
as he does not, it will grate. Snodgrass grated badly in passages like
this from the title poem of his first book, *Heart's Needle*:

> In their smooth covering, white
> As quilts to warm the resting bed
> Of birth or pain, spotless as pages spread
> For me to write,

Or this, from the same poem:

> Like nerves caught in a graph
> the morning-glory vines
>    frost has erased by half
> still crawl across their rigid twines.
>    Like broken lines
> of verses I can't make.

Years later, in the work collected in *After Experience*, the same slate
is scratched:

> Now I can earn a living
> By turning out elegant strophes.

The reader's first and sound reaction is that he does not want to hear this: just read the news, please. The reaction is sound because this new habit of calling attention to the practical business of putting words on paper is the trivialization of what for some centuries has correctly been regarded as a divine act, an act which no decent practitioner should regard as his own preserve. The effect is childish, even in a poet of Snodgrass's abilities: he is joined in this to those academically-environed hordes of giftless poets who utterly fail to realize that man is not the measure of art. But before we come to that general point, it can be put beyond doubt that Snodgrass is a poet capable of extraordinary effects. His acute, sparely employed (in fact under-indulged, metaphorical sense can put an era into an image:

> This moth caught in the room tonight
> Squirmed up, sniper-style, between
> The rusty edges of the screen;

Faster and neater than that you don't get: a whole background comes over in a flash. The well-known virtuoso effort 'The Examination' (once 'the Phi Beta Kappa ceremonial poem at Columbia University', save the mark), detailing the ghastly victimization of a generalized Otherness and recalling the eery dismemberment of angels in the film by Borowczik, has an exquisitely schooled timing in its local effects that creates for the reader a nightmare he cannot stop.

> Meantime, one of them has set blinders to the eyes,
> Inserted light packing beneath each of the ears
> And calked the nostrils in. One, with thin twine, ties
> The genitals off. With long wooden-handled shears,
>
> Another chops pinions out of the scarlet wings.

You can see how each line of the stanza infallibly brings something worse to life, and how, after the qualification 'wooden-handled', has placed your own garden-shears in your hands, the jump across the gap to the next stanza tells you that the next thing is the worst of the lot. In an age of fake rough-stuff turned out by those youngish poets who seem fascinated by greased hair and high boots this poem,

and another called 'A Flat One' about an old man dying, are evidence
that Snodgrass is capable of genuine tragic power – a power that
the fashionable preoccupation with violence tends to dissipate. And
it is not accidental that in these two instances the viewpoint is
impersonal: the crippling assumption that one man can be a world
is not in evidence.

Of those poems referring to a life meant to sound like his own the
best are those in which the experience has a general applicability
to a time, to a culture. 'What We Said', a gently singing reminiscence
of estrangement, is a good example. When he tries extra hard to
supply the specific detail which will give the sense of a particular
life (this is really *me* talking) he tends to be in the first place flimsy
('Mementos I' fades right out beside Larkin's poem using the same
properties, 'Lines on a Young Lady's Photograph Album') and in the
second place dishonourable, since the theme, reduced to the loss of
happiness, seems to assume a *right* to happiness – which for sound
reasons has never been counted among an artist's legitimate expectations. Betraying themselves technically by a prevalence of shakily
cantilevered rhymes (bringing the reader as near as he will ever get
to groaning at poetry of this accomplishment), such poems demonstrate that a necessary consequence of abolishing the distinction
between private life and public life is that ordinary privacy ceases to
exist as a concept: characterized with a ruthless hand and unable
to answer back, the true sufferers in 'confessional' poetry are the
poets' wives.

The contradiction inherent in 'confessional' poetry which goes
beyond its scope is damagingly evident in Snodgrass's attempt at a
poem about Eichmann, 'A Visitation'. Technically very interesti ng
it creates an effect of jammed dialogue by interlacing two mono-
logues, one by Eichmann, the other by the poet. (This exceedingly
difficult trick of stereo voicing is used by Snodgrass elsewhere in
'After Experience Taught me . . .' and he may be said by now to
hold the copyright on it.) But examined close to, the poem reveals
itself to be dependent on all the usual weary banalities that would
trace the phenomena of mass-murder to tendencies in the artist's
own soul, provide the illusion of debate and flatter the pretensions
of the liberal spirit towards a forgiving generosity. In view of this

it is particularly unfortunate that the poem should carry as an epigraph a quotation from Hannah Arendt, who has certainly declared (in the very book from which Snodgrass quotes) that these events can be understood in the long run only by the poets, but who equally certainly, and as long ago as the appearance of her monumental *The Origins of Totalitarianism*, made her views known about those who thought 'that inner experience could be given historical significance, that one's own self had become the battlefield of history'.

'Confessional' poetry has taken a small, previously neglected field among all the possible fields of poetry and within that field pushed on to a new adventure. It becomes absurd when it usurps the impersonal fields with the language of the personal – when it fails to recognize its limitations. Eichmann's crimes, for example, were in the public realm; they are not to be traced to the sadistic impulse which is in all of us or to any other impulse which is in all of us; they can be understood only in history. When the poet pretends to contain, mirror or model history within his own suffering, his talent gives out for just as long as the folly lasts; the better he is, the worse the work he does; and even a first-rate talent like Snodgrass's produces the smoothly 'distinguished' work which is the bane of our lives and to which we do not normally expect a man of his powers to contribute.

(1969)

## I I

# A Reason for Translation

Ted Walker's *The Night Bathers* is more than a quarter translations – from Neruda, Verlaine, Rilke, Leconte de Lisle, Montale, Lorca, Hölderlin, and Lope de Vega. They are not the brutal jobs of reinterpretation and covert distortion that Robert Lowell goes in for, possibly on the grounds that Pound said it was allowable, probably with the self-generated sanction that one's own intensity added to somebody else's intensity yields *more* intensity. Ted Walker's efforts are quite the other thing: painstakingly faithful to the original's movement and humbly committed to its author's characteristic tone. Which makes them, as translations, excessively unexciting; until you ask yourself why he takes on the task at all.

The main reason he does so much translating is probably that his own poems are limited, as well as fuelled, by his extraordinary penetration of nature, and the seed-catalogue specificity of terminology that seems to go with the cast of mind. Take this couple of stanzas from his poem 'Bonfire':

> All afternoon was the waft
> from blue fields, the stubble-scorch,
> pricking me to this. I crouch
> like an ancient to my craft,
> knowing this moment to lift
>
> dry leafage to little twigs
> and lean to a locked apex
> the slats of a smashed apple-box.
> Gripping broken ladder-legs,
> the blaze skips up to long logs
>
> of old, wasp-ruddled fruitwood.

There can't be more than one reader in a hundred who would know whether or not 'ruddled' is a misprint for 'raddled' ('riddled'?), but who's objecting? One relaxes in the safe hands of somebody who really knows his way around a garden. It's a quality of disciplined seeing that Richard Wilbur shares; the quality that Andrew Young so well embodies. And over and above the quality of seeing there is the quality of the performance.

But *right* over and above both the seeing and the way the things seen are put together, the conclusions come pat: the poem's argument is all too plainly a vehicle for its particular images. As a consequence the satisfactions are many – gratifyingly many, and let there be no doubt that Mr. Walker is a good poet – but the surprises are few. Of the following two stanzas from 'Snow asthma', each is a satisfaction, but only the second is a surprise, the incongruous photographic vocabulary lifting the proceedings out of their naturalist rut.

Bullfinches were in bloom
  On a bough of dead apple;
As though the moon made daylight,
  Shadow was purple.

Seldom as bereavement
  Came snow. For a brief
Morning my mother's face
  Looked underlit with grief.

From the make-up of this collection it's permissible to assume that Mr. Walker has sensed his danger and consequently stiffened his own work with translations of poems which attempt and achieve a greater amplitude of utterance – poems which may start out from nature but which get something said without being dragged down into the concrete detail of chaffinch-husks and the precise pitch of a bloodwort's warble.

'The heart of Hialmar' is a case in point. The attentive reader may track down the original in Leconte de Lisle's *Poèmes barbares* and note how Mr. Walker has tried to meet the challenge of reproducing not only the movement of the quatrain (which pretty well means adding something of his own every four lines) but also the disturbingly familiar tone of Hialmar's address to the raven.

Unfortunately one can't successfully *tutoyer* in English by using the grammatically acceptable, but effectively counter-productive, *thou* and *thy*, so things go wrong: 'Come, bold raven, eating men is thy art, Pick my breast open with thy iron beak', is not the same as 'Viens par ici, Corbeau, mon brave mangeur d'hommes/Ouvremoi la poitrine avec ton bec de fer'. But at least the attempt to capture the purely human tone is there – and with all its naturenotes which may very well have attracted Mr. Walker's attention in the first place, *Le Coeur de Hialmar* is nevertheless primarily a poem about a man speaking. It's a dramatic poem, with a man up front and the scenery in the background: it exactly reverses its translator's own usual priorities.

The same argument applies to 'To the Fates' ('An die Parzen', a tub-thumping Hölderlin anthology piece) and pre-eminently to 'Bring me a sunflower . . .' (Montale's 'Portami il girasole'), which retains (and even, Lowell-style, amplifies) the spoken urgency of

the original while abandoning – this time – both the movement
and the detail. In fact this effort features some good rousing mis-
translation in the barbaric modern mode: Montale would be amused
to hear that he had written anything like 'Bodies are consumed in
floods of *shade*' since at that point he was actually plugging away at
his trusty theme about things being broken down into *colours* – 'si
esauriscono i corpi in un fluire/di tinte' – a theme he finally pinned
down in 'Carnivale di Gerti' with the hair-raising image about the
wrist-watch.

(1970)

# 12

# Augustan Wattle

Against modernism and for classicism; against the bloodlessly
refined and for the sensuously robust; backing the past against the
present and both against the technological future; and yet with all
this, backing the undernourished and perhaps crippled Australian
culture against a European civilization run to seed: there were all
these reasons, as well as the sheer quality of his poetic performance,
that A. D. Hope should emerge as the most distinctive poetic voice
in Australia since Slessor stopped writing. With as much going for
him as Slessor ever had – imagination, authority, touch – and a
greater range than Brennan, Hope is by now established as the poet
who matters most in all of the largest island's short but variegated
cultural history.

Yet Hope doesn't fit into that history any better than Brennan
did. His alignments against, his contests with, a tradition, are all
against or with a *European* tradition. The regional emphases don't
really matter much. It's far more pertinent to ask why he approves
of Swift's rage (and why he approves of that rage as *reasonable*)
than to ask about his precise attitude to current Australian society,
for although that society might be the immediate stimulus of his
opposition it is a whole modern era he objects to. In making this

objection he writes two main kinds of poetry, one a choleric railing against all dunces in which the powder flies off his wig, the other a bitter and desperate taking of solace either in the contemplation of past greatness (Swift, Yeats, and notably in this volume Baudelaire) or in the embrace of unnamed ladies who emerge from his heroic imagery as tending to be on the strapping side.

Both strains in his work long ago became predictable. But neither strain has ever become predictable as to the actual handling of it, and each continues to throw up a remarkable number of excellent poems. For anybody who first owned the beautiful Edwards and Shaw edition of *The Wandering Islands*, and later slipped the *Collected Poems* into the shelf beside it, and now must add this latest volume (*New Poems*), it is the combination of bulk and solidity that impresses. There have been plenty of Australian poets who have had bulk, in the same way that a trailer-load of sponge-rubber has bulk. Similarly there have been more than a few Australian poets responsible for a handful of intense, solid performances. But Hope has managed to add density to density, and already, with a lot of writing left in him, he has established the kind of presence we associate only with truly formidable talents.

It's ironic that he should have won his way through to the European poetic tradition by the sheer cogency and power of his contesting almost every one of its manifestations in the modern age, and also won his way through to a pre-eminence in Australian cultural history while never once going in search of an heroic Australian past, as James McAuley did, or getting himself identified with the soil, as Judith Wright did. It shows just how hard it is to get the individual talent taped, when the talent is there.

Hope's twelve 'Sonnets to Baudelaire' are at the physical and thematic centre of the new book. Baudelaire is addressed as an equal, which takes nerve:

> For we are fellow travellers in a land
> Where few around us know they walk in hell.
> Where what they take for the creating Word
>
> Is a blind wind sowing the sand with sand.
> Brother, it is our task of love to tell
> Men they are damned, and damned in being absurd.

As in his earlier alliances with Swift, Blake, and Yeats, Hope has
here found a way of ducking back into the past in order to recruit
reinforcements for an attack on his own present. Baudelaire's
position vis-à-vis his critics becomes, by adoption (presumption?),
Hope's own:

> He warms my heart, your Monsieur Monselet;
> – Such culture addicts, such genteel amateurs
> As scold us for 'abominable verse.'
> While, savage with joy, we let them have their say –
>
> Poor fellow, I see him scan your lines, his eyes
> Moist with fine feeling, till they meet the words
> About the hanged man's belly ripped by birds:
> 'His dangling bowels dribbled down his thighs!'

'What else could I do?' Hope has Baudelaire say: 'A poem is not
a game; the image I chose/Was what my theme required.' The
implication, in part justified, is that Hope himself has had to say
some superficially horrible things in order to penetrate to hidden
truth. But to write, as Baudelaire indeed did, 'Les intestins pesants
lui coulaient sur les cuisses', is one thing: he was out to show that
Cytherea was a trifle disappointing. To write, as he also wrote, 'Là,
tout n'est qu'ordre et beauté/Luxe, calme et volupté', was definitely
another. When Baudelaire mixed these two thematic worlds it was
by force of circumstance – because the facts said so. 'Les Petites
Vieilles', for example, gets its huge force because the pitiable facts
batter through all such cheap defences as superiority, disdain, even
art: it's a compassionate poem. But with Hope these worlds are
scrambled into one from the start, and that one world is acutely,
narrowly personal. He sees the skull beneath the skin right enough,
but his trouble – and it's his limitation as a poet – is that he expects
us to fall down in astonishment on being told that life is made up
of bones, blood, gristle, guts, and unpalatable, rank juices. He can't
leave it alone. He's really much more like Swift than like Baudelaire:
the thing that gets him is that Celia shits. And the answer to that
one is still Lawrence's: how much worse it would be if she didn't.
Finally Hope overcomes his repugnance and utters 'the heart's
unhesitating: Yes!' to life. But his contemptuous objection to *this*
life, the one we are trying to lead now, is that we are all busy trying

to deny the harsh facts. Hence the condescension of tone, and the regression in time, of almost everything he writes. The only consolations offered are fatalistic, and then you see that the fatalism is private too.

(1970)

# 13

## Seamus Heaney

Of all the newer tight-lipped poets Mr. Heaney is the hardest case, and the tight-lipped critics whose praise is not usually easy to get have been sending quite a lot of approbation his way. His technique is hard-edged: a punchy line travels about two inches. The subject matter is loud with the slap of the spade and sour with the stink of turned earth. Close to the vest, close to the bone and close to the soil. We have learnt already not to look to him for the expansive gesture: there are bitter essences to compensate for the lack of that. *Door into the Dark* confirms him in his course, its very title telling you in which direction that course lies. I will show you fear in a tinful of bait. It should be said at the outset that poetry as good as Mr. Heaney's best is hard to come by. But it is all pretty desperate stuff, and in those poems where we don't feel the brooding vision to be justified by the customary dense beauty of his technique we are probably in the right to come down hard and send our criticism as close as we can to the man within. The man within is at least in some degree a chooser. If he chose to be slick, to let his finely-worked clinching stanzas fall pat, there would be a new kind of damaging poetry on the way – squat, ugly and unstoppable.

But first let us demonstrate the quality of the poetic intelligence with which we have to deal. This is the first stanza of his two-stanza poem 'Dream': it should be quickly apparent that his virtuoso kinetic gift can find interior equivalents in language for almost any movement in the exterior world, so that the mere act of sub-vocalizing the poem brings one out in a sweat.

With a billhook
Whose head was hand-forged and heavy
I was hacking a stalk
Thick as a telegraph pole.
My sleeves were rolled
And the air fanned cool past my arms
As I swung and buried the blade,
Then laboured to work it unstuck.

All the correct chunks and squeaks are caught without being said.
But where does it get us? It gets us to the second stanza.

The next stroke
Found a man's head under the hook.
Before I woke
I heard the steel stop
In the bone of the brow.

He had a dream, you see, and his skill brings you close to believing
it – but not quite. This deadfall finish is really a conventional echo
of the professional toughies, 'realistic' about violence, who have
been giving us the jitters for some time. Most of the other symptoms
in the syndrome are manifest somewhere or other in the book.
Human characteristics tend to be referred back to animals and
objects. As with Ted Hughes, it takes a visit to the zoo, the game
reserve, or an imaginary dive below the sod before the idea of
*personality* gets any showing at all. The people themselves are mostly
clichés disguised in heroic trappings. A stable vacated by a horse
('Gone') offers more character than the smithy still occupied by the
smith ('The Forge'). This latter poem, surely fated to be an anthology piece for the generations to come, can usefully be quoted
in full:

All I know is a door into the dark.
Outside, old axles and iron hoops rusting;
Inside, the hammered anvil's short-pitched ring,
The unpredictable fantail of sparks
Or hiss when a new shoe toughens in water.
The anvil must be somewhere in the centre,
Horned as a unicorn, at one end square,
Set there immoveable: an altar
Where he expends himself in shape and music.

Sometimes, leather-aproned, hairs in his nose,
He leans out on the jamb, recalls a clatter
Of hoofs where traffic is flashing in rows;
Then grunts and goes in, with a slam and flick
To beat real iron out, to work the bellows.

The numbered questions in the back of the school anthology are obvious. What is the attitude of the smith to modern civilization? Is it the same as the poet's attitude? And (for advanced students) would you consider the Leavisite views on the organic relationship of work to life relevant? But it should also be obvious that the interest of the poem drops considerably when the human being replaces the object at stage centre. Those hairs in his nose don't do much to establish him, except as a character actor sent down at an hour's notice from Central Casting. If he were more real, his attitudes towards mechanized culture might not fall so pat. Get through that doorway in the dark and you might find him beating out hubcaps or balancing the wire wheels on a DB6 – both jobs which can be done with as much love as bending your millionth horseshoe. There is no conflict here: there is just a received opinion expressed in hints and cleverly overblown in unexpected places – that altar, and the unicorn's horn, which ought to be a rhino's only that's too easy. On the page the refined poem has its attractive spareness: it's the implication, the area of suggestion, that worries the reader through the ordinariness of its assumptions about culture. Self-employed artisans are usually tough enough to see reality straight: given the chance, the leather-aproned subject might well remind Mr. Heaney that there ain't no pity in the city.

Things live; animals almost live; humans live scarcely at all. The inverse progression holds disturbingly true in well-known efforts like the poem about the frozen pump, 'Rite of Spring'.

That sent the pump up in flame.
It cooled, we lifted her latch,
Her entrance was wet, and she came.

It's a roundabout way for passion to get into print. The obverse poems to this are 'Mother', in which the lady ends up wanting to be like the pump, and 'The Wife's Tale', a brilliantly tactile poem in which you touch everything – cloth, stubble, grass, bread, seed and china cups – except flesh.

Mr. Heaney's 'A Lough Neagh Sequence' forms an important section of the book and could well be pointed to if one were asked to isolate a thematic area absolutely his.

> They're busy in a high boat
> That stalks towards Antrim, the power cut.
> The line's a filament of smut
>
> Drawn hand over fist
> Where every three yards a hook's missed
> Or taken (and the smut thickens, wrist-
>
> Thick, a flail
> Lashed into the barrel
> With one swing). Each eel
>
> Comes aboard to this welcome:
> The hook left in gill or gum,
> It's slapped into the barrel numb
>
> But knits itself, four-ply,
> With the furling, slippy
> Haul, a knot of back and pewter belly
>
> That stays continuously one
> For each catch they fling in
> Is sucked home like lubrication.

Evocation could go no further: the eels ('hatched fears') are practically in your lap. Similarly in poems like 'Bann Clay' and 'Bogland' his grating line, shudderingly switched back and forth like teeth ground in a nightmare, finds endless technical equivalents for the subject described: he really is astonishingly capable. And in 'Bogland' there is an indication that he can do something even more difficult – state the open statement, make the gesture that enlivens life.

> They've taken the skeleton
> Of the Great Irish Elk
> Out of the peat, set it up
> An astounding crate full of air.

The spirits lift to the flash of wit. There ought to be more of it. Nobody in his right mind would deny that Mr. Heaney's is one of

the outstanding talents on the scene, or want that talent to settle
in its ways too early.

(1969)

# 14

## The Wheeze Incarnadined

The evening is probably not far off when Steed will recite verses
through the dressing-room door to Tara King as she dons her
fighting suit for a new adventure: when he does, George MacBeth's
*The Night of Stones* could be his text. 'The Avengers' is fancy telly
and this stuff is fancy poetry, stylelessly stylish, unoriginally new,
each tuneless phrase poised and punctuated so that it *must* mean
more than it seems to do. The unwritten guarantee which comes
with 'Avengers' drama assures the viewer that nothing, no event,
image or show of character, will force itself upon the memory –
only a general air of chic will remain. With the blood-stone-light-
bone poetry here under consideration, the reader is assured that
the words will stay safely on the page. Though the most appalling
scenes of carnage and nuclear holocaust are visited, it is only for
the run of the book; usually only for the length of the page. Atomic
bombs go off with soporific regularity, scorching the *stone* with
*light* and playing hell with the *blood*, not to mention the *bone*. But
these atomic bombs are Material for Poetry, and the killed are
Material for Poetry too – their deadness is thematically handier
than their lost aliveness. As in grand guignol, the only genuine
casualties – once breathing, now rigid – are the words themselves.

> Old, asleep,
> Washing slow hands in water, she was there,
> Grey-haired and guilty, waiting for their thumbs
> To choke her blood and stone. . . .
> Like a dog
> Blood ran between them with its nose to the ground
> Sniffing for a scent. . . .

> Somewhere a faucet dripped
> Water, blood, water on stone. Inside her brain
> The blood beat back.
> Fire was the sign of blood. . . .
> So he drove on,
> Wading in blood. . . .

(In this last piece one assumes that the car has a very long pedal travel, thus inducing a wading sensation when changing gears.)

In the longish poem, 'Driving West', which opens the book, the word *blood* occurs eighteen times, although to some extent monotony is avoided by supplying it in a variety of colours and textures – red, black, soupy, oily, watery and with its nose to the ground. In the book overall the word receives several more mentions than any of *flame*, *silk*, *ice* and the ever-popular *groin*, and towards the end manages to race away even from its stable-mates *bone*, *stone* and *light* to amass a total of twenty-five mentions – surely a record for a single substantive at the distance.

Suspended in this non-evocative vocabulary float inert namings of gadgets and gimmicks, mostly leftover properties from low-budget SF serials like *Captain Video*: hypodermics, electric coils and inevitably the dread laser.

> O, my dear one, tempered
> by the beam of the laser, torn
> by the stone body of the gorgon, the man-child
> *lighten my darkness, I*
> *need you now*

None of the *O.E.D.* definitions of *tempered* accords with the actual properties of a *laser*, but no matter: prop gimmicks cost money and must be put to a variety of uses, as when Captain Video employed his personal oscilloscope (the Optic Inscillometer) to detect the political affiliations of the invaders from the Red planet Mongo. The pun count for the book is low, but the instances are revealing. This one is about a German dog.

> his
> jaw swivels, and:
> schnapps!

*Schnapps*, you see, because the dog is German; and his jaw *snaps*; and *Schnapps* is a German drink. One's response to such felicities sharpens at a second reading, causing, in the fit reader, a tendency to drum the heels on the floor. Nevertheless, this sequence of mini-poems about dogs (called 'At Cruft's') is the best thing in the book: 'characteristic' pix of your favourite pets, taken with one of those cameras which develops the film instantly and gives you a slightly wet but reasonable sharp impression of what the outside of things looks like.

There are a few trick poems included, based on 'vowel analysis' and 'numerical analysis' of other people's work: a dangerous game for this poet, since a blood-stone-light-bone analysis of his own poems would uncover the precisely recurring clotted patterns of a radar screen sweeping a herd of tortoise. A poem about Malta which conflates imagery of the two great sieges (1565 and 1940) seems to contain a moment of genuine memory:

> With paired wings, three remain
> Holding the gold walls. . . .

These are Faith, Hope and Charity, the three Gladiators (they were biplanes, hence the 'paired wings') which defended the island at one desperate period. The poet's emotions are at least temporarily involved here, so the verse comes to life for a while: a writer so tough about Death, though, should have avoided giving the planes' pilots

> clean, grey eyes
> Behind the wings, mounting in honour

Biggles, Ginger and Algy fly again, as technical advisers to *Malta Story*.

The combination of recondite information and predictable emotion is characteristic – a narrow intensity of curiosity shared by stereo fiends and those people who wear opera capes and green eyeshadow and who can name you the directors of every Bette Davis movie if you give them half a chance. To draw upon the flat characters, contrived situations and ramshackle properties of B-pictures, Sam Katzman serials and comic strips is the only way to

talk about poetry of this type. It is media poetry. It has a great air
of living and struggling in the true world of Hitler, Himmler,
Stalin and Beria, but a close look reveals that it has been trans-
formed by fright-wigs and plastic incisors into the process-shot
world of Bela Lugosi, Boris Karloff and J. Carroll Naish, each lit
uncannily among the zapping electric coils. Like horror films, this
kind of poetry is the art with which frivolous people fulfil their
seriousness quota. 'I was terrified', said the old lady emerging from
*Psycho.* 'It was wonderful.' And in all that spookery ('all that' is
one of this poet's favourite soggy specificities), not a single haunting
phrase.

(1968)

## PART THREE

# Carry that Weight

# 15

## Roy Fuller's Magisterial Thumb

In the fourth of his very fine collection of Oxford poetry lectures, entitled *Owls and Artificers*, Roy Fuller, praising Wallace Stevens, at one point writes:

I wouldn't want to leave this aspect of Stevens without saying that he himself was perfectly aware of the objections to his existence as the existence of a poet which many of you have no doubt been silently raising. Mentioning his forthcoming collection of poems, *Auroras of Autumn*, in a letter of 1949 he said: 'I don't know how the book will be regarded,' adding: 'It is not easy to experience much in the rather routine life that I lead. While one is never sure that it makes much difference, one is equally never sure that it doesn't.'

Of course, Stevens was not speaking here of his avoidance of a superficial Bohemianism (if that adjective is ever really needed to qualify that substantive).

One is certain that Mr. Fuller can think of cases, in the past if not in the present, when the substantive needs to be left not only unqualified but untainted. One is equally certain that for his current purposes Mr. Fuller prefers not to try to think of them. As well as providing a great deal of first-rate criticism and professional commentary, he is conducting a polemic – a polemic in which the dedicated balancing of art and life, the long-term professionalism in a poet like Stevens, is to be emphasized to the extinction of any enthusiastic conception of the poetic whatsoever. A director of the Woolwich Equitable Building Society salutes the memory of a vice-president of the Hartford Accident and Indemnity Company: the tone is level, the words select, the hand dry-palmed.

In asides, in paragraphs, and sometimes in whole pages, this polemic is kept up throughout the lectures, on the assumption that a substantial part of the audience is in the grip of error. The error is unreasoning, indiscriminate enthusiasm (if those adjectives are ever really needed to qualify that substantive), and for the purposes of this polemic (or perhaps because Mr. Fuller really thinks so) it is assumed to be not only a common affliction of the immediately post-pubescent age group at all times, but uniquely prevalent at *this* time, among all age groups.

The enthusiasm may have any or all of the following phenomena – culled from the book's index – for objects: BEATLES, THE; BOND, JAMES; CREELEY, ROBERT; GINSBERG, ALLEN; HORNSEY COLLEGE OF ART; LIVERPOOL POETS, THE; MAOISM; OLSON, CHARLES; PATTEN, BRIAN; STOCKHAUSEN, KARLHEINZ; YEVTUSHENKO, YEVGENY. The enthusiasm distorts and corrodes what is genuine, both sets trends and is swayed by them, and is a prey to fashion at the very moment of plundering the serious. It is a good argument to make and always has been: it can even be said that Mr. Fuller is correct in judging that it is a particularly necessary argument to make now. What might be worth considering, however, is whether Mr. Fuller has not done too thorough a job of ignoring the admittedly simplistic political assumptions on which this enthusiasm – among the young, at any rate – is largely based. By his own account (and here reference is made to an autobiographical note he contributed to the anthology *The Poetry of War 1939–45*) it took a good deal of hard experience before Mr. Fuller substituted reality for illusion in his own mind.

Among the vast majority of the young people who harbour them, the current illusions about the dysfunctionality of traditional art (and the functionality of a projected, revolutionary art) are part and parcel of a political view that is very generous: it can be argued that it is self-defeating, but scarcely argued that it is entirely unprincipled, and never argued that it is unprovoked. Like many of his generation of illuminati – and several of them are in Oxford on a permanent basis – Mr. Fuller has difficulty in realizing that in young eyes the social order is likely to go on needing justification in great detail. In supplying such a justification, even for the impregnable verities of artistic discipline and rigorous education, the merest hint of the tones of the Warden of All Souls is apt to prove ruinous.

The first lecture is called 'Philistines and Jacobins' and draws deeply on propositions first put forward by Matthew Arnold, a previous occupant of the Oxford chair of poetry. Arnold's anguish at the prospect of a victory for prosperous Philistinism is by no means out of date. But now the Philistinism has some added features. First, the young who rebel against it are likely to produce a separate Philistinism on their own account. Second, the prosperity, if prosperity it be, has not spread so far as to put the intellectual out of his misery – he might earn his living as an intellectual, but only through a nominal, media-desensitized exercise of his function. This second point is obviously broadly true. The first, however, immediately needs the qualification that it is not mere 'affluence' that the young are in rebellion against. In supposing their dis-affection to be based on only that, Mr. Fuller sets the terms for his sub-argument on this topic which extends throughout the book. The penalty paid is to strike at the outset the tones not of analysis but of obfuscation:

Even the offspring of the intelligentsia revolt, by way of dropping out from education, rash erotic alliances, crumminess of appearance, and so forth, perhaps because they see their parents more and more obsessed by the gadgets of affluence and less and less convinced that anything can be done by way of principle and belief.

And perhaps because they see their parents becoming more and more prone to abandoning, not only the conviction that anything can be done by way of principle and belief, but principle and belief as such. Be that as it may, the sub-argument is allowed to rest temporarily at this preliminary point, because Mr. Fuller wants to get on to another aspect of contemporary Philistinism – its ability to infect the adult intelligentsia itself.

Not only does kitsch flourish in parallel to culture, it increasingly is promoted – by the very people who ought to know better – as a substitute for culture. On this point he has some incisive things to say. Many of them have been said before (notably by Dwight Macdonald in *Against the American Grain*) but they bear being said again. It turns out, though, that most of the kitsch in question is provided by the young, who are promptly dragged back into the argument and treated as the culprits of whom the trendily treason-able adult clerks are merely the accomplices. Here, surely, is a clear case of the real argument being simplified, and in being simplified falsified, by a reflex invocation of the sub-argument. It is barely considered (and then only through a quick suggestion that modern poetry gave in too quickly to its status as a minority art) that poetry had entered a crisis of standards well before any youth rebellion had ever been heard of. Admirers of the Beatles are soundly trounced, but with scarcely a hint that the high musical tradition had at some time previous got itself into a crisis of acceptance.

Obviously these are large problems and it is a work of professional application – which is in itself one of the problems – to understand them. Nobody could mind if they had been sketched in and left unsolved. The trouble here is that Mr. Fuller, by an action more automatic than conscious, has had a shot at solving them. He has managed to propose that it is the audience which has instigated these crises of standards, of acceptance, of appreciation: you would have needed keen ears at this lecture to find out that modern creativity in its most intense forms had ever put itself beyond reach of amateur comprehension and caused critical, pedagogical, and sociological problems by doing so. The steady message of Mr. Fuller's book is that the true line of descent in modern art is the line of unenthusiastic, fully conscious clarity of aim. This squares well with Mr. Fuller's own production. It squares well also with the tendency of metropolitan (but not necessarily academic) criticism of poetry over the past decade – obviously it is the line of modest clarity which is being reasserted in the present and rediscovered, when it is there to be rediscovered, in the past. But when you are rebuilding comprehensible, universally applicable standards of meaning, it may be polemically justified, but it cannot be justified in fact, to talk as if those standards had been there all along.

The second lecture, '"Woodbine Willie" Lives!', is an acute exploration of sentimentality in verse. Reactionary emotion, anti-scientific feeling and deficiency of realism are held to be sentimentality's characteristics. One can think of more, but in the personal battle of Mr. Fuller's generation against the successive prevailing fashions these were clearly the characteristics that mattered. He asserts that sentimentality was latent in the ideas that dominated 1930s poetry and surfaced when those ideas lost their dominance, somewhere around the end of the war. No surprise, then, that Dylan Thomas began to be valued for what was worst in him. And no surprise either that the Movement did not stop the rot: 'The clear aims, logical thought, modest subject matter of the Larkins and the Thwaitses (*sic*) became superannuated . . . once more a poetry marked by sentimentality was let in.' Mr. Fuller then proceeds to do an abrupt razor-job on Brian Patten. In the face of the successful emergence of the Liverpudlians, is it not clear that *Practical Criticism* was written largely in vain?

But one can welcome the accuracy and force of Mr. Fuller's attack on all this trendy sludge without necessarily accepting his interpretation of modern literary history in general. To show that issues have now become clear, is it really desirable to pretend that they were always clear? 'As the 'forties succeeded the 'thirties, so the 'sixties succeeded the 'fifties', Mr. Fuller states. But this is to speak with a neatness of which only the old guard who have fought their way through to the 1970s are capable.

The propensity of modern art to run away with itself – to be unclear in aim, to be illogical in thought, and to be the reverse of modest in subject matter – was well established in the 1920s and could be defensibly regarded as central to the modern achievement. Indeed the question of the relationship of intellect to the creative imagination (and particularly whether that relationship was a *governing* one) was raised by modern art to the status of a problem. Mr. Fuller reduces it again to a mere difficulty – the difficulty being that corrupt taste among the consumers feeds back to vitiate the scrupulousness of the creators. You wouldn't get all this high-flown tat if the yokels weren't so easily impressed.

'An Artifice of Versification' is the third lecture and pretty much of a classic: it is in work like this that *Owls and Artificers* transcends even the best parts of *The Crowning Privilege*. The topic is syllabic verse. Marianne Moore and Elizabeth Daryush are the two main subject poets. All the traps of syllabics are clearly seen (including the paradoxical tendency of the freedom from regular stress to induce a greater complexity of diction) and yet finally the approval comes, especially for Miss Moore's achievement, by which Mr. Fuller is manifestly enchanted. 'It is hardly necessary for me to add', he adds, 'that it is syllabic verse's extreme formal element that above all else gives one confidence in its validity.'

But this conclusion is not wholly satisfactory even when tested by the lecture's own terms. He has been fairly careful to distinguish, in Miss Moore's work, between the form that is merely intellected and the form which is felt. But simultaneously he has been very careful to distinguish between the syllabics he approves and those, sanctioned by Olson and Williams, which have come to nothing and are in no way the product of skill. Isn't it the formlessness of these last that leads Mr. Fuller to endorse the 'extreme formal element', and allow the 'validity' of the syllabics employed by Moore, Daryush and Auden? Because if it is, the tendency of this lecture to be suspicious of coldly intellected form has been artificially checked. The lecture is really trying to say that its 'extreme formal element' can't possibly be the reason why we should have confidence in the validity of syllabic verse. But the lecturer, thinking suddenly and uncomfortably of his archetypal shaggy opponent, almost by instinct steps on the brake. The theme is once again altered ihto a polemical weapon. It is only half allowed throughout the lecture, and completely disallowed at its end, that a preoccupation with form can be self-defeating – that under pressure of expression the notion of formal rules must be forced to give way to the notion of formal characteristics, these being discernible only *ex post facto*. And it is probable that Mr. Fuller takes this stance because he is all too aware of what has happened when, under the pressure of no expression worth speaking of except an advanced case of *scribendi cacoethes* (Dr. Johnson's term, borrowed from Juvenal, for the unfortunate desire to write), formal rules have given way to sludge.

The fourth lecture, 'Both Pie and Custard', is the one on Wallace Stevens mentioned above. Critically, it is the only lecture in the course which is expansive rather than proscriptive, and excitement accrues as a consequence. One can imagine hirsute undergrads translating themselves at a rate of knots from the Sheldonian to the Bod in order to get acquainted with more than the few lines quoted of 'The Comedian as the Letter C' and 'Notes Toward a Supreme Fiction'. One subsidiary virtue in Mr. Fuller's excellent trans-

mission of Stevens's specific quality is a realization that the in-
auguration of the Modern had implications beyond those the lecturer has elsewhere allowed:

On the purely literary side we can see now that in the poems of *Har-
monium* Stevens was liberated from explicit meaning, from the common-
places of the tradition of his youth, through his reading of the French
symbolists, a process similar to that undergone by T. S. Eliot.... 
Though a good deal of Stevens is not really as difficult as was once – as,
indeed, is often still – thought, the 'nonsense' side of the modern movement in verse – the arbitrary symbols, the private references, the unex-
plained personae and fragmentary plots – persisted with him, in fact,
until the end.... But, of course, if this were all there were to him he
would merely share a place with a score of others. As it is, the conviction
grows that he must be placed with the two or three greatest English-
speaking poets of the twentieth century.

Making due allowance for the nonsense side, that must still
leave quite a lot of inexplicit meaning at the centre of Stevens's
achievement. This, however, is a floodgate of argument that Mr.
Fuller does not propose to open. Instead he pushes the line that
Stevens's attention to the details of his everyday office job held him
comfortably close to reality. One says 'pushes the line' because it
plainly *is* a line, a fact made further evident by this peculiar
passage:

I wonder whether it is too fanciful to suggest that Stevens's long lifetime
of secular sensitivity to reality was sustained by his day to day absorption
in business affairs. Certainly the relations between reality and poetry to
be found everywhere in his work are paralleled by the relations of his
office and his evening pursuits, and I don't think the analogy necessarily
glib or superficial. Many artists are, through the very success of their art,
led away from the tensions and sources that brought it into being. And
absorbed in the world of art they can become a prey to idealistic notions
that their earlier years in the realer world would simply never have
entertained. Spot illustrations are apt to be crude but the cases of D. H.
Lawrence and T. S. Eliot spring to mind. It would be absurd to say that
when the former left the Midlands, and the latter Lloyds Bank, decline
set in, but it can hardly be denied that what is unsatisfactory in the later
careers of both writers stems from a slackening of their hold on reality
and the importation into their work of ideas that we can't help but feel
to be false or at the least inappropriate.

Does this mean that in the case of Eliot we missed getting a major poem called, say, *Four Overdrafts*? What we actually did get, for better or for worse, was an apprehension of a reality which Eliot considered to extend, both in time and space, well beyond the confines of the daily task. Is there anything 'unsatisfactory' about *Four Quartets* that is not also part and parcel of it, central to it? Surely that poem is a salient case of a modern work in which what is clear and what is not clear, what is rigorously perceived and what is gropingly envisioned, cannot easily be divided up? And by now it has become apparent that in his determination to argue for an unpretentious discipline of vocation, for a harmony of art and life, Mr. Fuller has inadvertently let in a mild variety of Philistinism on his own account. He has been redrawing the past to make it look more controllable than it was, and perhaps inadvertently giving the illusion that the modern movement in art, and beyond that the modern age in politics, offered few problems that force of character could not have dealt with. The magnetic attraction of the sub-argument has diverted the theme towards the simplistic. Short back and sides, a good steady job, and concoct your supreme fictions in the evenings: a straight-arrow formula if ever there was one.

'The Filthy Aunt and the Anonymous Seabird', the fifth lecture, faces the problem of difficulty in verse front on: of all these lectures it does the best job of keeping a balance between the theme and the sub-argument. Poets have a right to their difficulty, so long as it is genuine – if this means that poetry is for the few, then so much for the many. There is no refuting this. The question of what difficulty is genuine and what is not is the eye of the storm in modern criticism: Mr. Fuller tends to peg genuineness to accuracy of perception, but he leaves room for what is inexplicable – for what is not merely condensed but transmuted.

This, however, does not mean that anybody will be allowed to create poetry by accident. The fashionable highbrow is foolish (the sub-argument again) to expect, in the field of the pop lyric, any kind of 'new start' for simple, resonant poetry. The reason, apparently, is that 'the great simple poets' of the far past were formidably intelligent – pop lyricists, of course, not being that. It would be interesting to know what Mr. Fuller thinks might happen if they were. It's a possibility that he dismisses too quickly. Real poetry retreats to the enclave. Fake poetry sweeps the new mass poetry market off its feet. No bridge-building, it appears, is feasible.

Such a stance allows for very direct, persuasive argument, but it denies the possibility (and it could be admitted that most of the evidence to date denies the possibility just as vehemently) that some of these guitar-plunking ragamuffins might, if they have something to express, develop disciplines to express it. In Mr. Fuller's view the apostolic succession goes on within the enclave. Outside the enclave it seems to be a toss-up between the two things that can happen: real talent is blasted in the bud, and no-talent is a raging success.

The last lecture, 'How to Stuff Owls', is a study of bad verse vastly entertaining in its examples (generously, some of his own mistakes are included) and, within certain limits, analytically exact. Once again the anatomizing of sentimentality; once again the identification of faulty or diffident technique as a sign of forced feeling. The theme is carried through impeccably and the lecture will stand as an exemplary treatment of the subject. But as well as completing the course's major argument about the nature of the art, this lecture also brings in the sub-argument for its final airing:

One thing a new anthologist would want to make clear – *The Stuffed Owl* demonstrates it unconsciously – is how from time to time in English poetry a school of poets arises which despises the intellect and elevates the feelings. The Della Cruscans at the end of the eighteenth century, the Spasmodics in the middle of the nineteenth – and in our own day the New Apocalyptics of the 'forties and that beat or underground movement unfortunately still with us: all these produced an amount of dangerous bad verse.

So finally it comes down to the balance kept between intellect and feeling – good hard news for the undergraduate audience to be supplied with, we may be sure. Crummy of appearance and prone to rash erotic alliances, current youth is anti-intellectual as well.

To a large extent it obviously is, and needs such a doggedly sustained polemic as *Owls and Artificers* to shake it up. But to the witlessly rebellious present, just how valuable, how reliable a picture of the artistic past, of the *story* of art, does this book supply? The answer needs careful framing.

Mr. Fuller will not admit relativism into the discussion of artistic merit, and in that he is right. Neither will he admit eclecticism, and he is right in that too. But when such commendable rigour becomes rigid, it does not become over-rigorous – it becomes not rigorous enough. It is relativistic, and therefore something less than rigorous, to promote the notion that artistic excellence is of necessity connected to a sane, balanced and verifiable view of the real. Such a notion may come in handy for squashing Beatles, but it can't make much of, say, Yeats.

When talent occurs within an unstructured intellect, the evidence suggests that it may well go on to structure that intellect along its own lines. When such a process takes place it is doubtful whether we can relate intellect to the creative imagination in any meaningful way at all. Logically it might be said that there has to be a separation in order for there to be a connection, but equally it can be argued that we are dealing with a unity. Statements about the provenance of creativity in given groups of people should consequently not be proscriptive. It is probable that burgeoning artists in all fields will go on acquiring as much education as they need. To say that they have always done so in the past is of course tautologous – if they had not, they would not have come to our attention.

And here is where the Beatles come back in, still defiantly crawling after the magisterial thumb is lifted. It is not relativism and it is not eclecticism to enjoy the best of their songs – it is merely pluralism. Mr. Fuller is afraid that the achievement in the song of Schubert, Brahms, Duparc, Debussy, Strauss, Rachmaninov and Poulenc is threatened by the recognition accorded to four trogs who crawled out of a cave. It is not made clear whether this is a sociological argument or an aesthetic one. If it is a sociological one, it can be countered by pointing out that for those who know those names there is no threat, and as for those who do not know those names, it is hardly fair to take the Beatles away from them too. If it is an aesthetic one, we should like to know by what criteria the Beatles' songs are so confidently dismissed from the same plane of achievement as Rachmaninov's. Certainly it is a pity that their

rudimentary formal training set limits to their development and
that trendy pressures diverted them towards the bogus. But it is a
greater pity still that young men with all the formal training in the
world go utterly to pieces. While Mr. Fuller hunts bugs, the house
burns down.

The Beatles are only one case in which Mr. Fuller has under-
estimated the generation he is attempting to instruct. He has very
sensitively and very correctly detected the intellectual vacuum, but
he has made the error of assuming that no art can breathe inside it.
But it is there, both actually and potentially: it presents difficulties
with which only an open mind can grapple.

The real problem is to supply it with a criticism which can deal
with what is promising in it without complying with what is retrogressive, virulent or inane. Total dismissal is too neat. For what it
deals with, *Owls and Artificers* is a penetrating work. For what it
fails to deal with it is more symptomatic than diagnostic – but still
personal, admirable and, finally, liberal in a way that the generation
it castigates will live to respect.

(1971)

# 16

## Love, Help and the Performing Self

There's a monster loose, and its name is English Studies. Will the
professor and his beautiful daughter manage to immobilize the
beast before it knocks over New York?

English Studies cannot do what it most often does to literary works and
pretend that these works still belong unto themselves or to English
literature. They belong, all marked up, to English studies.

This key passage occurs early in the second section of Richard
Poirier's *The Performing Self* – the section which is the book's real
beginning. It sets the tone for a spectacular razor-job on American
pedagogy: PhD-mills, symbol-mongering, the lot. This section may

be read with great profit. Like Edmund Wilson assessing the out-
pourings of the MLA, Mr. Poirier is able to point with certainty to
various ways in which culture can't be transmitted. What's worrying
in his case, though, is the conclusion which is made to emerge about
how culture *can* be transmitted. Apparently it can be done by
paying the appropriate attention to the Performing Self.

English studies cannot be the body of English literature but it can be at
one with its spirit; of struggling, of wrestling with words and meaning.
Otherwise English studies may go one of two ways; it can shrink, in a
manner possibly as invigorating as that which accompanied the retrench-
ment of Classics departments; or it can become distended by claims to a
relevance merely topical. Alternatively, it can take a positive new step.
It can further develop ways of treating *all* writing and *all* reading as
analogous acts, as simultaneously developing performances, some of
which will deaden, some of which will quicken us.

It's to be the quick and the dead, then. For the rest of the book,
which is subtitled 'Compositions and Decompositions in the
Languages of Contemporary Life', Mr. Poirier goes on to talk about
the Beatles and to anatomize the non-comprehension extended to
the young by the entrenched culturalists. Here he is very much on
the side of the angels: as he has revealed before in other writings,
his appreciation of rock music is passionate, non-trendy and unashamed without being complacent. He is correct in mounting an
attack against a hierarchy of creative categories. But it is remarkable
how he manages to be almost as dull about these new Performances
as the uptight old guard are dull about Eng Lit. Could it be that
it was not English Studies, but English Literature itself that failed
him, loosing a great deal of hungry love to go searching for an
object?

The answer is a qualified Yes, and lies in the first section of the
book – a section which Mr. Poirier thinks outlines what has been
happening to literature, but which in fact outlines what has been
happening to his appreciation of it. Mr. Poirier is intelligent enough
to realize what rampant academicism has done to the way we
'approach' literature – we approach it over fields of boredom,
nattered at from all sides. But somehow he seems to have forgotten
that he is in on the act, that as well as being Richard Poirier, Sixth

Beatle, he is also Richard Poirier, Professor of English and Chairman of the Federated Departments of English at Rutgers University, contributor to *Harvard Studies in English* and author of *The Comic Sense of Henry James: A Study of the Early Novels* and *A World Elsewhere: The Place of Style in American Literature*. One of his main subjects, and very rightly, is the place of such 'studies' in the nearest garbage bin. But old habits die hard, and we regretfully get the sense that it is the literature which has been discarded, while the attitudes which helped make it a burden have been retained – especially that old itch to explicate.

Mr. Poirier's first section starts well:

Given the now monumental amount of interpretation lavished on the academically entrenched works of modern literature, it has largely escaped notice that most of these works are self-analytical to a degree that might have warned against further efforts in the same direction.

Just because metropolitan men of letters have been trying to get that news over to academics for decades is no reason to disparage Mr. Poirier for his tardiness in cottoning on: and anyway, it was perhaps to his advantage that these facts largely escaped notice until he had completed his work on Henry James's comic sense and tracked down Style's place in American Literature. But Mr. Poirier doesn't go on to draw the further conclusion that the contemporary literature that really matters might itself be escaping attention through failing to provide academicism with its required stimuli. The further conclusion he does draw is that the contemporary literature that matters is the stuff which concerns itself with parodying all the symbolisms and structures that academicism previously found, or claimed to find, in the old masters. Pynchon, Barth, Borges and Mailer's (apparently much-misunderstood) *An American Dream* – those are the works to contend with. They are works that in some way have *got literature's number*: they reassure you, through parody and conscious excess, that all those formidable-looking old structures the academics used to burble on about were never that serious in the first place.

As the previous chapter suggests, John Barth seems to me a writer of evident genius; I wrote a long and enthusiastic review of *Giles Goat-Boy* when it came out, and I'd take none of it back now. Even while writing the review, however, I was conscious of forgetting what it had been like at certain moments to read the book, what a confining, prolonged, and even exasperating experience it had sometimes been. Now and again I'd been bored and disengaged, and if I hadn't promised to review it I might not have finished it at all. To say this isn't really to disparage Barth or his achievement, surely not to anyone sufficiently honest about his own experience of 'great' books. How many would ever have finished *Moby Dick* – read all of it, I mean – or *Ulysses*, not to mention *Paradise Lost* or other monsters of that kind, if it weren't for school assignments, the academic equivalent of being asked to write a review?

Now it's perfectly possible that the majority of intelligent readers are bored and disengaged when reading parts of *Ulysses* or *Paradise Lost*, and the reader who has not gone to sleep over some parts of *Moby Dick* is not worth listening to when he's awake. But that isn't the same as saying that you wouldn't have finished those books if you hadn't been paid to. To anyone sufficiently honest about his own experience of these great (no inverted commas) books, doesn't that experience run roughly thus: that you hit passages in them which give you the excuse to put them down for a while and look around you at life before getting back into them? And that this process of assimilating large and complex works of art into your own mentality at the proper time *and at a decent rate* is interfered with, not by anything in the works themselves, but by exactly that academic mill which Mr. Poirier is eager to discredit?

Mr. Poirier can't get the right conclusions from his own discoveries, and to say this really is to disparage his achievement. It's the academic mill that *stops* you finishing great books, by making you read them faster than they can be read, or by driving you to the commentaries and explications. But Mr. Poirier doesn't draw the appropriate conclusions about the state pedagogy has got itself into. He draws tendentious conclusions about the state literature was supposedly in all along. He decides that it is useless to try to recover the capital works of the past by re-creating their historical context; and indeed it is true that if their historical context was the only thing defining them, they would be irrecoverable. But they are alive, and worth having, in themselves – which is the reason why scholarship and criticism in the best sense of those activities have always gone on, and will go on even if their thick, fervent and worthless imitators bring pedagogy to ruin. It is really a bit much that Mr. Poirier, who has been engaged in these activities most of his life, should now want to demote literature along with the parasitism which has accrued to it. Charitably, though, it should be said that Mr. Poirier could scarcely have meant his argument to come out sounding like this: it sounds like this only because he is trying to make a point at the top of his voice. Teaching has gone wrong because its explanatory functions have hypertrophied, but in wanting teaching reformed he has forgotten that there are irreducible explanatory functions which teaching must retain, or else the autodidact will be left prey to the supreme academicism – his own.

This first section of the book would not be so bad if Mr. Poirier did not presume to find the germ of his 'decreative' aesthetic in Eliot and Joyce. The idea starts well enough:

The literary organizations they adumbrate only to mimic, the schematizations they propose only to show the irrelevance of them to actualities of experience – these have been extracted by commentators from the contexts that erode them and have been imposed back on the material in the form of designs or meanings.

A good, if painfully obvious, point to make. And Mr. Poirier is adequate at showing that the main force of Eliot's criticism was not to reinforce historicism but to undermine it, and so reintroduce the idea of the permanent contemporaneity of past works. He forgets to add, though, that Eliot in a good deal of his creative work (and Joyce in nearly all his creative work) gave academicism the courage to expand – that they invited the emergence of the monster which eventually flopped crushingly on top of them.

It is *necessarily* an historical contention that there were certain kinds of prestige Eliot was eager to acquire. And some of the strains in Eliot which Mr. Poirier considers parodistic pure and simple were in fact more ambitious than that – it is an elementary logical mistake to assume that artistry reduces forms to structures or themes to material, or the artist to a tactician. The academic industry which has grown up out of Eliot and Joyce has now come to a crisis in which the qualities of those writers can no longer be transmitted. But that does not mean that once the industry collapses their difficulties will be swept away or resolved into a simplistic formula. Eliot, for example, really is both personal and impersonal; his 'schematizations' really are relevant to the actualities of experience; and these things are true even though – especially because – the wrong people have been saying so. Mr. Poirier is properly scornful about easy notions of the impersonal artist. But this does not stop Eliot being, at a profound level, the impersonal artist.

Eliot exists for understanding at an impossible remove, perhaps, from the kind of mind, the liberal orthodox, for whom thinking and even suffering consists in the abrasions of one abstraction on another. But anyone of genuinely radical sentiment can find in him an exercise of intelligence and spirit for which to be humanly proud and grateful.

We can imagine what Eliot would have said about 'genuinely radical sentiment' and 'exercise of intelligence': thanks, but no thanks. In the production and confident employment of terms like those, Eliot might have isolated one of the elements to be incorporated in his own definition of liberal orthodoxy.

Mr. Poirier's liberal orthodoxy has turned against itself, but has not changed its character. The most vivid part of his book, once the 'de-creative' aesthetic has been established and life has been breathed into the notion of the Performing Self, is about rock music. Unfortunately Mr. Poirier has not got the patience to be a true pluralist. It is a work of patience, of taking pains, to attack categories while insisting on values, and there is no valid way of speeding the job up: the hasty man tries to get it done by hitching himself to the bandwagon of history. The old guard incorporates categories into values: *Lieder* are good because they are *Lieder*, whereas a Beatles song is just a song. The too-hasty pluralist ditches values along with categories, and usually finds himself being historicist in the pejorative sense: so-and-so's songs are good because they express this, that and the other about being young today. In spite of his engaging enthusiasm for it, Mr. Poirier shows no evidence of being able to criticize rock – he merely approves of it, and lavishes on it the explicatory attention he has withdrawn from literature. It largely escapes his notice that most of these works are self-analytical to a degree that might have warned against further efforts in the same direction. His expository prose is numbingly recognizable.

The audience in Albert Hall [*sic*] – the same as 'the lovely audience' in the first song [of *Sgt. Pepper*] whom the Beatles would like to 'take home' with them? – are only so many holes: unfilled and therefore unfertile holes, holes of decomposition, gathered together but separate and therefore countable, inarticulately alone, the epitome of so many 'assholes'. Is this merely a bit of visionary ghoulishness, something seen on a 'trip'? No. . . .

Isn't this merely the kind of crumb-dumb/clever prose that generations of students have been turning out about *Ash Wednesday* when they should have been down in the garage doing something more useful, such as building hot-rods or actually reading *Ash Wednesday*? And does anyone who admires the Beatles' music really think that they, even when adulation had driven them almost to distraction, ever thought of their audience with quite that contempt? The Beatles have found a rhyme by filling the Albert Hall with pot-holes: a good joke that can't be soured except by the ponderous attention Mr. Poirier extends to it. And where is all that mistrust of 'relevance' now? What happened to all that talk about extracting structures and schemes and reimposing them?

Ringo, helped by the other Beatles, will, as I've already mentioned, try not to sing out of 'key'. He will try, that is, to fit into a style still heard in England although very much out of date.

This marvellous idea is part of Mr. Poirier's attempt to give *Sgt Pepper* the kind of schematized unity those silly old academics tried to engineer on to *The Waste Land*. It takes no account of the fact that Ringo Starr does (or did, before voice lessons and before Phil Spector) sing out of key, needed 'help' to fit into the vocal line-up, and that this was part of his appeal (apart from the fundamental appeal of being one of the best rock drummers in the business). Mr. Poirier's instinct to go to what the song might just conceivably be peripherally about – instead of to what it simply and fundamentally is about – is ineluctable. He's a metaphysician by nature.

They are a group, and the unmistakable group identity exists almost in spite of sharp individuation, each of them, except the now dead Martin, known to be unique in some shaggy way.

He probably means Epstein, or perhaps Stu Sutcliffe, but it could be more metaphysics: perhaps George Martin is 'dead' on the aesthetic plane, an un-person of the new revolution.

The last few chapters of the book are about politics, and they convey a proper anguish about what is happening in the United States. Mr. Poirier is eager not to align himself with cheery youth-worshippers like Roszak and Reich, but can't help doing it.

And before trying to make my fellow countrymen accept the burden for the pain and suffering they have caused I would want to do something else. I would want to investigate the degree to which, despite any claims to higher culture, most men brutishly do not feel the burdens of complicity and brotherhood. Forced at last by the great mass of mankind now clamouring for our love and help, for our fellowship and charity, for our food, perhaps we shall have to decide that the humane values cultivated from study of the great works of art are values meant to apply only to people like ourselves, that they are wedded at last to privilege, class and race. I make these statements in the spirit not of accusation but of inquiry.

At this point refutation must stop. There is nothing to say except: if you are not serious about the great works of art, get right away from them and leave them to those who are – who are far more likely to be doing the suffering, incidentally, than inflicting it.

(1972)

# 17

# F. R. Leavis in America

With 150 pages of text devoted to only four pieces, *Lectures in America* by F. R. Leavis and Q. D. Leavis is far from being a collection of writings by-the-way. In spite of the ambling tone, perhaps too faithfully retained from its original lecture form, each piece is a distillation, rather than a dilution, of complexities of thought brought into being by one or the other of these two highly original minds and worked over for a long time: the book would take about four hours to read out, and took about four decades to think up. The first three pieces are general ones on the unity of culture, on Eliot and on Yeats: all these are by F. R. Leavis himself. The fourth and last piece, a fusion of two lectures, deals closely with *Wuthering Heights*, has four appendixes, and is composed by Q. D. Leavis. Reading from the back of the book to the front (there is no reason why you should, but it is revealing), you will proceed from criticism that opens and looks hard at a single book to criticism that closes books and gazes above and across them at the contemporary scene. The gaze is unfriendly. It is a brave, not a weak unfriendliness, but it is most unsettling. *Lectures in America* is a disturbing book, difficult to sum up and easy to distort, and it has mostly been reviewed favourably rather than well.

It is not that F. R. Leavis ranges beyond his reviewers' competence as literati, but that he ranges beyond their preparedness to discuss cultural issues as matters of life and death – of what life should be like, of what furthers it, what cheapens it and what defeats it. Although he has always made a point of disclaiming philosophical rigour (most specifically in the fine essay 'Literary Criticism and Philosophy' in *The Common Pursuit*) he is a philosopher in the true sense, and has been recognized as such by all who have read him since he first began to work, in the intensity of their acceptances and rejections if not in their vocabulary. In Britain in this century Croce's old rule about the philosophical spirit has been obeyed: if it can find no home in the philosophy schools, it will descend to, and take up residence in, the nearest activity in which men are committing their whole understanding. As anyone capable of grasping the issues is well aware, in Britain the mental battles that matter, the battles which involve the intellectual passions, have for a long time now been fought out in the field of 'literary criticism' in the first instance, with the result that literary criticism has constantly seemed, to those intent on providing it with habitable professional limits, to be getting above itself. The descent of scholarship to data-processing they can just live with – jokes can be made, and there's no denying those machines are impressive. The ascent of criticism to philosophy, however, looks more damaging – and *is* more damaging, since diffidence is denied its due respect.

F. R. Leavis's objection to practising criticism in what he conceived to be a philosophical way was that criticism could not afford to be pre-occupied with method. He could equally have said that *philosophy* could not afford to be preoccupied with method. As things have turned out, he has been far more free than professional philosophers to speak on issues. He has been able to identify the issues as they come up and go on to get them right, get them wrong or get them confused. This is the work that philosophy is bound to do or else pay the penalty of falling back upon the investigation of its own ways and means. When F. R. Leavis says that the English school should be the centre of the university (he says it again here, in the first lecture 'Luddites? or There is Only One Culture', a piece in which many often-heard themes return as in the last minutes of a *Ring* cycle rather scrappily conducted), the assertion sounds at first absurdly pretentious. But rephrase it in terms of his own intellectual commitment, say that the first concern of the university should be to create philosophers, and it makes, on a traditional view, more sense – while being even more subversive of the modern order as he characterizes that state, or tendency, of affairs. He might accept the victory of 'the blind enlightened menace' (magnificent phrase) as inevitable, but he refuses to accept the inevitable as the good. The bravery of this stand remains to be admired even if one does not agree with his diagnosis of the present, his interpretation of the past, or his premonition of the future.

The reinstatement of a truly embracing concept of culture; a reversal of the 'alienating' tendency of industrialism and a restoration of the unity of work and purpose; the dismissal of the debilitating 'leisure' concept – it probably can't be done. F. R. Leavis admits it probably can't be done but doesn't cease to press for it, to point to the danger even as the danger becomes an unstoppable reality. His enormously complicated (and always knottily expressed) view of historical change has been strong in so far as it has enabled him to give a clear account of the changing conditions of creativity, and weak in so far as it has slid towards pessimism – towards an impression, implicit in even his finest work, that the conditions of life are working now towards the utter defeat of the creative spirit. Britain's political continuity has perhaps saved him from a more thorough pessimism (that and his own temperament): like his equal in America, Edmund Wilson (for whom he seems to have had little time), he has benefited from an early disinclination to identify the coherence of culture with the political integrity of Europe, and his continuing rage is not to be equated with the resigned despair of the European panoptic scholars who compared the ruined present with the supposed unity of the past and forgivably reached the conclusion that the thread was at last broken. As he is once again at pains to avow, he is not to be saddled with the advocacy of a return to the past:

We [he and Denys Thompson in *Culture and Environment*] didn't recall this organic kind of relation of work to life in any nostalgic spirit, as something to be restored or to take a melancholy pleasure in lamenting; but by way of emphasizing that it was *gone*, with the organic community it belonged to, not to be restored in any foreseeable future.

And as well as not being nostalgic about the wheelwright's shop, he is of course even more emphatically not misty-eyed about the disappearance of a supposedly integrated Christendom. As a consequence, F. R. Leavis is not vulnerable to an attack on his bases in the past. Nevertheless he has a view of the flow of history in recent times which is open to attack. He sees the tide of mediocrity, of second-rate work and inhuman charity, rising ever higher. He consistently underestimates the capacity of the productive spirit, both creative and critical, to survive and flourish, and faced with the spectacle of a swarm of seaside trippers listening to pop on transistor radios he reacts in the very tones of Malcolm Muggeridge, his phrases differing only in their cost per word. Beethoven's name coming up, F. R. Leavis does not suggest that these people would have listened to his music once upon a time, but he does suggest that some kind of conspiracy, some inexorable rigging of the circumstances, is getting in the road of their doing so now. Well of course it is, but what are the factors? This is where we have only the famous tone of voice, and not the much more important clarity of statement, to answer us. Whether nostalgically or not, the past is vaguely invoked – an organic unity then that is not an organic unity now. Standards. Life. For life. But suppose that culture were one factor in a plurality, had always been and must always be one factor in a plurality, ranged then, now and for always *against forces that are ranged against it*. Suppose that, and you will quickly see that when we ask a man of F. R. Leavis's stature to beware of pessimism, we are not asking him to embrace optimism. The choice is not between pessimism and optimism, but between both these things and truth.

It is no more polite but a lot less trivial to attribute to a calculated pessimism, rather than to a quirk of temperament, those recurring themes in his work which do most to cheapen the level of discussion and whose wholesale adoption infallibly marks the more bone-headed of his disciples. The dread 'modish literary world' is with us again in this book, once again working in far-flung, intricately connected conspiracies across modish literary London for the downfall of standards and against life. Well, there's something in it, but you'd be amazed to know how often the singleness of utterance among mediocrities is to be explained not by their clubbing up but by their being mediocrities. F. R. Leavis is unable to give a clear account of the second-rate or to show that he has any idea of how culture needs to be staffed and run by differing orders of intellect in proper relationship to one another. Pessimistically, he is always assuming that the gangs are increasing their grip, buying their way to power with cocktails and flattery or fingering the independent operator for a quick, lethal dose of 'misrepresentation'. Even more nebulous and rapidly fatal than the modish literary world is the much-feared social world. 'Eliot's intelligence doesn't show to advantage in the social world. . . . I don't think I need spend time over shades and transitions of meaning.' Of course you don't. Your audience is already rippling with knowing laughter and nodding agreement, just as it did at Eliot. Or perhaps you do.

This shying away from detail, while at the same time giving a tremendous air of having the social realities well weighed up, leaves the problem sign-posted but invisible, like a whale between death and destruction. In fact it is not possible for life, in the past, the present or the future, to offer us the example of great men moving in a milieu which is equal to them: if it were, it would not be a milieu, and the men would not be great. It's sad but necessary to say that F. R. Leavis's view of society (if something so subtle can be designated by that term) is very seriously hurt by pessimism, to the point that his feeling for language deserts him and actual bromides – not just characteristic turns of phrase – turn up in a prose otherwise free of dead talk.

But as for the actual working-class people who *can* be regarded as characteristic, it's not anything in the nature of moral indignation one feels towards *them*, but shame, concern and apprehension at the way our civilization has let them down – left them to enjoy a 'high standard of living' in a vacuum of disinheritance.

Well, our civilization can only have 'let them down' if it was at some time possible for our civilization to have seen and wilfully neglected to pursue a better course. But for 'our civilization' or anybody else's such a choice never reveals itself as a choice at the crucial time. Also (and this is a cliché, but the point being made here is that in this passage he let himself in for it) those ideas of disinheritance are handed down from above. In reality (and reality includes *all* the passions that drive society) the transition from that condition of 'inheritance' (it probably means 'organic kind of relation of work to life') to the 'high standard of living' is a neutral one. As a neutral transition, it can be analysed infinitely, or at any rate down to the level of the individuals concerned. But once judged pessimistically, it ceases to yield information about the present *or* the past. History acquires a downward curve. It becomes possible to write a sentence beginning, 'The problem is to reestablish an effective educated public . . .' Just 'establish' would have done.

The essay on Eliot is called 'Eliot's Classical Standing' and leaves nothing to be desired except a few pages on *The Waste Land*, which was by-passed to save time but which might very well be treated in future editions of what really is a superb essay – no, lecture; one forgets. Not many lectures, and few enough essays, go so far towards tracing the main course of a creative life while never ceasing to emphasize the impossibility of simplifying it. When speaking of Eliot's poetry, F. R. Leavis isolates his concept of significance by marking the difference between the 'sincere' and the 'social' Eliot – the 'social' being whatever force it was that induced him to infiltrate superstition into *The Cocktail Party*. He sees Eliot's creative career as 'a sustained, heroic and indefatigably resourceful quest of a profound sincerity of the most difficult kind', a quest which finds realization in 'one astonishing major work' (*Four Quartets*). In fine, all Eliot's poetry can be read as one longish poem getting, aberrations aside, progressively better. This is not a startling conclusion to reach – the quotable judgments in the lecture sound quite ordinary – but the way of reaching it is wholly original and will have to be contended with from now on. The measure of the 'sincerity' is daringly made dependent on subtly implied estimates of the poet's personality, the poet in his creative manhood having been regarded by the lecturer as a polar intellect over a period of decades.

Whether or not in discussing that necessity of fully human life which is wanting – discussing as Eliot evokes it that which might meet human spiritual need – one finds oneself dealing in Christian theology depends on who one is. I myself think I am paying a high tribute to the genius of the poet when I express my conviction that as literary critic one had better not find oneself doing that – and that it needs literary criticism to do justice to Eliot.

By thus leaving a theological approach out of the question he makes room for judgments upon Eliot's *personal* truth to the spiritual needs and lacks he presumes to deduce from a long contemporaneous study of the work in its development. It would be interesting to see how steadily these judgments would hold if all the major work, and not just a few selected passages, were to come under close discussion. But even in this restricted space, the approach makes possible some revolutionary statements, as when he abruptly decides to 'risk saying crudely that in relation to his own quest, Eliot over-valued what Dante had to offer him'. The inference is

that Shakespeare would have been better than Dante at helping
Eliot in what 'should' have been of importance: to deal with 'the
creative relation between the sexes in all its significance'. To come
to grips with the implications of this short but heavily scored line
of argument it is not only necessary to know exactly what you think
of Eliot, it is necessary to know exactly what you think of Dante.

'Yeats: The Problem and the Challenge' isn't up to the Eliot
piece for several reasons. To begin with, it is too restrictive: 'Sailing
to Byzantium', 'Byzantium' and 'Among School Children' are the
only qualifiers for the title of 'fully achieved thing'. This *has* to be
wrong. In outflanking the dreaded 'fully equipped commentators'
F. R. Leavis is concerned with identifying and isolating the major
poems (not just the many Yeats poems 'worth having') which do
not require 'that one should bring up any special knowledge or
instructions from outside'. But here one of his most valuable strains
of thought, the one which has always been able to evaluate academic
pressures and characterize rampant scholarship as a cultural threat,
has been mightily over-asserted. Yeats's poems explain each other
where they do not explain themselves, and it is possible to go a
long way towards a full understanding of his work without ever
once opening any ancillary volume by him or anybody else: his
intention of writing a magic book of the arts was fulfilled.

F. R. Leavis's whole argument – it is intricately developed –
about the extra-poetical in Yeats could as well be detached from
that poet and attached to, say, Eliot – in relation to whom, it seems
plain, some *very* extra-poetical considerations are gone into in the
lecture next door. Looking at the two essays in conjunction, it
seems likely that such considerations are rationalized when admiration is total and developed into a limiting commentary when
it is not.

It is characteristic of Yeats to have had no centre of unity, and to have
been unable to find one. The lack is apparent in his solemn propoundings
about the Mask and the Anti-self, and in the related schematic elaborations.

Not the same, apparently, as being solemn about the Etruscans.

Throughout this piece on Yeats, the appreciation of the few

poems does not link up with the limiting of the many: the appreciation and the limiting do not spring from the one impulse, despite the vigour with which singleness of viewpoint is asserted. It can be added, perhaps impertinently, that this lecture, like the others, contains several endearingly familiar turns of speech and all on its own offers us one of the master's most memorable put-downs.

I remember vividly the impact of *The Tower*, of which I have a first edition, acquired in the way in which I have acquired such first editions as I have had – I bought it when it first came out.

What a burn! Yet here again you see what he is driving at; rejecting the fashionable, recalling the essential.

I don't believe in any 'literary values', and you won't find me talking about them; the judgments the literary critic is concerned with are judgments about life.

When a man offers 'the friction, the sense of pregnant arrest, which goes with active realizing thought and the taking of a real charged meaning', he is not offering something he will be honoured for in any conventional way. But as a living force in the plurality of society his recognition is assured, and his name becomes a known quality. *Lectures in America* helps to define that quality even more closely.

(1969)

PART FOUR

# Past Masters

# 18

## D. H. Lawrence in transit

If one were to take a wax pencil and trace Lawrence's travels on a globe of the world, the result would be an enigmatic squiggle: a squiggle that started off minutely preoccupied in Europe, was reduced still further to a fat dot formed by the cramped war-time movements within England, broke out, enlarged itself to a bold transoceanic zig-zag which at one wild moment streaked right around the planet, and then subsided again into more diffident, European vagaries – still restless, but listless, tailing off. The pencil should properly come to a halt at Vence, in the Alpes Maritimes, although if we substituted for it another pencil of a different colour we might legitimately add one last, sweeping leg to the journey, as Lawrence's mobility recovered in death and his ashes rode back mindlessly to New Mexico.

In a few minutes we could map the wanderings of nearly two decades. It wouldn't tell us much, apart from the obvious fact that he liked to move about. He was in search of something, no question of it. Headquarters, the fissure into the underworld – it had many names. But one is permitted to doubt whether it could ever have been found, the doubt being engendered less by the world's nature than by an assessment of Lawrence's insatiable hunger for meaning. There is a tendency, once Lawrence's odyssey has been identified as a spiritual quest, to suppose that Lawrence had a firm idea of his spiritual object: hence the notion that he was in revolt against twentieth-century society, or post-Renaissance Europe, or post-Columbian America, or whatever you care to name. Lawrence was in revolt all right, but the revolt encompassed almost everything he knew in the present and nearly all the past he ever came to know, and this ability to exhaust reality through intimacy shows up in his travels as much as in anything else he did.

It was not so much that familiarity bred contempt – and anyway,

there were some familiarities of which he never quite tired – as that
it bred unease. Never to find things important enough is the mark
of a dreamer. Lawrence, thoroughly practical and businesslike in
matters large and small, was no ordinary dreamer: nevertheless he
could get no lasting peace from his surroundings, and as time went
by felt bound to look upon them as an impoverished outwardness
implying a symbolic centre – and this despite an unrivalled ability
to reflect the fullness of physical reality undiminished onto the
page. Lawrence is beyond the reach of any other modern writer
writing about what can be seen, since whatever could be seen he
saw instantaneously and without effort – which is probably why he
could regard it as nothing but the periphery of the real. If he had
lived longer, his novels might well have lost any touch at all with
worldly objects: the sense of actuality which other men serve long
apprenticeships to attain was for him a departure point. And again
if he had lived longer, he might well have exhausted the earth with
travel. Had he not placed such an emphasis on turning inwards to
the dark, fiery centre, we could by now have been tempted to
imagine him turning outwards, away from the tellurian cultures
depleted by the ravenous enquiry of his imagination and towards
an uncapturable infinity that actually exists – orchestrations of
dark suns, unapproachable galaxies peopled by Etruscans who
stayed on top, nebulae like turquoise horses, the ocean of the great
desire. Quetzalcoatl's *serape*! Sun-dragon! Star-oil! Lawrence was
in search of, was enraged over the loss of, a significance this world
does not supply and has never supplied. For a worldling, his
symbolist requirements were inordinate. As a spaceman he might
have found repose. Heaven knows, he was genius enough not to be
outshone by the beyond. He could have written down a supernova.

Supposing, though, that this was what his journeyings were all in
aid of – home. The supposition is at least part of the truth, although
by no means, I think, the largest part. If home was ever anywhere,
it was at the Del Monte and Flying Heart ranches in New Mexico
– whose mountains seemed to be the place he could stay at longest
without feeling compelled to move on. Yet there were still times
when he missed Europe, just as, in Europe, there were so many
times when he missed America, and just as, on either continent,

there were troubled times when he missed England. Headquarters tended to be where Lawrence was not. Places abandoned because they did not possess the secret could be fondly remembered later on – perhaps they had had the secret after all. But it never occurred to Lawrence that there *was* no secret. Out of all the thousands of pages of his incredibly productive short life, the great pathos which emerges is of this extraterrestrial unbelonging – far more frightening, in the long run, than the social challenges which by now we have absorbed, or else written off as uninformative propositions. Critical unreason often occurs in creative genius, but creative unreason rarely does: for a talent to be as big as Lawrence's and yet still be sick is a strange thing. It's easily understandable that people equipped to appreciate his magnitude as a writer should take the intellectually less taxing course, declaring Lawrence to be a paragon of prophetic sanity and the world sick instead.

Lawrence's first travels were to London, Brighton, the Isle of Wight, Bournemouth. Readers of the early letters will be rocked back on their heels to find the same descriptive power turned loose on Brighton as later reached out to seize the dawn over Sicily, the flowers in Tuscany, the Sinai desert, the sperm-like lake in Mexico and the ranches after snow. Then, in 1912, the first run to Metz, in Germany: Waldbröl in the Rhineland, Munich, Mayrhofen in Austria. A walk over the Tyrol. Lake Garda. Back to England in 1913, then back to Bavaria. Lerici. England again. The war confined these short European pencil strokes to a fitfully vibrating dot within England, covering Sussex, Hampstead, Cornwall; an angry return to London after being hounded from the coast and possible contact with the High Seas Fleet; Berkshire, Derbyshire.

In 1919, free to quit England, he broke straight for Italy: Turin, Lerici, Florence, Rome, Picinisco, Capri. In 1920, Taormina, in Sicily. Malta. In 1921, Sardinia, Germany, Austria, Italy, Taormina again. (Taormina is a node, like – later on – Taos, and the Villa Mirenda at Scandicci, outside Florence.)

In 1922, the emboldened pattern struck outwards to Ceylon. Australia for two months. Then America: Taos, the Del Monte ranch, the mountains. In 1923 he was in Mexico City, New York, Los Angeles, Mexico again and . . . England. In 1924 France,

Germany, New York, Taos. The Flying Heart ranch, alias the Lobo, alias the Kiowa. Oaxaca, in Mexico.

The year 1925 ended the period of the big pattern. After a wrecking illness in New Mexico he returned to London. Then Baden-Baden. Spotorno. In 1926, Capri, Spotorno and the Villa Mirenda in Scandicci – his last real place to be. Germany, England, Scotland. Italy.

In 1927 he toured the Etruscan tombs. A score of names cropped up in his itinerary: Volterra, Orvieto, Tarquinia – short strokes all over Tuscany and Umbria, the Etruscan places. Then to Austria and Germany, and in 1928 to Switzerland, with the Villa Mirenda abandoned. Gsteig bei Gstaad, Baden-Baden (the Kurhaus Plättig) and the Ile de Port-Cros, Toulon. From low-lying sun-trap to *Höheluftkurort* the short strokes moved trembling. Bandol, in the south of France. He was in Paris in 1929, then Palma de Mallorca, Forte dei Marmi, Florence, Bandol again. In 1930 Vence, and death.

Even in Vence he wasn't too sick to use his amazing eyes. There isn't a place on the list that he didn't inhabit at a glance. And yet as we read on and on through the magnificence of his travel writings, a little voice keeps telling us that the man was never there. The man, the spaceman, never travelled except in dreams. Dreaming, while dying, of India and China and everything else that lay beyond the San Francisco gate. Dreaming of altogether elsewhere, of an England that was not England, of a Europe that was never Europe.

It was a great day, Frieda said, when they walked together from the Isartal into the Alps. Lawrence wrote it down, in a way that takes us straight there. But where was he? 'We stayed at a Gasthaus', he wrote to Edward Garnett, 'and used to have breakfast out under the horse-chestnut trees, steep above the river weir, where the timber rafts come down. The river is green glacier water.' Compare this to one of the famous opening sentences of *A Farewell to Arms* – 'In the bed of the river there were pebbles and boulders, dry and white in the sun, and the water was clear and swiftly moving and blue in the channels' – and we will find Lawrence's descriptive prose both more economical and less nostalgic, the effortless reportage of an infallibly observant visitor.

Still on the same descriptive trail, go south to Italy ('I love these people') and look at Lerici. 'And in the morning', he wrote to Lady Cynthia Asquith, 'one wakes and sees the pines all dark and mixed up with perfect rose of dawn, and all day long the olives shimmer in the sun, and fishing boats and strange sails like Corsican ships come out of nowhere on a pale blue sea, and then at evening all the sea is milky gold and scarlet with sundown.' The fake-naïve rhythms, suitable for consumption by titled ladies, can't mask the searing power of that simplicity. 'The mountains of Carrara are white, of a soft white blue eidelweiss, in a faint pearl haze – all snowy. The sun is very warm, and the sea glitters.' It still does, even though polluted with a thoroughness which even Lawrence would have hesitated to prophesy. 'The Mediterranean is quite wonderful – and when the sun sets beyond the islands of Porto Venere, and all the sea is like heaving white milk with a street of fire across it, and amethyst islands away back, it is too beautiful.' It's small wonder that Lawrence could talk about art having characteristics rather than rules, and even disparage the idea of art altogether. He had it to burn.

Reality offered Lawrence no resistance. Mysticism did, and it was into mysticism that he poured his conscious energy. Turning to *Twilight in Italy*, we can find something on every page to match the descriptions in the letters. Here is Lake Garda at dawn.

In the morning I often lie in bed and watch the sunrise. The lake lies dim and milky, the mountains are dark blue at the back, while over them the sky gushes and glistens with light. At a certain place on the mountain ridge the light burns gold, seems to fuse a little groove on the hill's rim. It fuses and fuses at this point, till of a sudden it comes, the intense, molten, living light. The mountains melt suddenly, the light steps down, there is a glitter, a spangle, a clutch of spangles, a great unbearable suntrack flashing across the milky lake, and the light falls on my face.

But superb as this is, it isn't what this book or any other Lawrence book is about. *Twilight in Italy* is about north and south, hill and dale – it is the tentative prototype for a great sequence of increasingly confident polarities, by which Lawrence the traveller was to go on splitting the world in two until there was nothing left of it but powder. The Bavarian highlanders, it appears, 'are almost the only race with the souls of artists . . . their processions and religious festivals are profoundly impressive, solemn, and rapt.' Again, they are 'a race that moves on the poles of mystic sensual delight. Every gesture is a gesture from the blood, every expression a symbolic utterance.' Your Bavarian highlander 'accepts the fate and the mystic delight of the senses with one will, he is complete and final. His sensuous experience is supreme, a consummation of life and death at once.' Whether drinking in the Gasthaus, or 'hating steadily and cruelly', or 'walking in the strange, dark, subject-procession' to bless the fields, 'it is always the same, the dark, powerful mystic, sensuous experience is the whole of him, he is mindless and bound within the absoluteness of the issue, the unchangeability of the great icy not-being which holds good for ever, and is supreme.' Yes, it was all happening in Bavaria – or rather, it was all to happen later on in Bavaria. But the thing to grasp here is that word 'dark'. Not only (as is well known) is it the key adjective in all of Lawrence, but Lawrence's travels can usefully be summarized as an interminable search for a noun it could firmly be attached to.

No sooner is Lawrence in Italy than we discover that the Italians have dark interiors too. 'The Italian people are called "Children of the Sun". They might better be called "Children of the Shadow". Their souls are dark and nocturnal.' A feature of the dark soul is unconsciousness, as in the spinning-woman, whose mind Lawrence can apparently read. 'She glanced at me again, with her wonderful, unchanging eyes, that were like the visible heavens, unthinking, or like the two flowers that are open in pure clear unconsciousness. To her I was a piece of the environment. That was all. Her world was clear and absolute, without consciousness of self. She was not self-conscious, because she was not aware that there was anything in the universe except *her* universe.'

But the darkly unconscious haven't got it all their own way. Much later in the book, during the fascinating passage that deals with the local production of *Amleto*, Lawrence spies a mountain man in the audience: he is of the same race as the old spinning-woman. 'He was fair, thin, and clear, abstract, of the mountains. . . . He has a fierce, abstract look, wild and untamed as a hawk, but like a hawk at its own nest, fierce with love . . . it is the fierce spirit of the Ego come out of the primal infinite, but detached, isolated, an aristocrat. He is not an Italian, dark-blooded. He is fair, keen as steel, with the blood of the mountaineer in him. He is like my old spinning woman.'

To reconcile this mountain-man with the spinning-woman, we must assume she was never dark-blooded, when a good deal of what we were told about her when we were reading about her suggested that she was. And indeed, looking back, we find that she *hasn't* been given a dark soul or dark blood – she is simply 'the core and centre to the world, the sun, and the single firmament.' Lawrence hasn't at this stage entirely identified the dark soul with the earth's centre, so it's still possible to combine abstractness with being at the centre of the world, and, presumably, dark-bloodedness with *not* being at the centre of the world. What's difficult to reconcile, however, even when stretching the idea of poetic consistency until it snaps, is a Bavarian highlander's dark-bloodedness with a mountain-man's clear abstractness: if these conditions are both different from an ordinary Italian's dark-bloodedness, are they different in different ways?

The awkward truth is that Lawrence left his Bavarian highlanders behind in his opening chapter and forgot about them while writing the bulk of the book, which even without them would still be extremely difficult to puzzle out. The confusion confesses itself in the passage about Paolo and Maria. Paolo is a native of San Gaudenzio, and therefore a hill man – fair, eyes-like-ice, unalterable, inaccessible. Maria is from the plain – dark-skinned, slow-souled. 'Paolo and she were the opposite sides of the universe, the light and the dark.' Nothing could be clearer. 'They were both by nature passionate, vehement. But the lines of their passion were opposite. Hers was the primitive, crude, violent flux of the blood, emotional and undiscriminating, but wanting to mix and mingle. His was the hard, clear, invulnerable passion of the bones, finely tempered and unchangeable.' As an opponent to, or complement of, the passion of the blood, the passion of the bones was evidently judged by Lawrence to be somewhat unwieldy – it never again made such an unabashed appearance. Pretty soon, the blood's passion became the only kind of authentic passion you could have.

In *Twilight in Italy*, though the destructive mechanization of the world had already clearly been perceived, Lawrence still had something to say for abstractness, intellectuality and cognate non-dark attributes. In 1915 he wrote to Lady Ottoline Morrell from Ripley, in Derbyshire: 'It is a cruel thing to go back to that which one has been . . . . Altogether the life here is so dark and violent; it all happens in the senses, powerful and rather destructive: no mind or mental consciousness, unintellectual. These men are passionate enough, sensuous, dark – God, how all my boyhood comes back – so violent, so dark, the mind always dark and without understanding, the senses violently active. It makes me sad beyond words.' It's not the first time that the word 'dark' is used like a comma, but it's one of the few times – all early – when Lawrence freely admitted the possibility that the dark soul could be as murderous on its own as intellect could. The emphasis was still on keeping a balance, on checking the word against the thing it was supposed to stand for. Lawrence's later history is the story of darkness being awarded a steadily more automatic virtue, the periodic calls for an equilibrium of forces degenerating into unfathomable proposals about establishing the correct relationship between the components of darkness itself.

Lawrence's 'dash' (his word) to Sardinia produced a book – *Sea and Sardinia* – which clearly shows his untroubled ability to uproot all the attributes he has just so triumphantly detected in a place, move them on to the next place, and then condemn the first place for either not having them in sufficient strength or never having had them. In Cagliari the men 'stood about in groups, but without the intimate Italian watchfulness that never leaves a passer-by alone.' Looks as if the Italians' dark blood wasn't dark enough, an impression confirmed by the menacing loins of the Sardinian peasant, 'a young one with a swift eye and hard cheek and hard, dangerous thighs. . . . How fascinating it is, after the soft Italians, to see these limbs in their close knee-breeches, so definite, so manly, with the old fierceness in them still. One realises, with horror, that the race of men is almost extinct in Europe . . .' Plainly the war period has helped sour Lawrence on Europe altogether, but even taking that convulsive time-lag into account, it's still difficult to square up *Sea and Sardinia* with *Twilight in Italy*. The real difference, it appears, is that Italy is *connu* and therefore sterile, whereas Sardinia is unknown and therefore isn't. 'There are unknown, unworked lands where the salt has not lost its savour. But one must have perfected oneself in the great past first.'

Whether in the vegetable market near the start of the book or at the peasants' procession near the end, Lawrence's colour sense is at its sumptuous best, and in general *Sea and Sardinia* is a remarkable piece of visualization. 'When we came up, the faint shape of land appeared ahead, more transparent than thin pearl. Already Sardinia. Magic are high lands seen from the sea, when they are far, far off, and ghostly translucent like icebergs.' Beautiful writing, but no lasting pledge. Lawrence was in and out of Sardinia in a hurry, and spent a good half of 1921 sitting in Taormina getting sick of Europe, which can't be said to exclude Sardinia. Just as Sardinia had it over Italy, somewhere else had it over the whole of Europe. 'I would like to break out of Europe,' he wrote to Mary Cannan. 'It has been like a bad meal of various courses . . . and one has got indigestion from every course.' He was thinking of 'something more velvety' – Japan, perhaps, or Siam. The south of Europe was better than the north, but there was no denying that even the south had gone off: 'I can't get the little taste of canker out of my mouth,' he told Catherine Carswell, 'The people –' A few days later he was telling E. H. Brewster that they were *canaille*, *canaglia*, *Schweinhunderei*, stink-pots. 'A curse, a murrain, a pox on this crawling, sniffling, spunkless brood of humanity.'

In his mind Lawrence was already embarked for Ceylon, and in another few days Mabel Dodge – by inviting him to Taos – had made it possible for him to project his mental journey right around the globe. Europe was promptly pronounced to be 'a dead dog which begins to stink intolerably.' England (in the same letter, written to S. S. Koteliansky) was declared 'a dead dog that died of a love disease like syphilis.' Bad news for Koteliansky, who was living in it at the time. (This letter also featured the Lawrentian pearl about 'one of those irritating people who have generalized detestations. . . . So unoriginal.')

'I feel I can't come –' Lawrence wrote to Brewster in January

1922, 'that the East is not my destiny.' Later in the same month, destiny doubled back, and Lawrence decided to go via Ceylon after all. 'I feel it is my destiny', he wrote to Mabel Dodge, 'to go east before coming west.' Destiny pulled another double-cross in Ceylon, where Lawrence found the velvety Orient inane. 'The East, the bit I've seen,' he told Mary Cannan, 'seems silly.' As he frequently did when off-balance, he thought of England, telling Robert Pratt Barlow that 'the most living clue of life is in us Englishmen in England, and the great mistake we make is in not uniting together in the strength of this real living clue – religious in the most vital sense – uniting together in England and so carrying the vital spark through . . . the responsibility for England, the living England, rests on men like you and me and Cunard – probably even the Prince of Wales . . .' The Prince of Wales was indirectly responsible for Lawrence's 'Elephant' poem, the most tangible result of the Singhalese sojourn apart from a disillusioning close-up of in-scrutable platoons of dark people with dark eyes – 'the vastness of the blood stream, so dark and hot and from so far off.'

As far as the East went, darkness was a dead loss. Not that the contradiction with many things he'd said before, or with nearly everything he said later, ever slowed him down. The task was to push his mystical system around the planet until it clicked; there was no obligation to explain why it kept going wrong.

Australia was a country Lawrence couldn't characterize . . . 'the spell of its indifference gets me.' Mystical content, zero. 'This is the most democratic place I have *ever* been in,' he wrote to Else Jaffe, 'And the more I see of democracy the more I dislike it . . . You *never* knew anything so nothing, *nichts, nullus, niente,* as the life here.' The situations in *Kangaroo* are mainly imported, and it's doubtful if Lawrence ever gave Australia much thought after the first few days. Nevertheless the settings in *Kangaroo* have small trouble in being the most acutely observed and evocative writing about Australia that there has no far been – bearing out my point that Lawrence could reproduce reality with no effort whatsoever. Trollope, Kipling, Conrad, Galsworthy and R. L. Stevenson all visited Australia at one time or another, but if any of them was capable of bringing off a piece of scene-setting like the opening chapter of *Kangaroo*, he didn't feel compelled to. The moment he got to Thirroul, Lawrence despatched letters announcing his longing for Europe – the dead dog lived again. The central situation in *Kangaroo* looks to be about Italian fascism – the Australian variety, which emerged much later, was very different. But *Kangaroo* is a bit more than a European play with an Australian set-designer. It has an interesting early scene in which Lawrence makes Lovat out to be a prig, reluctant to lend Jack Callcott a book of essays in case it bores him. '"I might rise up to it, you know", said Jack laconically, "if I bring all my mental weight to bear on it."' There is a hint, here, that someone might have shaken Lawrence by urging him to lay off the intensity. It's a rare moment of self-criticism, and almost *the* moment of self-deprecating humour. Lawrence was perhaps a touch less certain about the aridity of the Australian spirit than he let on.

America. Lorenzo in Taos – it was a giant step. It rapidly became clear that the most dangerous item of local fauna was Mabel Dodge, the hostess who favoured will over feeling – a priority always guaranteed to grate on Lawrence, whose will and feeling were united in Destiny. 'My heart still turns most readily to Italy,' he told Mary Cannan – a strong sign of unease – and 'I even begin to get a bit homesick for England . . .' A certain sign. At this stage Lawrence had decided that the Indians couldn't be copied. 'And after all, if we have to go ahead,' he wrote to Else Jaffe, 'we must ourselves go ahead. We can go back and pick up some threads – but these Indians are up against a dead wall, even more than we are: but a different wall.' And to Catherine Carswell: '*Però, son sempre Inglese.*' Even after moving to the Del Monte, putting a helpful seventeen miles between himself and the Mabel-ridden Taos, Lawrence was detecting the same *innerlich* emptiness in his surroundings as had wasted his time in Australia. Mexico, however, worked differently, and he was soon telling the much-maligned Middleton Murry that if England wanted to lead the world again she would have to pick up a lost trail, and that the end of the trail lay in – Mexico.

*The Plumed Serpent* is a work of uncanny poetic force which manages to keep some sort of shape despite intense distorting pressures from Lawrence's now-rampant mysticism. Kate, with her European blood and conscious understanding, is outdistanced by dark-faced silent men with their columns of dark blood and dark, fiery clouds of passionate male tenderness. In addition to the oppressive symbolic scheme, there are moments which lead you to suspect that the author might simply be cracked – as when he suggests that Bolshevists are all born near railways. Yet Chapter V, 'The Lake', is one of Lawrence's supreme stretches of writing. The boatman 'pulled rhythmically through the frail-rippling, sperm-like water, with a sense of peace. And for the first time Kate felt she had met the mystery of the natives, the strange and mysterious gentleness between a scylla and charibdis of violence: the small poised, perfect body of the bird that waves wings of thunder and wings of fire and night in its flight.' Frail-rippling – what a writer. The transparent purity of the book's descriptions is inseparable from its symbolic structure, which is an opposition between principles which no ordinary mortal will ever be able to clarify, since Lawrence himself could only grope towards them with incantatory phrase-making.

The book's incandescent set-pieces – the burning of the images, the execution of the traitors, and so on – are spaced apart by impenetrable thickets of unmeaning. 'But within his own heavy, dark range he had a curious power,' Kate learns of Cipriano. 'Almost she could *see* the black fume of power which he emitted, the dark, heavy vibration of his blood . . . she could feel the curious tingling heat of his blood, and the heavy power of the *will* that lay unemerged in his blood.' What the Bavarian highlanders and plains Italians had lost, the sons of Quetzalcoatl had gained.

Lawrence learned about Indians during the hiatus between writing chapter ten and chapter eleven of *The Plumed Serpent*. His mystical conclusions are distributed between the later part of that novel (e.g., the snake in the fire at the heart of the world) and *Mornings in Mexico*, a travel book of unusual difficulty, even for Lawrence. Certainly he no longer pleads for a balance between the disparate consciousnesses of the white man and the dark man. You can't, it appears, have it both ways. The most you can hope for is to harbour a little ghost who sees in both directions. Yet ghost or no ghost, Lawrence seems to be trying hard to belong to the Indian way, to the 'abdomen where the great blood-stream surges in the dark, and surges in its own generic experiences.' What we seek in sleep, Lawrence says, the Indians perhaps seek actively, 'the dark blood falling back from the mind, from sight and speech and knowing, back to the great central source where is rest and unspeakable renewal.' Relieved by some of his most brilliant descriptive passages, the rhetoric is short of totally suffocating, but still fearsomely turgid. It takes the letters to remind us that he could write in an unfevered way during this period. 'Here the grass is only just moving green out of the sere earth,' he wrote to Zelia Nuttall, 'and the hairy, pale mauve anemones that the Indians call owl flowers stand strange and alone among the dead pine needles, under the wintry trees. Extraordinary how the place seems *seared* with winter: almost cauterized. And so winter-cleaned, from under three feet of snow.' A cold towel for the reader's forehead. Green glacier water.

Back in Europe to stay, Lawrence unpacked his mystical machine and set about applying it to the Etruscans. At the same time, and without any disabling sense of contradicting himself, he started rehabilitating Europe, even the long-forsaken north. 'I am very much inclined to agree', he wrote to Rolf Gardiner in July 1926, 'that one must look for real guts and self-responsibility to the Northern peoples. After a winter in Italy – and a while in France – I am a bit bored by the Latins, there is a sort of inner helplessness and lack of courage in them . . .' Writing from Lincolnshire to E. H. Brewster, he claimed to have rediscovered 'a queer, odd sort of potentiality in the people, especially the common people . . .' The common English people, back in the running at long last! Whether or not the Prince of Wales qualified wasn't stated.

As a traveller through ordinary space, Lawrence got back on slanging terms with his repudiated Europe. Baden-Baden, for example, was a *Totentanz* out of Holbein, 'old, old people tottering their cautious dance of triumph: *wir sind noch hier* . . .' As a traveller through time and thought, he moved on a grander scale. *Etruscan Places* is a gentle book, endearingly characteristic in its handy division between Etruscan and Roman and disarmingly uncharacteristic in its emphasis on delicacy and humour: it's the book of a strong man dying. 'We have lost the art of living;' he writes, 'and in the most important science of all, the science of daily life, the science of behaviour, we are complete ignoramuses.' The Etruscans weren't like that. Their art had the 'natural beauty of proportion of the phallic consciousness, contrasted with the more studied or ecstatic proportion of the mental and spiritual Consciousness we are accustomed to.' The contrast, as always, is asserted with a degree of confidence which is bound to draw forth a preliminary nod of assent. It remains a fact, however, that this kind of argument has practically nothing to do with post-Renaissance art or pre-Renaissance art or any kind of art, since art is more likely to depend on these two sorts of proportion being in tension than on one getting rid of the other. Lawrence's binomial schemes were useless for thinking about art, as those of his disciples who tried to employ them went on to prove. Without them, though, we wouldn't have had *his* art.

In January 1928, Lawrence told Dorothy Brett that he still intended coming back to the ranch. 'It's very lovely,' he wrote to Lady Glenavy, 'and I'd be well there.' But his seven-league boots were worn through, and he was never to get out of Europe alive. We have only to read 'Reflections on the Death of a Porcupine' or the last part of *St. Mawr* to realize that his ashes ended up on the right spot. The mountains were a cherished place. They weren't home, though. Home was at the Source, and the Source – he said it himself – is past comprehension.

(1972)

# 19

## The Perpetual Promise of James Agee

The two volumes of Agee's bye-writings called *The Collected Poems of James Agee* and *The Collected Short Prose of James Agee* don't add anything revolutionary to our picture of the author, but what they do add is good and solid. The *Collected Poems* volume re-issues the whole of the long-lost 'Permit Me Voyage' and tacks on about three times as much other material, thereby vastly enlarging the field in which Agee can be studied as a poet. The results of such a study are likely to be mixed, since his disabling limitations as a poet are revealed along with the continuity of his dedication and seriousness: poetry just didn't bring out the best in him. The *Collected Short Prose* volume, on the other hand, is a book which demands to be considered – some of the pieces collected in it are as weighty and as rich as scraps and shavings can well get.

'He had so many gifts,' Dwight Macdonald once wrote of Agee, 'including such odd ones, for intellectuals, as reverence and feeling.' Very true, and what is more he had them at an early age. The early *Harvard Advocate* short stories included here are quite astonishing in their moral maturity: the emotional wisdom that other men must strive to attain seems to have been present in Agee as a gift, and it's easy to see why he impressed his contemporaries as some kind of Rimbaud of the understanding – the range of sympathy inspires not just awe, but a certain dread. Indeed it's possible to argue, in the light of these early efforts, that to have it all is to have too much. Men whose minds and talents grow through the recognition and correction of error probably find it easier to shape their lives. Agee had a deficient practical sense, largely bungled his career, completed only a tenth of what was in him and habitually overwrote – economy, for an artist with a faculty of registration as fertile as his, didn't mean weeding the garden so much as chopping the orchids down with a machete. Only the kind of sensitivity which develops can come up with a novel like *The Great Gatsby* – to produce a book like that in its maturity, it has to be capable of writing *This Side of Paradise* in its youth.

A saving obtuseness was simply never part of Agee's equipment. With his entire creative life stretching ahead of him, he had almost nothing left to learn.

'Death in the Desert,' from the October, 1930, issue of the *Harvard Advocate*, is the story of a young man hitch-hiking through the slump. At first glance it's anybody's story of a college boy going on the bum to discover America, and turns on the seemingly elementary moral point that the kind couple who pick him up won't stop for a Negro in serious trouble. But the control of the narrative, the modulations of the tone, the registration of speech-patterns and the presentation of character combine to turn the story away from neatness and towards complexity, judgment permanently suspended. The narrator (Agee in thin disguise) has a boil in his ear. At the beginning of the story, where he waits an eternity to be picked up while crippled hobos get lifts with ease, the boil looks like a comic device.

For a while I talked with a peg-legged man of perhaps sixty; he spent his winters with his niece and her husband in St Louis. In the summers he got out of their way. His luck was always good, he said – too damned good. This summer he'd been through St Louis twice already. Unless he did something about it, he'd be there again inside of a week. Did I have a cigarette? Thanks. . . . All the while, as he talked, he watched the cars come up the road, and flicked his thumb eastward as each one approached. He stood always with his peg leg towards town. Before long a Chandler, after running a half-mile gauntlet of men, slowed down for him. He took another cigarette and was gone.

For the rest of us, rides came more slowly. My ear was too sore, by now, to make talking a pastime. I sat down on my coat and decided that it was rather less than necessary on days like this. After a couple of hours, I considered the manifold advantages of being conspicuously a cripple. After another hour I had the idea of holding up a sign:

SORE EAR

PLEASE

The humour reminds us of one previous writer, Lardner, and of several subsequent writers, especially Salinger, whose early stories like 'This Sandwich Has No Mayonnaise' echo the tone precisely (consider the way that story's platoon sergeant translates his man-management problems into movie marquee slogans like FOUR MUST GO – FROM THE TRUCK OF THE SAME NAME). But the sore ear turns out to be a lot more than just a comic device. It's because of the nagging twinges he is suffering that the narrator decides to make no protest when the driver who picks him up eventually steps on the accelerator instead of the brake and races past the desperate Negro's outstretched arms. Agee is making the subtle point that we are likely to treat ourselves as a special case when we are in pain, and defer our duties on the assumption that the Fates, or our better selves, will understand. Like the bad tooth in *Darkness at Noon*, the boil resists all attempts to make something symbolical of it – it's just a fact, leading to more facts, in a sequence of marvellously analytical probings and worryings. Agee was twenty when he wrote the story. An ounce more talent and he would have sunk into the earth.

Another *Advocate* story, 'They That Sow in Sorrow Shall Reap', is similarly . . . well, precocious is the wrong word: prodigious. The young Agee character is immured in a dreadful boarding-house, whose master is an aging and barely repressed queer. They strike a silent bargain, in which the old man is allowed to adore but not to touch, beyond the occasional friendly squeeze of the shoulder. Agee introduces a young acquaintance into the boarding-house. The old man tries the friendly squeeze and gets slapped in the mouth. All the tacit understandings upon which the house has previously run, and especially the relationship between the old man and his wife, promptly collapse. Agee the character is reduced to tacit agonies of self-recrimination and regret, while Agee the writer records the to-ings and fro-ings in the shattered household with customary mastery. Supposing Agee had dropped dead the following year – wouldn't we be justified, on this showing, in the conjecture that he might have been one of the great writers of the century?

The real tragedy, looking back, is not in the presence of *Let Us Now Praise Famous Men* or *A Death in the Family* or all the other part-realized things, unsatisfactory though they are, but in the absence of that sequence of novels which might have recollected his life – a sequence for the writing of which he had qualifications rivalling Proust's. Unfortunately an 'autobiographical novel' (his inverted commas) was only one among many of the long-term Agee projects. Recollection was fundamental to the cast of his mind, but it wasn't his creative obsession. He wasn't neurotic enough. If people had hated him more he might have taken revenge; if he had hated himself sufficiently, he might have made redress; as it was, he had only love to drive him forward, and love makes poor fuel in its pure state. It's a heavy irony that through Agee the 'positive' creative attitude which people like Archibald MacLeish were currently calling for could well have established its own tradition. That it failed to come about was not just MacLeish's loss but everybody's, not least those who had seen the disingenuousness of the 'positive' propaganda but who would be compelled in the future to watch the American novel wave goodbye to everything Agee represented. It's been said that Agee wasn't bored by virtue – another way of saying that he could see what was interesting about normality. When he went down, he took three or four decades of ordinary American life with him, and the middlebrow salvage operations – O'Hara, Cheever and the like – got nowhere near lifting the hulk.

The two 'satiric' pieces included in *The Collected Short Prose* are from later in the day and are in a familiar Agee vein of phantasmagoria: the letter from Agee to Macdonald quoted in Macdonald's 'Jim Agee, A Memoir' (printed as an appendix to the excellent critical essay on Agee in *Against the American Grain*) gives a better idea of the referential lushness of his intelligence when he allowed it to run wild. There was something compulsive about the way he piled on the detail, and friends who received such letters might well have frowned through their delight – why take so much time and trouble, and to what purpose? Here are some scraps from the letter to Macdonald:

I think *The Brothers Karamazov* deserves the co-operation of all the finest talents in Hollywood and wd. richly repay all research & expenditure. A fullsized replica, complete down to the last topmizznmst, of the Mad Tsar Pierre (Charles Laughton). Papa Karamazov (Lionel Barrymore). His comic servant Grigory (Wallace Beery). Grigory's wife (Zazu Pitts). Smerdyakov (Charles Laughton). Smerdyakov's Familiar, a cat named Tabitha (Elsa Lanchester, the bride of Frankenstein). Zossima (Henry B. Walthall) ... Miusov (Malcolm Cowley) ... in Alyosha's Dream: Alyosha (Fred Astaire). Puck (Wallace Beery). Titania (Ginger Rogers or James Cagney). . . . Routines by Albertina Rasch. Artificial snow by Jean Cocteau. . . . Entire production supervised by Hugh Walpole. . . . To be played on the world's first Globular Screen, opening at the Hippodrome the night before *Jumbo* closes. . . . Artificial foreskins will be handed out at the north end of the Wilhelmstrasse to anyone who is fool enough to call for them.

Stuff like this reminds us of the many reasons why Perelman was unassailable – to begin with, he was far funnier. And Perelman wrote his madcap collages as therapy: Agee at this time (1936) was not involved in Hollywood and had no frustrations to work off, except perhaps the frustration of not being part of it all. There is something cancerous about this side of his talent. It produces cells uncontrollably, and the longer satirical piece included here (called 'Dedication Day', and nominally given over to goosing the scientists and politicians responsible for the first atomic bombs) runs away with itself in a fashion simultaneously boring and worrying.

As convincing demonstrations of just how sensitive Agee was there are two small fragments – 'Run Over', about a cat hit by a car, and 'Give Him Air', about a human car-crash victim dying – which are strictly unbearable: you'd need nerves of steel to read them twice. At the end of the first piece Agee notes in parenthesis that 'Things like this are happening somewhere on the earth every second.' It's one of the peculiarities of Agee's writing that he can achieve delicacy and subtlety but never distance. He took everything right on the chin. This doesn't mean that all his material presented itself to him as having equal value, but it did present itself with equal impact. If he'd cared less, he might have been able to shape things more easily. A man who doesn't know which way to turn finds it hard to get his head down. His doomed application for a 1937 Guggenheim grant is printed here – there are 47 separate projects.

For the Guggenheim people it must have been like trying to estimate Leonardo da Vinci in an early period. What were they to make of 'Extension in writing; ramification in suspension; Schubert 2-cello Quintet'? ('Experiments, mostly in form of the lifted and maximum-suspended periodic sentence. Ramification (and development) through developments, repeats, semi-repeats, of evolving thought, of emotion, of associatives and dissonants.') Don't ring us: we'll ring you. The awkward truth is that the capacity for general thought which Macdonald praised in Agee worked mainly as a drawback, blurring his creative focus. His comparatively low productivity isn't sufficiently explained by pointing to his chaotic style of life, and it's even possible to suggest – tentatively, remembering we are strangers – that the style of life might have been in part a reflection of a gift continually troubled by the search for the one idea that would temporarily suppress all the others. Where can will-power come from in a mind so short of limitations?

Travel notes and movie projects end the book. The fragments of filmscript bear out Macdonald's acute remark that Agee's scripts were the work of a frustrated director – details of camera angles and lighting (precisely the stuff that no film director ever wants to see in a script) are gone into at numbing length. As it happened, Agee spent the 1930s a long way away from the Hollywood salt-mines, toiling naked in a salt-mine of another type – the Luce magazines. The long (57 page) and praiseworthy introduction to the *Collected Short Prose* book is by Robert Fitzgerald, a friend of Agee's, and valuably complicates the story of Agee's connections with *Time*, *Life* and *Fortune* (or *Dime*, *Spy* and *Destiny* as Philip Barry called them) which Macdonald recounts with forbidding plagency in his memoir. (As demonstrated most notably by his embalming job on Hemingway, Macdonald has a tendency to wrap up a dead body and throw away the key to the sarcophagus: all done in the name of preservation, but a touch too slick.) 'Under a reasonable dispensation', Mr. Fitzgerald writes,

a man who had proved himself a born writer before he left the university could go ahead in that profession, but this did not seem to be the case in the United States in 1932. Neither in Boston nor New York nor elsewhere did there appear any livelihood appropriate for a brilliant President of *The Harvard Advocate*, nor any mode of life resembling that freedom of research that I have sketched as ours at Harvard. In the shrunken market the services of an original artist were not in demand. Hart Crane and Vachel Lindsay took their lives that spring. Great gifts always set their possessors apart, but not necessarily apart from any chance to exercise them; this gift at that time pretty well did. . . . Agee thankfully took the first job he could get and joined the staff of *Fortune* a month after graduation.

Which settles the question of why Agee joined Luce in the first place. Nevertheless, Macdonald is surely right in arguing that the Luce ambience did Agee crippling damage by offering him the illusion of being able to do serious work. The years clocked up and words went down the drain in thousands – nothing to be much ashamed of, but nothing to be proud of either. It was the state, familiar to all young writers in harness, of doing well without doing anything properly. Perhaps Hollywood would have been better, but he was without bargaining power and without that you stood an excellent chance of getting yourself killed. It took prestige like Faulkner's to be able to use Hollywood: failing that, Hollywood used you. As it was, Agee became the supreme critic of the period's films, and began to participate only after the industry had embarked on its long and agonizing modification of the studio system.

Even then, results were not robust. Apart from the charming *The Bride Comes to Yellow Sky*, there is nothing substantial except the largely unknown and fiercely underrated *The Night of the Hunter*, one of the key works in the whole Agee canon. The one and only film directed by Charles Laughton (who in his last years was playing Captain Bligh opposite Abbott and Costello and stands with Peter Lorre as an example of what the Hollywood mill could do to the European intellectual), it incarnates Agee's conception of the struggle between love and hate – Robert Mitchum, as the homicidal preacher, has the letters of these two short words inscribed on his knuckles, and stages a wrestling match between his two hands to mesmerize his victims.

It is a unique film, a taste of what Agee might have done. But he spent too much of his time and hopes involved with John Huston, a semi-artist of overwhelming personal charm who launched Agee's career as a script-writer by getting him to 'lick the book' of *The African Queen*, which as a Bogart-Hepburn vehicle won its Oscars but did not add up to very much. Reputedly it was an early morning, killer-diller tennis match with Huston that first put a strain on Agee's heart. Certainly it would be neat symbolism: Agee was not equipped to stay in the running with men like Huston, whose lives were geared to turning out work just above (never too far above) the Hollywood norm and who put their real creativity into the life-style that stuns and the pace that kills. Creatively, Agee had no gear except top – he could never have worked Faulkner's trick of giving them nothing but a refined and characteristic version of what they wanted. Sometimes they were right, too. In a film like *The Big Sleep*, some of the most memorable Chandler dialogue isn't Chandler's but Faulkner's, written with his left hand: of Bogart's famous line 'She tried to sit in my lap while I was standing up', the first half is Chandler and the second half – which precisely fits the lightened, racy tone Hawks gives the film visually – is Faulkner. Faulkner, who took the money and ran, got more out of Hollywood and put more back than Chandler, who gave it every-thing he had as a writer, saw little on the screen to show for it and was well-nigh consumed by bitterness.

In a cooperative enterprise you play percentages or lose all. The difference between the two men (a temperamental difference in the ability to see what was likely and possible) is worth drawing, since Agee was a larger and more complete example of Chandler's type – all artist and nothing but an artist. Hollywood ate men like that for breakfast. It's remarkable, given Agee's psychology, that he got as much done out there as he did.

Closing these two books with that mixture of gratitude and regret which any writing by Agee seems invariably to call from us, we can vary Tolstoy's question and ask – how much talent does a man need? 'He could get magic into his writing the hardest way, by precise description', says Macdonald, and quotes this passage from *A Death in the Family*:

First an insane noise of violence in the nozzle, then the still irregular sound of adjustment, then the smoothing into steadiness and a pitch as accurately tuned to the size and style of stream as any violin . . . the short still arch of the separate big drops, silent as a held breath, and only the noise the flattering noise on leaves and the slapped grass at the fall of each big drop. That, and the intense hiss with the intense stream; that, and that same intensity not growing less but growing more quiet and delicate with the turn of the nozzle, up to that extreme tender whisper when the water was just a wide bell of film.

He could write, all right. But Macdonald didn't draw attention to the underlying pathos of paragraphs – stanzas? – like this. 'Words cannot embody', Agee wrote in *Let Us Now Praise Famous Men*, 'they can only describe.' Yet he poured torrents of energy into making them embody. He was beyond words. Everything he wrote, and not just the scripts, was the work of a frustrated director: the page was a wrap-around screen with four-track stereophonic sound. Fundamentally anti-economical, it was the approach of a putter-in rather than a leaver-out, and all too frequently his prose had a coronary occlusion right there in front of you. It's the reason why even his famous essay on the silent comedians is somehow debilitating, and by extension the reason why his film criticism as a whole was finally less influential than Parker Tyler's (who couldn't write half so well): too much of his effort went into making the prose re-create, point for point, what he had seen.

Agee's inability to be narrowly professional was part of his humanity. He was versatile in an age that doesn't understand versatility. Yet it's possible to imagine him getting more things finished – or would be possible, if it weren't for the suspicion that something was wrong from the start. Half the reward of being an artist is becoming one. Agee missed out on that.

(1972)

## 20

## A Dinosaur at Sunset

Like the first, the second volume of what will eventually be a four-book set of Shaw's correspondence looks and handles like a doorstop from Valhalla. Nearly a thousand pages of it, most of them unskippable: the reader must forge on in a kind of despairing delight, overwhelmed by the abundance and vitality of what is on offer and secretly grateful that he knows only as a statistic what Professor Laurence knows for a fact – the complete set will contain a mere hundredth of the communications Shaw actually wrote. Compared with Shaw, Dickens is Ronald Firbank. Here is writing as a form of breathing, industry as a form of rest. In the last couple of weeks I have read both volumes and been convinced all over again that Shaw was out of this world, not least in his ability to understand the world so well. In this volume, covering the twelve years (1898–1910) in which he revolutionized the theatre, his grasp of affairs – big and little, world-wide and domestic – is as true as it is powerful. Not until a long time later did garrulity displace eloquence and brainwaves insight. For the present, he is making history, and so we read on with the unsettling certainty that he is helping to make us: a character-building experience, relieved by the high entertainment value of his style as a correspondent.

'All genuine intellectual work,' he wrote to Florence Farr, 'is humorous,' and whatever the truth of that in general, in his own particular case he was at this time busy proving it. Apart from the pamphlet-length letters to his biographer, Archibald Henderson, the book is marked by compression, cogency and a vivid epigrammatic brio. Gags abound, all of them emergent from a penetrating realism. 'Like a greengrocer and unlike a minor poet,' he tells the concussed Henderson, 'I have lived instead of dreaming.' Everybody knows about Shaw's ability to immerse himself in the detail of activity: it's the quality which provides the solid underpinning of *Music in London* and *Our Theatres in the Nineties*, securing those six volumes as the finest critical achievement in the language. And for years now there has been a growth industry in exploring Shaw's interests: books like *Shaw the Chucker-Out* amplify the picture sketched in monographs and biographies by men like Chesterton, Pearson and (still a central book) Eric Bentley. But what this selection of correspondence uniquely provides is the feel and force of all Shaw's enterprises raging forward simultaneously from day to day: the Goethean artist-philosopher, the intellectual omnivore, is right there in front of you. By the beard of the prophet, was there nothing the man could ignore?

He goes up in a balloon, and within weeks is already an expert on balloons. He buys a car and becomes a leading authority on cars. He commences an international correspondence with photography fanatics: this lens, that lens, wet plates, dry plates. The virtues and failings of a new pianola are sorted out and communicated to fellow pedal-pushers. These minor themes of his intellectual formation multiply in a steadily more complicated counterpoint. Surging through them are the major themes, most of them developed in an earlier period but still involved in an endless process of receiving their final elaborations. His socialism by this stage had become complex, tirelessly analytical and cleansed of utopianism. 'Of course an artificial city, so to speak, is no more impossible than a canal is,' he writes to Edward Rose in 1899, 'but the thing should be kept clear of philanthropy and utopian socialism because people (the tenants) will not stand being kept in a nursery.' It could be contended that his judgments are sound because he is relying on what he sees rather than on (as he did at a later stage, about Soviet Russia) what the Webbs thought they saw. But the contention won't quite do. Shaw in this period was able to make reliable generalizations about America, which he had never visited, and when the Fabians split over the South Africa question he put himself above the battle by providing an analysis of the situation prophetic in its clarity – in fact, South African history is now working itself out along lines which Shaw deduced from documents seventy years ago without setting foot outside London. Prophecy is not the test of analysis, but as supplementary evidence it's hard to ignore, and the reader of this volume will find himself encountering it every few score pages.

His power of generalization from detail – not only from observed detail, but from reported detail collated and pondered – is at its peak. It's only one of the ways in which he resembles Croce in the same period: one grows more and more convinced that they are the twin master-minds over that stretch of history. Like Croce, Shaw had read Marx before Lenin did, and again like Croce he had gone on to a vastly more complicated analytical position. Shaw's cyclic theory of history, in which events swung back and forth like a clock's pendulum but civilization went forward like a clock's tick, bore a piquant resemblance to Croce's, in which all occurrences ran in Viconian circles but the human spirit was carried forward by Providence. Both men had sought to discard the vulgarities of historicist metaphysics while retaining an ideal of progress. And to cap the resemblance, Shaw was as obviously (and remains to this day) the greatest prose stylist in English as Croce was and remains the greatest in Italian. Such a comparison isn't meant to imply that Shaw is Croce's equal as a philosopher: in fact, the difference between the two men is a precise demonstration of why the artist-philosopher is finally engaged in something other than philosophy. But it is meant to imply that this was the last modern period in which super-minds could grasp the world whole, with confidence of purpose as well as of ability. This purposive element is what now

makes them look like dinosaurs – dinosaurs at sunset. Croce thought
evil was simply error, and that no movement totally devoid of constructive ideas could possibly affect history. Shaw's view was
perilously similar and ran into the same kind of difficulty. The
arrival of totalitarianism settled the hash of their ideas of progress
as effectively as they themselves had discredited the materialistic
determinism of their predecessors – an irony compounded by the
fact that the new callousness was a throw-back to those predecessors.
The consensus now is that Shaw was a fool to understand totalitarianism so slowly. My point in bringing up Croce is that Shaw
was not alone in being so unhorsed. It was the very magnitude of
their minds that misled them. They thought that unreason could
be reasoned out of countenance. A great, a truly great, mistake.

In these years occur the first productions of all Shaw's early plays.
He was involved in the practicalities of theatrical business to the
uppermost bristle of his eyebrows. There are brilliant letters to
Ada Rehan on the changing character of the stage since Ibsen
which show the kind of trouble he was prepared to take to convince
actors that they were doing something serious. Ignore such instruction as they might, the actors were unlikely to brush lightly
aisde the accompanying bombardment of technical advice: the nuts
and bolts of performance and production stick out tangibly everywhere in the volume, re-creating in the most abrasive way what a
Shaw matinée at the Royal Court must have been like – an act of
dedication, and not just because scarcely anybody got properly
paid. These were the days before Shaw became the 'overwhelming
force in the theatre' that the Penguin blurbs were later to call him.
Commercially, it was small-time: but the planning that went into
the presentation was the full complement of the thought that went
into writing the plays, and anyone who doubts that Shaw's humility
was as endless as his conceit should look at the relevant letters and
see the lengths that selfless toil can go to. A visionary, he was yet
the opposite of a dreamer. He was responsibility incarnate. As a
vestryman of St. Pancras he fights to keep the district's solitary free
women's loo open; as a playwright he strives to convince his translator Trebitsch that arbitrary variations on words play havoc with
construction; as an author he controls everything from the renting

out of his own electrotypes to the width of his margins and the founts of his title-pages. Nothing, but nothing, is let slide. It will be a rare contemporary reader who contemplates this perfection of character without wishing a plague on the man's ashes.

Orwell somewhere calls Shaw an empty windbag and somewhere else confesses that he has read practically every word Shaw has written. Such ambivalence is inevitable. The superhuman is inhuman in the end, and only a dolt could admire it without misgivings. But that doesn't mean we should go on trying to cut Shaw down to size. It's widely supposed that Shaw wasn't capable of sex, but a less comfortable and more likely supposition is that he was above it, like Leonardo. He could certainly be an interfering busybody, but only because as a totally truthful man he couldn't readily conceive of someone intelligent not wanting to hear the truth. Poor Erica Cotterill was allowed to entertain her hopes of conquest too long, but one doubts whether it was because Shaw was toying with her affections: he probably believed that by an application of common reason he could fill her head with something else besides passion. Shaw's friendships were so disinterested as to be hardly recognizable as friendship. He lent money to acquaintances of good character but would never grant a loan to his friend Charles Charrington, whose bad character he would forgive but not abet. He supported Wells in the Fabian power struggle until the moment when Wells's reckless indolence was proved, whereupon he destroyed him overnight. Shaw can appear callous only to the selectively compassionate – i.e. to nearly all of us. Most of us love unreasonably, tell half-truths and favour our friends. The world is like that – which is what I mean by saying Shaw was out of it. He was a moral genius.

'His correspondence alone would fill many volumes,' St. John Ervine wrote in his now reissued *Bernard Shaw*, 'and the task of editing it will not be enviable.' Enviable, perhaps not. Vital, certainly. Professor Laurence, half-way home, has already proved himself fully equal to the task.

(1972)

## 21

# The Last Amateur

The notes at the back looking as long as a book, and the book at the front looming as big as a house, Mr. Mizener's new opus is to be approached with a trepidation only slightly eased by the fact that we are here plainly in the tradition of one-volume giganticism exemplified by Mark Schorer, rather than the tradition of multi-volume elephantiasis exemplified by George Painter and Leon Edel. As it turns out, the span of the average train strike is just sufficient to get the book read. This feat accomplished, the immediate temptation is to hail a masterpiece. *The Saddest Story* is in fact something less than that, but it is still very good. Arthur Mizener has taken time (years) and pains (infinite) to root out every possible fact about Ford Madox Ford, a job complicated severely by Ford's inability to tell the truth about anything for more than two seconds running. If Ford has talked about crossing the Channel on a certain boat, Mr. Mizener checks up in the shipping records to see if Ford has got the boat right: invariably Ford has got it wrong. As with *The Far Side of Paradise*, the research data are interpreted with admirable level-headedness and written up in a flat style that does little to draw you forward. 'It is one of the sad ironies of Ford's life that, with all his scorn of businessmen and his belief that as an artist he had risen above the vulgar pressures of money, he was constantly at the mercy of his need for money.' The best you can say of a sentence like that is that it limps in a straight line. Nevertheless the book bubbles and sings. Ford Madox Ford – novelist's novelist, editor of editors, fascinator of gifted women, seer, saint and arch-twit – is here given. It's a fantastic show.

Even when the actuality was more than good enough to get by on, Ford was compelled to improve the truth: he was a walking credibility gap. Mr. Mizener does not attempt to trace the trauma but he does a thorough job of tracing the results – a job that would have been devastating if he had not managed to hold fast to his correct estimate of Ford's quality as a creative mind. Carlos Baker's admiration of Hemingway trembled on its base as the facts came out; Lawrance Thompson's admiration of Frost was destroyed by them; Mizener's admiration of Ford seems to go on climbing as the buffoonery mounts beyond farce into the empyrean. It's a valuable corrective to Hemingway's mean-spirited estimate in *A Movable Feast*. With the single important exception of his neglectful bad faith with abandoned loves, Ford was titanically generous in everything: even his paranoid dealings with agents and publishers were on too wildly impractical a scale ever to appear less than prodigal. An opulently charming nutter who wound up as a bore, an eccentric who lived to be pathetic, he did everything he could to dissipate his marvellous talent, but on at least two occasions things defeated him by going right: *The Good Soldier* and the Tietjens tetralogy are two clear white spaces in a copy-book consisting almost entirely of blots, permanently valuable hiatuses in a literary life that swept inexorably towards the evanescent.

Brought up among Pre-Raphaelites, Ford suffered agonies of humiliation as the frightful Rossetti children outshone him in parlour pageants: little Arthur Rossetti starred as Theseus while Ford wilted. From that day until the end of his life, Ford favoured a medievalism purged of aestheticism: the image of Rossetti in a dressing-gown conducting sexual intrigues amidst litter and cold bacon fat haunted him through a long life of dressing-gowns, sexual intrigues, litter and cold bacon fat. He dreamed an ideal of plain dealing while living a chaotic actuality of tortuous evasiveness. He went to a school run by a man called Praetorius: later on he called it Westminster. He put it about that he had a golf handicap of three. He said that W. E. Henley had called him the finest living stylist in the English language: what Henley had actually said was: 'Who the hell are you?' Ford's war record was sound enough for a man 42 years old who didn't need to go – he really was blown up by a shell at Bécourt-Bécordel – but he made it all incredible by promoting himself from the support lines to the trenches and claiming that the Government had plotted against him to suppress his ideas for the peace terms. Ford needed fantasy the way he needed sexual adventure. Both needs are characteristic of mother's boys, and one could wish that Mr. Mizener had explored this question further.

The women succeed each other sensationally throughout the book. Even at his youngest and trimmest Ford looked like an earless Bugs Bunny on stilts, and by his own admission he was more interested in chat than sex: nevertheless the Grade A crumpet came at him like kamikazes, crashing through his upper decks in gaudy cataracts of fire. Violet Hunt took him away from his first wife, Elsie. Violet had already gone through the contemporary literati like a flame-thrower, only Henry James escaping unsinged. She ate arsenic for her looks and already had tertiary syphilis when she got off with Ford. A woman who had somehow managed to hit the sack with Somerset Maugham was a sexual force of primal urgency. Ford was the one she settled down with, ruining her social acceptability: Ford, still called Hueffer at that stage, fantasized a German divorce and Violet was besotted enough to swallow it.

It wasn't all she swallowed: in 1912 they were both on Adalin and went about crashed out of their skulls. After the war Ford got involved with the Australian Stella Bowen, retiring up-country to become an expert on the Sussex Large Black Pig and exercise his gifts, too long repressed, as a simple artisan: he built a rickety oaken sty in which the pig promptly caught a chill and croaked. Violet spied on them over the fence. Stella gave way to the young novelist Jean Rhys, but bore no grudge: she was intelligent enough to realize the falsity of Ford's posturings as a gentleman, and enough of an Australian woman to give thanks for having met a gentle man, under whatever circumstances. Stella stuck with Ford through his further liaison with an American, Rene Wright, but finally lost him to America itself: the Tietjens novels were a biggish success there, making just enough money to tempt Ford into total ruin. Finally he met fiery little Janice, who loved him as they all did and helped him fight his misjudged battles. From first to last, it's an uncanny record of female sacrifice on the part of all of them. Their only reward was his companionship, which must have been sheer magic.

Ford was a great editor, though not a practical one: his magazines were doomed from their inception, immortality being their only earnings. The first number of the *English Review* had Hardy, James, Galsworthy, Hudson, Wells and Conrad. Ford edited during the second house at the Shepherd's Bush Empire, the only place he could be alone. Business management was carried out with the same hard-headed practicality which led him to wash his Panama hat and place it in Jessie Conrad's oven to dry, thereby fumigating the Sunday joint. Ford's admiration for other good writers was total: Conrad's for his old collaborator rather less. Conrad was a calculator and therefore a concentrater: Ford helped him learn how to write English but couldn't match what he did with it, except with *The Good Soldier* and Tietjens, where his fantasies about himself (the Tory radical, much put upon but never complaining) were so brilliantly realized they became the foolishness of us all. Always precisely wrong about his own character, Ford's vaunting of his professionalism gives us the clue: he was the last amateur. He loved literature and literature will always love him. Fellini's Guido Anselmi – similarly a liar, similarly a host of hosts – called his own life a festival. So was Ford's. Here it is.

(1972)

PART FIVE

# Clerical Treason

# 22

# Cuter than a Cub Koala: Richard Neville's
## *Play Power*

Three hundred and sixty one pages bound in boards, a Martin
Sharp funny-paper wrapper stamped with the holy initials of a
leading establishment publishing house, and a price tag of 38s
(£1.90) net in UK only: this is the *underground*? But before we smile
wryly, let's leave aside for the moment the essential question of
who the book is supposed to be for (with its related question of
what the author is trying to promote himself as), and deal rapidly
with the incidental question of what the book is. Ordinarily this
last question would be the central one, but in this case it's peripheral: there isn't much in the book that you won't have come across
in one trendy place or another. What's unusual is to have this information on play-politics and the new sex and the dope culture, these
polemics on system-erosion and generational confrontation and Do
Your Own Thing, and these clue-charts on where to score and when
to squat and how to fool slot machines, all wrapped into one parcel.

I should also mention that Richard Neville can write. *Oz*, the
intermittently active magazine he edits, never has enough of his
own writing: among the sleepy drone of the acid heads and the
foam-flecked rhetoric of the loonier Situationists his own voice rings
out clear but seldom. Over the length of *Play Power* one gets to
know and like him. Within the terms he sets himself he speaks with
a welcome balance of constructive cheek and admonitory caution,
giving the book something of the air of an up-dated *Boys' Com-
panion* with the knot-tying and daily cold showers left out and
healthy screwing and safe smoking put in. But of course we're
already sliding into the question of who the book is for.

*Play Power* is for new recruits and for the older unconverted who
will remain unconverted but may become tolerant. The first group
can be considered statistically negligible, at any rate until the

paperback comes out. It's the second group that's interesting, both in what they represent and the kind of play Neville makes for their attention. This group is straight and likely to remain so. Neville is a straight freak. In *Oz* he edits freak material for freak consumption. In this book he is bringing the freak world to straights: as cute on the page as he is in life, he explains, he cajoles and he dedicates the book to mum and dad. Although ostensibly aimed at extending the experience of those who already share his style of life, Neville's book is in fact cunningly slanted towards those who have missed out on it but whose understanding of it is essential if the life-style is to consolidate itself. He isn't altogether clear about whether he is identifying the state with the capitalist system in this country, he isn't altogether clear about whether he is identifying this country with the United States, but in fact his book tends to separate these things and has its real force in seeing what is possible *here*. The global pot-trail trotting and the salutes of solidarity to pig-baiting Yippies are treated as inspiring exotica. What matters (and I think he sees this is what matters) is that given the right conditions an alternative society can survive and even expand in this country without either an attempt to overthrow the state or a fruitless straight/freak confrontation.

In pointing out that Neville hasn't written the book as an incitement to bloody rebellion one isn't necessarily contending that he's a quietist. He believes in radical change all right – but a change by Hash Cookie subversion, by a general turning-on of children. Compared with the concrete proposals, or even the tone of voice, of young American radicals in an equivalent position of influence, he sounds about as dangerous as a provisionally licensed pixie. But then Britain and the United States are not equivalent societies. Britain is the more advanced; which is one of the reasons that Neville is here instead of there. In the United States the alternative society (you couldn't use the term 'play power' in *that* context) is inextricably mixed up with revolution: a revolution it can't make without ditching its fundamental values by assuming power, and a revolution it now seems it can't afford *not* to make without being pressured into quietism.

The lesson in the United States is that capitalism can give ground to the new life-style but that the state can't. The lesson here, so far, is that they both can. In the United States the straights have no give, so the freaks have no room to turn around in: play becomes a gesture at best and pack-drill at worst, the fuck-you rhetoric escalates to scare the straights even further, and cool is blown in vast quantities on either side. In Britain the straight/freak confrontation is softened to the point of workability by the presence in government and the media of the meritocratic elite – the older alternative society which identified absorptive flexibility as the essential characteristic of British politics and furthered the work of institutionalizing it. Consciously or unconsciously (mainly unconsciously: their rhetoric ran the other way, towards revolution) the underground here separated state from system and began to throw up ideas, not all of them feeble, for effecting social change without overthrowing the power structure.

For anyone regarding Capitalism with a capital C as the enemy this was an alarmingly quietist trend of thought. But in fact there's nothing quieter than a shout against the wind, and even though several unreconstructed revolutionaries have found a platform in *Oz*, the underground trend runs nowhere near the barricades. The important thing to remember is that in the underground here the revolutionaries are the exceptions: they're a straight influence which survives among the freaks only so long as their stance remains rhetorical. Half-articulated but far more powerful, the real drive in the underground is to survive and expand in an unpolarized straight society. The great strength of Neville's book is that he has recognized this drive and realized that if the underground has any power, this is its power. His naïvety resides in his breathless recounting of the underground life-styles in the United States as if *all* these phenomena were *ipso facto* cures, palliatives, creative advances. His sophistication resides in not trying to import the American situation – or the Dutch, the French or the German – holus bolus. He thereby dodges the hopelessly contradictory one-worldness (*one* fight against *one* system) which has so vitiated underground writing from the beginning. *Play Power* is consequently realistic in the sense that matters – its dreams of peace are really dreamable.

Does it make sense to argue that simply by surviving the underground is a force for change? In the British context I think it does, though it's easy to imagine other contexts in which the argument would have no political meaning at all, or at best would be a gentle plea for tolerant pluralism. The underground in Britain, unlike the American version, has no single issue to guarantee its solidarity: it has a solidarity beyond single issues, which means it really *does* have a style – a complex of attitudes which criticize and subvert established values without insisting on their immediate disappearance.

You can sum up Neville's key proposition thus: don't turn on the cops with your fists, turn their sons on to pot. In the United States there wouldn't be much sense in proposing this at the moment. But it does make sense here. There's at least a slim chance of the meek inheriting this part of the earth and profoundly modifying both capitalism and the state simply by growing into them. It's an extension of the principle by which the system and the state can be played off against one another as soon as you recognize they are separable. What you *can't* usefully do is call them both the one thing and talk the necessary majority of the people into mounting a frontal attack: nor can you hope to induce the conditions of polarization which would radicalize the populace as it now is. But of course the one thing the populace can never do is stay as it now is. It has to replace itself. And it's very significant that at this particular point in time a scene-chief like Neville should come forward and help to guard this process of replacement by presenting it in as flattering a light as possible to the straight generations who are called upon, in the view of the underground, to do nothing except die.

The last thing I want to suggest is that Neville has figured all this out. But the fact that something like this is the general drift of his work, even though arrived at instinctively, is of far greater interest than the choleric sperm-in-the-streets programmes of imported revolutionaries like Angelo Quattrocchi. Neville is not only an underground figure in his own right – there's no denying that – he's also a mini-capitalist in his own right, not to mention an aspiring moderator of television chat-shows. To the 'old' New Left he must look riddled with contradictions. But he and others like him are modifying the system as they take it over. And here is the real advantage of being an outlander, in this case an Australian. He can see that the system *is* modifiable. By managing *Oz* in Australia he was able to give a practical demonstration that the repressive feedback of the state into the economic system was a good deal less than 100 per cent. By simply being an Australian he manages to slice through the British class-system even faster than the emancipated indigenous meritocrats who long ago spotted that Communications was the class swindle's breaking-point.

Let these be the trends. Then what are the chances? I don't believe, myself, that a society of Love is coming: as with most of the immediately pre-underground generation of lefties my one last hope is in the possibility of a society of Rights. Basically it's the claim to rights which forms the substance of the underground's real style but it's all unnervingly mixed up with the promotion of moods, emotional abstractions like Love which to the underground seem concrete but which logically extended could lead to anything. But if Neville hasn't completely unscrambled the dreamable dreams from the disguised nightmares, at least he's scrambled them no further. As a universal compendium the book's a bust. As a text of local application it has real value. He's come to the right place.

(1970)

# 23

## After the *Oz* Trial

The *Oz* trial went overhead very slowly, like a fair to middling episode of *Monty Python's Flying Circus* running at the wrong speed. Suddenly, a far-off crunch: our faces fall. The news arrives that there has been an almighty pile-up and three of the madcap aviators will have to walk back – one of them might not be back at all. End of joke.

In the heyday of censorship in Australia's comic State of Victoria,

you always knew what you were up against: nobody pretended to
wisdom or even common reason. Inspector Eulenspiegel, or whatever his name was, simply asked the court to hang, draw and quarter
the editors of the *Oxford English Dictionary* on the grounds that it
contained certain words: whereupon the judge instructed the jury
to show no mercy and awarded Eulenspiegel a fourth bar to his
Surf Lifesaving Association's Bronze Medallion. The Returned
Servicemen's League (95 per cent of the male adult population of
the country) would then commandeer every existing news medium
to remind the other 5 per cent that the lonely voice of the true
digger had at last been heard and that these poms from Oxford
were a mob of cockatoos and poof-dahs. There was none of this
misleading veneer of common sense disguising the essential rat-
baggery and shoddiness of the proceedings: you knew where you
were – which was usually on the first available ship to England.

There is not much point in stoking the fire under Judge Argyle.
Despite the views of several of Fleet Street's most distinguished
leader writers (who seem to be of the opinion that he had sentenced
the *Oz* editors for corrupting and depraving minors), he most
definitely did not sentence the three intrepid flyers for something
the jury said they had not done. What he did was give them a
thundering sentence for what the jury said they *had* done. He
picked them up by the exposed scruff of the neck and dumped them
in the jug for something that in the normal course of events would
not have cost them anything but money. Several of Fleet Street's
most distinguished leader writers were acting on their own account
when they decided to flounce up and down outside the chokey
window patting themselves with power puffs and shrieking about
'corruption' – an idea the jury had already rejected, on the strength
of the prosecution's notable failure to produce expert evidence in
its favour. Whether something is obscene or not is a ponderable
which Judge Argyle treated as something empirically ascertainable,
like whether someone is dead or not or whether a shop has been
broken into or not: there is nothing in the law to dictate that he
should have done otherwise, and if Wittgenstein had been in his
place the instruction to the jury would still have had to be based on
an *a priori* assumption, although probably a better one.

For the same reason, there is no point in guying Brian Leary: he attacked the moral credibility of witnesses for the simple reason that the law encourages him to – the only way to falsify somebody's moral assertions is to prove him immoral. When the crime itself is all to be established, who among us is not guilty? Nobody, except (and here we see a dazzle of propeller, a flash of goggles and a stream of silken scarf) Lord Longford, the White Knight of the Air.

Similarly there are no prizes to be won by poking fun at Detective Inspector Luff of the Obscene Publications Squad. For all the restrictions it places in the way of the police interpreting people's intentions and evincing distaste for people's general attitudes, the law (which is the well-known double-whammy, the Obscene Publications Acts of 1964 and 1969) might as well be Article 58 of the old Soviet Criminal Code.

With all the world of obscenity to choose from – and everything is obscene which the police disapprove of – it is necessary to be selective. No wonder then, that Soho porn is left relatively alone and those areas are picked on which are not self-regulating, where rudery is claimed to be a means towards an end and where the end is something with which they are out of sympathy. The police would have to be Athenian philosophers, and several cuts above the ones surrounding Socrates, to do better than they do now. It's the law that's at fault. It centres on a concept that nobody has ever been able to define, and once a charge has been brought under it there is no defence against the ordinary prejudices of prosecution, judge and jury except to introduce a counterbalancing, equally undefinable concept, such as literary merit.

In the *Oz* case the counter-balancing concept turned out to be a version of the public good – a version involving the right to criticize, the right to question, the necessity for untrammelled evolutionary change. It didn't have a chance. It wouldn't have had a chance if George Bernard Shaw had stood there for five weeks reading his collected 'Prefaces' aloud and screening newsreels of Galileo on the rack. There is nothing that can happen in a courtroom which will give specificity to a vague law. It was a wise man who said that the Lady Chatterley acquittal gave the notion of obscenity substance and was therefore catastrophic.

Under the Obscenity laws it is possible to bring covert charges against political opinions, and the mere possibility should be enough reason to get these laws off the books in all haste. It makes no difference if the judge thinks it is not a political trial. It makes no difference if all the leader-writers in London think it is not a political trial. Once there is selection in deciding what to charge, it is a political trial, whatever happens at it and whichever way it goes. An underground publication can be wiped out simply by the cost of being hauled before a court. Once the charge is brought, the job is done. This is too much power for anyone to have, and what our leader-writers must realize – all at once if possible, but one at a time if necessary – is that *any* use of such power is an abuse.

I should say at this point that I myself have small sympathy for *Oz* in general, and scarcely any at all for the culprit issue No. 28: I laughed like a drain at the priapic Rupert the Bear but found the rest thick-witted and raucous in the usual *Oz* way. That it was produced by schoolchildren proved nothing to me beyond the fact that adolescent rhetoric had shifted away from class-ridden, British Empire rubbish towards revolutionary rubbish. The new brand of rhetoric, like the old, is there to be grown out of in the search for the real, and the one advantage it offers is that it at least tries to take account of a few salient facts about the condition of the modern world. On sex the new rhetoric is less obscurantist than the old, and the *Oz* editors (and their defenders both legal and journalistic) are on strong moral ground when they argue that an imposed ignorance is no control and that a compassionate concern for the world is closely allied to the shedding of sexual guilt.

Beyond that, in *Oz* No. 28, as in every other issue, there is just the usual earnest confusion about what the condition of the world actually is. Like equivalent confusions of previous eras it strikes me as being ineluctably middle-class in the political solutions it proposes. For the short term at any rate it's a phantom revolution, but at least it is not po-faced. At least it tries to be fun to belong to, and probably the objections of the Whitehouse–Longford brigade begin at this fact. Although the underground thinks quite otherwise, neither of these worthies is in the least political; they are sheerly and simply Puritan and wouldn't know a radical alternative from a limited-slip differential, and where the law allows them no scope they can have no influence beyond that conferred by innate authority: i.e., practically zero.

I have known Richard Neville for years and have always admired his honesty: his intelligence (which apparently earned him an extra three months in the slam, if I read Judge Argyle aright) is tenacious rather than quick, but he faces facts once he has worked them out. In his book *Play Power* there were already signs that he had recognized the dangers the underground might face through violent confrontation. He was already betting on establishing a plump, healthy parasite alternative within the body of a tolerant host. When people started jumping bail after he had posted his own money for them, he regretted fast enough – and in *Oz* too – that he had ever recommended sharp practice.

The editorial policy of *Oz* has always been to have no policy: they'd shove anything in, not excluding the ravings of the madder situationists or the bomb plots of crazed, desperate Americans. But I never heard that the *Oz* editors as a group had any idea of encouraging organized violence in this country. Their double-think about Britain was too impregnable for that: they never doubted that this hopelessly corrupt, repressive capitalist system was anything other than fundamentally reliable, tolerant and pluralist. Revolutionary in rhetoric, *Oz* and all its off-shoots are revisionist to the core.

Until recently there was an interesting situation evolving in the underground press. *Time Out* had moved up to a just-below-the-overground position where it started providing news and services in a recognizable and useful radical mode. *Ink* had been launched as an alternative newspaper and after a typically chaotic start (everything around Neville is pure Keystone Kops) had begun to improve. Below these, down in the old underground, *Oz*, *IT* and the rest were facing the possibility that the underground was here to stay – that it was part of the life of the country and needed to work out what kind of influences it could exert. I don't think I'm being optimistic or smug in saying that the underground was maturing. If society had rational interests it would have been within those interests to protect this maturing process by leaving it alone. But as the underground began to find out all over again, you underestimate your opponent if you attribute rational coherence to the 'system': it is not perfectly coherent, it is far from rational and it has no reliable means of knowing its own interests.

In late March a wave of prosecutions and book-shop raids began. It was left to the underground press to report the speed and weight of this wave, and now the underground press itself is starting to crumple under the pressure. The charge which made life difficult for *IT* was particularly piquant: the editors were pulled in on an obscenity rap for allowing homosexuals to signal to one another in the small ads. So far as I know, there is nothing that proscribes this in any law of the land, and by the same logic the police should be conducting lightning raids on public lavatories and carrying away van-loads of cubicle doors.

Under the obscenity law, young people are being charged with offences they will not be aware they have committed until they hear the verdict. This is against the whole spirit of the legal system in this country and has its proper place only in police states. Under the obscenity law, defence counsel is obliged to ask for a wider context to be taken into consideration (the public good, etc.) and so imply that in the narrow context the object in question may well be obscene. This places the defence in a difficult position and on occasion virtually aligns it with the prosecution. Under the obscenity law, the police are encouraged to behave like Dogberry, and the bench is obliged to indulge in philosophical investigations that are beyond its competence, and would be beyond the competence of Hegel and Aristotle trapped together for ten years in the Library of Congress.

The first penalty of thought control is to make the controller seem a clown. Already we are not far from the moment when some home-grown equivalent of Eulenspiegel will support the evidence of his latest pot-bust with books culled from private shelves. Neville has got his bail, which postpones the fateful moment, but if his appeal should be turned down, there might not be any need to cap his fifteen-month stretch by sending him home. Australia could already be here.

(1971)

# 24

## Another Dreamer

Theodore Roszak's *The Making of a Counter Culture* should have been the first contemplative study of the counter culture, or alternative society, to matter; so it's a pity that the book is not very good. Things we can forgive Richard Neville can't really be forgiven Theodore Roszak. He can draw upon sufficient intellectual resources to know a problem when he sees it. Having seen it, he raises it; and having raised it, skates around it. So *The Making of a Counter Culture* is shallow without being naïve, which is a lot worse than Neville's *Play Power*, which was shallow *because* it was naïve.

In the first and best two chapters of the book Roszak describes the counter culture at the same time as describing the technocratic culture from which it is supposedly trying to break free. His description of the counter culture is comprehensive: it ranges from the dropped-out to the wanting-in. He proposes here a common factor, but since the common factor is only a common attitude to the prevailing technocracy, it's hard to see how the common factor would stay common if a fluid revolutionary situation actually developed.

His description of the technocratic culture, though very wide-ranging, is really only a glorified characterization, at once too exclusive and too inclusive. It excludes institutions and hence removes the obligation to analyse them. It includes phenomena which should properly be isolated, and thus abets the bad intellectual practice (universal in the underground) of anathematizing the 'system' without defining it.

Throughout this twin-track description of the two cultures there are enough get-out clauses and implied qualifications to safeguard the author's claim to an objective view, but not nearly enough instances of close argument to justify his pretension to a capacity for analysis.

'And yet . . . there are manifestations around the fringe of the counter culture that one cannot but regard as worrisomely un-healthy.' There is enough in Roszak's own account of emotion re-placing intellect to give one confidence in asserting that some of these worrisomely unhealthy manifestations are not just around the fringe but bang in the centre. Roszak is well aware that irrationalism has a fly-blown history in this century. He is very eager to show that the counter culture is not Nazi. He attempts to show this by characterizing Nazism: predictably, in accordance with his whole intellectual style, he focuses on ideology and pays little attention to organization or institutions. But with the Nazis one of the con-sequences of irrationality was precisely that ideology was extremely flexible: anything could be presented for belief, and be believed.

Roszak says that with the counter culture there are first principles (feelings of compassion, awareness, sensitivity and so on) which place a limit to potential aberrations. Except around the fringe? Orwell once suggested that every revolutionary is forced to lie about the immediate future. With a sympathetic analyst like Roszak, for the movement but not of it, there is no necessity to lie: merely to ignore. He says little about what would have to happen if straight institutions and technologies gave way before the burgeoning counter culture at a rate which would entail an assumption of powers.

But to ignore the problem of the immediate revolutionary future means to skirt the question of the real nature of the relationship between the cultures. Is the counter culture the dependent part of a necessary dualism? If it is not, and is fated to replace the tech-nocracy, can it retain the indispensable benefits conferred by the technocracy without corrupting itself by developing the organ-izational structures necessary to retain them? And so on.

These, and dozens more like them, are the real issues. Some of them are raised, none is treated. Instead, Roszak 'develops' his argument (i.e., depressurizes and diverts it) by setting up a further dialectical expounding-and-balancing, this time of Marcuse and Norman O. Brown. Brown emerges a clear winner. And before going on to examine the questions of how Brown's insights could be put into action on a large scale, and what would happen to them if they were (questions which might well have given pause to Pareto),

Roszak's off again – this time into the Wisdom of the East. Once again he covers himself (as he covers himself when talking about Brown) by characterizing the counter culture's derivations from eastern religions as a mish-mash, but also once again he's wonderfully confident in announcing that the bias of the mish-mash is radiantly towards life-giving mind-expansion and healthily away from the tight-arsed European heritage that's had a hex on us all these years. Well, it passes for rhetoric but as analysis it's hopeless. In fact the book itself is a symptom of the American disease whose ravages Roszak is well able to see but whose nature he is incompetent to judge. He doesn't know what an institution is: he puts his trust in a change of heart.

(1970)

# 25

## The Green American

News of Charles Reich's *The Greening of America* has been filtering across the pond for some time. It has been reported that under its benevolent influence middle-aged pink-rinsed ladies have tossed aside their jumbo tubes of tranquillizers and embraced their hairy lost sons in a fit of understanding, kissing them noisily on the sweat-band. *Rolling Stone* ran an interview with Reich in which the interviewers seemed as delighted as he was at the possibility of reconciling the generations. The pipe of peace (spiked in this case with sweetly crumbling hash) was being passed, and gnarled, trembling hands were reaching out to take a hit. A piquant scene.

It would be a churl who failed to salute the spirit which informs *The Greening of America*, and this should hold true even when it is shown – as it quite easily can be – that the book's theoretical structure is something of a ruin and that its view of the emergent alternative life-style is simplistic and has already been outdistanced by events. A polemical writer is necessarily committed to portraying situations as rather simpler than they really are. It's the price he pays for the chance to alter them. The effect on the reader is often to convince him that the author is smarter than the book. There are elements in this book which are quite sensationally obtuse. I don't want to suggest that these elements are reflections of Mr. Reich's optimum performance on such mental tests as the Stanford-Binet, the Wechsler-Bellevue or the Minnesota Multiphasic: merely that they reflect a tendency to pursue an ideal by donning blinkers, plunging the head into the sand and subjecting the resulting field of vision to a pitiless scrutiny.

There is a great deal to be said for Mr. Reich's analysis of what has gone wrong with America – his critique is a bit like a large helping of C. Wright Mills with some stiffened Marcuse ladled over the top, but just because it is derivative and somewhat etiolated does not make it irrelevant. In his celebration of the youth movement, however, he is starry-eyed to a degree that can no longer be accepted even by the youth movement itself. He is fixed in time somewhere between Woodstock and Altamont, which means that he has omitted to mention the moment when the joyous tribe of children was joined by a pale rider. He is fixed in space between the separate family encampments of the Californian rock epicentre (Jefferson Airplane, Grateful Dead) and that other musical commune who solved the challenge of Sharon Tate's inimical emblematic status by translating her ferociously into oblivion. He waves a gay farewell not just to the bogus rationality which has created misery for so many Americans and caused so many Americans to create misery for so many others, but to rationality itself. He seems to think that the past can be dumped simply by wishing it, and in thinking this he underestimates the pervasiveness of the American tragedy; it is not timorous or spiteful, it is merely wise for an intelligent man to insist that the new American consciousness might just pose the same threats to *moderation* that America has always posed. They apologize for frightening us with their dreams, and in recompense send us another dream.

Of the book's theoretical basis – Consciousness I, Consciousness II and (jackpot!) Consciousness III – there is much effort to be expended in paraphrase, although little in dismissal. Briefly, Consciousness I is the pioneering, personal property-accumulating spirit which built the Republic and began the work of destroying it through exploitation. Consciousness II is the public spirit which attempted to govern this process but succeeded (principally through the New Deal) only in institutionalizing the destructive processes through codifying them into a corporate state. No degree, however generous and imaginative, of commitment to institutional reform will get you out of Consciousness II: conflicts within it are nugatory:

Consciousness II believes that the present American crisis can be solved by greater commitment of individuals to the public interest, more social responsibility by private business, and, above all, by more affirmative government action – regulation, planning, more of a welfare state, better and more rational administration and management.

Silly old Consciousness II. Consciousness III is the youth culture which knows (just as Lenin's peasants mysteriously 'knew') that none of this is going to work.

At this point Mr. Reich's argument, and most of his prose along with it, collapses quickly into self-deceiving rhetoric, although I should in fairness add that a lot of the rhetoric is very forceful and never less than humane. Mr. Reich says that the youth culture (and the older generations when they, too, are persuaded) will reject system, reject the idea of a career, and will use technology instead of being used by it. But clearly if this new Consciousness is to become the body of the animal, instead of the parasite, it will have to organize the appropriate changes; and equally clearly it can only organize these changes through rediscovering a rational public spirit.

To take only one example, what follows from Mr. Reich's analysis of the law's lawlessness except the conclusion that the law will have to be made law-abiding? To take another, does Mr. Reich seriously suppose that high-grade technology can be turned towards humane purposes in any other than a planned way? Or even run down in any other than a planned way? However, this is merely reasoning.

Conceptually, then, Consciousness III is part of Consciousness II and cannot be otherwise. There will either be a reform of institutions or the whole show will go under. Once the notion of seizing power is abandoned (and Mr. Reich very sensibly sees that the whole force of the youth movement is to set an example rather than to coerce) the revolution becomes a reformist movement willy-nilly. There has simply been a change of emphasis, although it is, of course, an enormous change of emphasis and quite probably already decisive.

Correctly viewed, the youth movement is a turning away from impersonal power and towards politics. Incorrectly viewed (and Reich's enthusiasm aids this view), it is a turning away from politics itself, towards a dream world in which identity will be painlessly recovered in a magically recrudescent Eden. In the land of Consciousness III/There ain't no apples on the Knowledge Tree.

(1971)

# 26

## Getting Married Later

Germaine Greer's first and very considerable book *The Female Eunuch* drops into the intelligentsia's radar accompanied by scores of off-putting decoy noise-sources: a panicky response is virtually guaranteed. Granada Publishing (the command group for Mac-Gibbon and Kee) have done an impressive job with the highbrow press, and weeks before publication date Dr. Greer was already well known.

If this makes it seem that the reviewer is too concerned with media reactions and media values, let it be made clear that there is little chance of any other kinds of reactions and values operating in the present instance. Germaine Greer is a storm of images; has already been promoted variously as Germaine de Staël, Fleur Fenton Cowles, Rosa Luxemburg and Beatrice Lillie; and at the time of writing needs only a few more weeks' exposure in order to reoccupy the corporeally vacant outlines of Lou Andreas-Salomé, George Sand, Marie von Thurn und Taxis-Hohenlohe and Marjorie Jackson (the Lithgow Flash). Media-hype is never sadder than when something decent is at the centre of the fuss. These forebodings might be wrong, and there could just be a slim chance that *The Female Eunuch* will be appreciated on its merits. But I wouldn't count on it.

The book's merits are of a high order. It possesses a fine, continuous flow of angry power which both engenders and does much to govern the speed-wobble of its logical progression; it sets out an adventurous analysis of social detail which does much to offset the triteness of its theoretical assumptions; and all in all it survives its flaws of style, falsities of assessment and excesses of sentimentality to present an argument of terrific polemical force. 'Now as before, women must refuse to be meek and guileful, for truth cannot be served by dissimulation. Women who fancy that they manipulate the world by pussy power and gentle cajolery are fools. It is time for the demolition to begin.' It's a revolutionary position from first to last, and a lot of people, many of them ladies, are going to be interested in taking the sting out of it, principally by institutionalizing the authoress. A six-foot knock-out freak don with three degrees and half a dozen languages who can sing, dance, act, write and turn men to stone with an epigram – what a target for the full media treatment!

Meanwhile the book's content demands summary and analysis, neither of which is easy to give. *The Female Eunuch* begins with a lushly overwritten dedication to various female companions in the struggle and ends with twenty pages of dauntingly erudite notes. In between are four main sections of argument and one minor section: 'Body', 'Soul', 'Love', 'Hate' and (the minor one) 'Revolution', which last I found to be mainly rhetoric. Of the main sections, the first one, 'Body', is the most ill-considered, so it's rather a pity that it sets the terms of the book as well as the tone. She argues very well in the 'Soul' section that the supposedly ineluctable differences of emotional and intellectual make-up between the sexes are imposed by stereotype and are consequently alterable, if not eliminable and indeed reversible. There was not the slightest need to peg this argument back to the 'Body' section and there pronounce that the differences of physical shape between men and women are likewise metaphysically determined. It makes for a poor start and surely a false one. The anthropological, ethnological, biological and chromosomal evidence adduced is scarcely convincing, and the notes given for this section are relatively thin – relative, that is, to the mass of reading which has been drawn upon to substantiate the arguments of the subsequent sections. The import of this opening section really amounts to the notion that women and men are more similar than they are different, which is unarguable, like its converse: like its converse it is merely a chosen emphasis, providing a preliminary to argument. It is one thing to say that 'the "normal" sex roles that we learn to play from our infancy are no more natural than the antics of a transvestite,' since that deals with the psychology of the business. It is another thing to say that in order 'to approximate those shapes and attitudes which are considered normal and desirable, both sexes deform themselves, justifying the process by referring to the primary, genetic difference between the sexes.' (Shapes? The *whole* shape? Everybody? All the time?) And it is a hell of a thing to say both those things in two succeeding sentences.

'But of 48 chromosomes only one is different: on this difference we base a complete separation of male and female, pretending as it were that all 48 are different.' Only if we are clowns. What we actually do is something far more insidious: realizing that differences based on physique are not seriously worth considering, we keep everything on a mental plane, and attribute to women intellectual virtues we do not possess, in order to palm off a mass of responsibilities we don't propose to handle. The same trick works in reverse: women flatter men in much the same way. The result, until recently, has been a workable (I don't say just) division of labour. A good deal of the woman's share (I don't say a fair share) of the labour centres on the fact that she has the babies – which is where the physical difference really does come in, or did. After Miss Greer has cleaned up the question of subsidiary physical differences (it appears that women wouldn't have so much subcutaneous fat if they didn't leave so much skin exposed on things like, for example, legs) and gets on to the social forms and structures which are governed by this one remaining, glaring physical difference, the book picks up. Because she instantly realizes that if women are to be free, the reproduction of the race is the rap they have to beat.

All the ensuing major sections of *The Female Eunuch* really amount to a brilliant attack on marriage and the psychological preparation for it, and on the nuclear family which is the result of it. This attack traces all the correct connections, from Barbara Cartland's powdered cleavage to the aspirin industry that thrives on frustration, from the doomed cosmetic ritual to the furtive adultery, and from the mother who sacrifices everything to the son who is grateful for nothing. The case has seldom been so well argued. One misses the wit that Dr. Greer wields in conversation, but the headlong rush of mordant disenchantment is all there. The book would be worth the price merely to read her anatomizing of the advice columns in the women's magazines – an effort comparable in approach (and, one hopes, in effect) to Gabriella Parca's masterly *Le Italiane si confessano*.

Passages of sympathetic fury like this constitute the book's solid worth: there are enough of them to establish Dr. Greer as an individual voice in popular social debate for some time to come. But suppose we take her condemnation of the received relationship between the sexes for granted – what alternatives does she offer? On this point, the book runs into trouble.

On a practical level – the level of *likelihoods*, of what might conceivably be brought about – Dr. Greer recommends little that you will not find equally well put (and put equally passionately) in the prefaces to *Man and Superman* and *Getting Married*. If the ideas of female freedom, liberation from the 'feminine' stereotype, and the economic key to sexual equality strike the new semi-intelligentsia as revolutionary, it will only be because of the thoroughness with which touch has been lost with the old radical tradition. Here as elsewhere in the wide spectrum of the currently fashionable revolutionary spirit, it's the theoretical atavism of the practical recommendations which strikes the concerned reader as extraordinary. One gets the sense, after a while, that living philosophical insights curve away from history to re-enter it later on as psychodrama, posturings and myth. Perhaps Pareto's diagrams on this subject were correct after all, and something like this has to happen before ideas take the form of action: but it is very eerie to be an onlooker. When Dr. Greer conjures up a loose-knit, 'organic' family, with several footloose fathers for the organic kids, and sets the imagined scene in Italy, we smile for two reasons. Not just because of the ill-judged setting (the courtyard would be stiff with the khaki Alfas of the *carabinieri di pronto intervento* before you could get the toys unpacked), but because the idea itself has already been and gone – the grass grew over it long ago in some abandoned phalanx, the kids grew up, moved out and went square.

But just because ideas like this have been and gone, it doesn't mean that the wished-for condition couldn't come again, and this time to stay. The question is: for how many? So far, only for a few. And for how long? Up to now, usually not long. The problem of substituting individual initiative for received social forms can be solved, but only at the cost of an extraordinary application of energy, and usually only in conditions of privilege.

The coming generations are obviously going to get many of the privileges that the old socialists fought for, prepared the ground for, but saw distorted, half-realized, and even abandoned. This is one of the reasons why the old radical hands are intolerant of the new bloods: the new bloods lack the intellectual preparation, the realization of continuous difficulty. The main message of the preface to *Getting Married* was that no matter how much she needed to be free, a woman needed to marry in order to protect herself socio-economically. Shaw had no illusions about what most marriages were. But equally he had no illusions about the currently feasible alternatives. The main message of *The Female Eunuch* is that the nuclear family is a menace, that the feminine role is a poisonous sham and that the farce ought to be wound up. If this position now looks tenable, it's not because Dr. Greer has a capacity for analysis superior to Shaw's, but because the socio-economics of the matter have changed. The opportunities for making a claim to individuality have vastly increased. But one can recognize this fact without being seduced by it – without forgetting that the benefits of living a liberated life are probably not to be measured on the scale of happiness. To do Dr. Greer credit in this regard, it is not an easier life she is asking for, but a more difficult, more honourable one.

She does not gloss over the fact that the alternatives will take a lot of guts. In my view, though, she seriously overrates the reserves of creative initiative that people have to draw upon. There is a sound assessment of their personal likelihoods behind the instinct of most people to settle for a quiet, unadventurous life. It's unusual for even highly gifted people to be original, to express a 'unique' self, in more than just a few areas. Dr. Greer argues that the female state of mind is enforced by the stereotype. She doesn't consider that the stereotype might have grown out of the state of mind – doesn't consider, that is, that the state of mind might be logically prior, historically evolved out of a steadily reinforced realization that most women, like most men, are not heroic.

Like most of the recent revolutionary ideologists, Dr. Greer glibly assumes that it is desirable for everybody to be not only fully aware of their condition, but fully politicised. This is to overrate the amount of originality a civilization can sustain, while simultaneously underrating the mass of people in it, whose ordinary affairs should rightly be regarded as consumingly complex and self-justifying, rather than as a poor substitute for the life of adventure which the genuine originals supposedly enjoy. Dr. Greer brilliantly uncovers the hoaxes governing ordinary feminine subservience, but always with the air that the millennium will arrive once these poor dumb ladies realize they are being conned. What just might happen, though, if the polemic message of her book gets through to a wide range of women, is something better: a further measure of equality. Getting a square shake is not as exciting to look at as blazing your way to immortality, but it counts.

*The Female Eunuch* states the case for altering all the conditions that leave women less free than men. In doing this, it creates several kinds of confusion about the amount and nature of the freedom conceivably available to either. But perhaps the case needs to be wrongly stated in order to take effect, to convince the next lot of guileless women seemingly predestined for a life of frustration and cheap dreams that there's no need to go through with it – you can just walk away from it, and hang loose. Getting married later, rather than sooner, would be a good start.

(1970)

# 27

## An Absolute Lady

Kate Millett's clamorous bestsellerdom in the United States has been running roughly parallel with Germaine Greer's similar success on this side of the pond. The time has now come for their books to change places. One has no certainty how 'The Female Eunuch' will go over there, but it would be within the bounds of credibility to suggest that it will go like a bomb. *Sexual Politics* should make the crossing OK, too: you couldn't say that its advent was exactly unheralded.

Women's Lib is one of those lonely little unsung struggles that refuse to be ignored, mainly because their key slogans are shouted at you from fleets of loud-speaker cars and beamed through your bedroom window from forty-foot neon signs rigged to the sides of dirigibles. At this rate the secret will soon be out. The veriest dullard must shortly realise that capitalism's celebrated capacity for repressing change through toleration has in this case sprung a leak. The demands of the marching ladies are both sensible and negotiable, and are seen to be so by all except the doddering fanatics of stasis. There is no reason why the movement should not push its way through to full equality of rights and the provision of those practical aids required for an equality of mobility and job-opportunity.

It can be argued that the only thing which could stop this would be for the movement to take seriously the rhetorical component in the works of its leading intellectuals and try for a drastic rearrangement in the power-structure, a fundamental rejigging (presumably attainable through brain surgery) of what is conceived to be male psychology, and the instigation by fair means or foul of what is naïvely looked forward to as a fruitful jettisoning of evolved institutions. The polemical force of the Women's Lib intellectuals is partly derived from the cultivation of myths. The fact that what they are recommending is in large part desirable doesn't make these myths any less mythical.

Kate Millett's myths are of a different type from those of Dr. Greer, who was guilty of some confusion but largely eschewed bad intellectual practice. She was dangerous, but in the right way: her revolutionary stance was really a call for reform. The danger in Kate Millett's book is of a deeper and darker kind: revolution is fundamental to it, reformism having apparently run its course. 'Sexual Politics' is a book of some power, but it is very tendentious; its arguments are boldly put and pushed through tenaciously to the end, but they are not sound; and although it advocates a change of consciousness, it is not conscious of its own hectoring, cantankerous and frequently plain boring characteristics. The crunching academic sarcasm tends to get you down.

In Dr. Greer's book men stood a chance of recognizing themselves. In Kate Millett's book they appear to be present only as a compound of Mighty Mouse, Caligula and the Creature from the Black Lagoon. John Stuart Mill and Engels come out of it all right, but the rest are just heavies. For Miss Millett, any male goodwill could now only be a cover-up, and the plausible smoothies could only be planning further humiliations designed to reduce all ladies to helpless, violated acquiescence. Our urge for dominance, it appears, is never more reprehensible than when masquerading as ordinary decency. We are patriarchs from the Id on up.

Apart from a catastrophic excursion into historical analysis (wherein it is established that Nazi Germany was the logical expression of Western sexual mores) Miss Millett draws her examples of the repressive male consciousness mainly from contemporary literature and especially from Henry Miller, Norman Mailer, D. H. Lawrence and Jean Genet. Her criticisms of all four are very keen and it is hard to see much wrong with them as far as they go. (As far as they really go, that is: they are made to go about a light-year farther than they ought.) She establishes that Lawrence was a male chauvinist in disguise, reducing women to a stereotype under the pretence of exploring their sexuality. She establishes Miller and Mailer as male chauvinists *without* the disguise, both hell-bent on using women as ash-trays, urinals, punching bags and stuffed sacks for bayonet practice: she is grateful to both for so copiously spilling the beans. Finally she sees the role of the passive queer in Genet as the essential statement of men's real attitude to women – the gloves are off, *mon vieux*, and the spurs are on.

All this adds up to quite a line of argument, and to obviate the possibility of our mistaking its force she goes right through it twice. Mailer has already replied on his own behalf and on behalf of all others present in the line-up: his reply took up almost an entire issue of *Harper's*, and as is customary with him it is a remarkable performance, although only fleetingly sane. But Mailer has succeeded in damaging her argument only in the detail. Its main drift stays recognizably true, even in the significance attached to Genet, which is a shattering analysis so long as it remains attached. What's wrong is the unquestioned, thumping assumption about the whole argument's applicability, leading to wool-pulling on the grand scale.

To begin with, she is assuming that because men wrote these books and some men read them, that most men are like that, totally and always. Apart from such an approach to literature being critically ruinous, it isn't even socially exploratory. And supposing that it *were* socially exploratory (i.e., supposing that a yodelling obsessive like Miller really did crystallize our hidden attitudes) it still isn't psychologically valuable or even interesting. Men's minds, like women's, are not monoliths: they may be full of secret drives without those drives being the key to us. Mentally we are not a monologue, we are a drama, and to suggest that we replace this supposed monologue with a better one is merely to transpose a tyrannous imputation from one end of the spectrum to the other.

Miss Millett's approach is really the etiolated, post-Marxist notion of System switched from the economic to the sexual sphere. Just as the earlier notion of System held that there could be no liberty at all until there was liberty everywhere (logically entailing that liberty cannot now be even conceived of, let alone extended) so the Sexual Politics notion of System holds that all men must necessarily continue to be repressive so long as they harbour drives towards dominance – which logically entails that nothing they can do, or have ever done, which is kind, generous and liberal, can have any meaning in the real world. Miss Millett wants to trade in one male robot for another, and in wanting to do that she wants to take away the possibility of our mastering ourselves – an aim which, if attained, would effectively demolish any tangible meaning in the idea of self-mastery for women.

(1971)

# 28

## Aquarius, Prisoner of Sex

Norman Mailer's *The Prisoner of Sex* started life as an entire issue of the magazine *Harper's*, appearing in America at about the same time Kate Millett's book 'Sexual Politics' – Mailer's main target – opened up shop in this country. Doing a radio programme on Millett and looking for ammo, I ploughed through an imported copy of the magazine with growing disappointment and steadily lessening velocity as the prose piled shoulder-high: if Millett's apocalyptic argument needed a counterblast, Mailer's metaphysical posturing wasn't it. The scene needed cooling out, not hotting up. But now that his long article has appeared in book form, Mailer's position starts to look more substantial.

It is often the way with him. I don't agree that he is a more interesting essayist than novelist – he has never written anything better than 'The Deer Park' – but certainly his essays have a way of sneaking up on you, usually long after you have finished shaking your head at the ego-tripping antics. His role-playing is a clownish tactic that has the effect of making you overreach yourself, so that you topple forward within range of a sudden welter of dizzying argument. He's been a Contender and a Candidate; he's been Aquarius; and in this book he kicks off as the Prizewinner. An opening statement like this one *has* to be disarming: if you took it at its face-value, you'd be honour bound to chuck the book out of the window:

Near the end of the Year of the Polymorphous Perverse (which is to say in the fall of '69) there were rumours he would win the Nobel.

Not bad for openers: old Aquarius is in the third person again, which is clinically appropriate to his proudly flourished paranoia. But the Prizewinner, having got us softened up with polite embarrassment, quickly metamorphoses into the Prisoner – the Prisoner of Sex. And to find out why he's behind bars, you have to read through to the end, by which time he's got his knees on your chest. Here is a bucketful of Stygian viscosity drawn from the last paragraph of the book:

Finally, he would agree with everything they asked but to quit the womb, for finally a day had to come when women shattered the pearl of their love for pristine and feminine will and found the man, yes that man in the million who could become the point of the seed which would give the egg back to nature, and let the woman return with a babe who came from the root of God's desire to go all the way, wherever was that way. And who was there to know that God was not the greatest lover of them all?

To get from the first quoted passage to the second in only 230 pages of large print is the work of a prince among line-shooters: on the terms he establishes in the book I find this flag-waving finale perfectly intelligible, yet I present it with utter confidence that the reader will understand not a word. How to summarize what has gone before?

There are two components in Women's Lib, the reformist and the revolutionary, and the reformist component is often put forward in revolutionary guise. We might call the first component realistic and the second rhetorical. Whether asking for the overthrow of all institutions or the complete restructuring of the male psyche the rhetorical component in Women's Lib seems to me counterproductive, spoiling the chances of the realistic component that all men of good will are bound to uphold. Mailer is ready to back the realistic component (he has good words for Betty Friedan) but only in the interests of a rhetoric of his own. And at the centre of his own rhetoric is a notion of the sexes' separate roles in . . . what is it? (Here one's powers of paraphrase down tools.) The search for the godhead? The furthering of destiny by Will? Anyway, it appears that a woman is mad to deny her Inner Space, for doesn't Mailer himself tell us that its very eggs are all agog to be favoured by selected spermatozoa (only two or three of the released millions are the true *herren*sperm) from a Man who is himself selected on principles that she, poor thing, might fail to understand with her merely conscious mind?

Strike me dead if it isn't true, but I now have it on Mailer's authority that the birthrate 'may' have gone up *because* of contraception – psychically bamboozled by technology, women have lost their erstwhile capacity to choose (by secret night-time mental processes unrevealed to their conscious minds or to any other agency than the Prisoner's snoopy-peepy back-pack detector) not to be pregnant! Good to have that cleared up.

No, (and here I help myself to the Prisoner's technique of tossing in a Yes, comma, or No, comma, at the very moment when the reader is yelling Hold On exclamation mark) Mailer isn't being as crass as all that. His argument can easily and neatly be attached by metaphysical sky-hooks to the perennial sense, which most of us share, that there is a natural dispensation which we are crazy to flout beyond a certain point. He has seen that the revolutionary component of Women's Lib is in thrall to technology: he is against it for that, and he is right. But in arguing that every act of love which is carried out without the possibility of conception in mind is a death-dealing waste, he is making the universe into a work of art whose plot-line is the working out of a purpose. Mailer once offered us the notion that hate, frustration and lies cause cancer. But good men and women get it, and children get it, too. Anyone struck by the arbitrariness with which divine favour is handed out will always find substance in the remark that the only excuse for God is that He does not exist. If He does, He can certainly be a clumsy lover.

There is a tragedy in *The Prisoner of Sex* that its author is not aware of. He deals with Millett's arid technologizing well enough, but he can make nothing much of Friedan beyond a pious regret that the possibilities of bringing about a social equity are small. It's a sad prospect: a social fabric unravelling towards ruin, while a good creative mind can find little to do except sling rhetoric in the void left by the banishment of realistic discourse.

(1971)

# 29

## Speed Writes: Tom Wolfe's *The Mid-Atlantic Man*

Most posh reviews of Tom Wolfe's books attempt to parody his style, demonstrating in the process that there is more to it than meets the eye, since they are hardly every any good. Wolfe has a lot more in the bag than conversational syntax, dots and dashes and pre-release vogue words. He has a fine sense of timing his detail and a sensitive foot on the accelerator: a steadily developing surge in the back propels you forward to the belief that the action is just over *there*, it's practically *here*, you're almost *in it* – it's ON!

That's the whole story of his success, though not necessarily of his literary importance: he's a colour supplement with the pix transmuted into prose, making the new scenes available to those who will live them in only a token way. Wolfe is a McLuhan Man even more than he himself realizes: not only does he condense pictures into an information beam of words which the reader's eye immediately converts back into pictures, but he embodies the point on which all McLuhan's theories about the simultaneous presence of information in the Global Village come to grief – information displaces experience, reportage obliterates reality. Wolfe writes best about people who don't need to read him. If you feel the urge to read him, you're probably plugged *out*. You're not getting it, you're boning up on it. Bad scene.

Without employing any (or not many – his prose has internal rhymes) of the lyric poet's techniques, Wolfe has the poet's gift of tuning in sonically to something fundamental in the brain – perhaps the alpha wave, or whatever it is that strobe lights and mainstream drumming also affect directly. In the strictest sense his writing makes compulsive reading. It is very difficult to stop the flow and question the attitudes that this latest and most hallucinating of the dandy monologuists undoubtedly has at some level or other.

As a cultural journalist it is difficult to type him, to find out exactly what lines he is pushing. His *role* is obvious enough: a kind of uttermost extension of the task which began to be performed much earlier by writers like Gilbert Seldes and Otis Ferguson, Malcolm Cowley's free-wheeling assistant on the *New Republic* of the mid thirties – the locating and analysing, with sociological over-tones, of the Lively Arts. All this and much more (he locates whole new life-styles, though it should be said he is not often first on the scene – merely loudest) Wolfe does well enough and sometimes brilliantly, but it isn't easy to find out where he stands in the maelstrom of what he describes and, by describing, helps towards a better-known, consequently self-conscious and arguably more vul-nerable existence. He is a dandy but not totally an unashamed one. In appearance he resembles Barry Humphries taking over Alec Guinness's role in *The Man in the White Suit*: the drag looks like a million, but the long hair carefully hints at all the brainy little wheels spinning underneath. He earns overwhelming, value-distorting amounts of bread even by American standards – the chapter on the automated hotel-room he took in order to finish some articles rocks you in more ways than one, since not many British journalists could earn in a whole day's writing what the room must have cost per hour.

He makes the scene, both the good scene and the bad scene: he has the precious gift of smelling out the power in a given set-up and taking it to lunch. A man with that much In *has* to be a smoothie – or else somebody cursed/blessed by the trick of identifying with any mood he runs into, in the way that some people can't help mimicking other people's accents. It's more than receptivity, it's a weakness: liberating in one way, but disabling in another, since only those capable of rejection can body forth a vision. But how many journalists have interviewed Hugh Hefner ('King of the Status Dropouts,' a key essay to Wolfe's strengths and weaknesses) actually *in situ* on his clownish revolving bed? And how many journalists have trotted along with Natalie Wood while she buys paintings? George Augustus Sala would have tipped his lid.

Yet it's exactly in these celebrity pieces that his pose of detached involvement (detached from the past, involved in the new permanent present) – his idea that these new 'statuspheres' need to be reported objectively without any prejudice deriving from the obsolescing life-style of the 'first industrial revolution – become attitudes in themselves. Regarded as an individual, Natalie Wood is not much more than a vapidly pretty face, and regarded as a representative of the overpaid film people who keep the heritage of European art out of circulation she is simply a pain in the neck. Take away the wowee prose and Wolfe's attentive regard for her reads like the ordinary highbrow slumming of those pro-popular, anti-mandarin intellectuals who spout hosannahs for Elizabeth Taylor when by some stupendous application of will-power she manages to be adequate. And surely Hefner is a joke and his magazine trash: whatever Robert Conquest says, and no matter how many millions of its readers are getting an intensity of attention paid to their dreams that has never happened in history before, *Playboy*'s status as pitiful tede is absolutely fixed.

Wolfe throws away his standards in order to liberate his receptivity for the New. To a great extent he has made an original job of this, but few of his exciting discoveries can really be claimed as a breakthrough in society with the same force as they can be rejected as further corruptions of it. Hefner! Custom cars! (He was *very* late on the scene there.) Pill-head Mods in groovy *Tiles*! (Featuring somebody called Larry Lynch, a kid just *made* to zip around cutely in the under-cranked sequences of a Clive Donner movie.) The Motorcycle Sub-culture! And here Wolfe doesn't hint at the obvious fact that one of the secrets is not that these people can ride bikes better than you and I ride buses, but that they *can't* ride bikes like Agostini: hence the overblown mystique, which true dedication in any field is usually free of.

Here as elsewhere the social pressure being fought is partly a meritocratic one, the anti-social pressure to be really good at something. To get around it, they form new social groups where the pressure to excel is reduced to an expression of minor gradations, such as lace ruffs and cuffs for the mods or the *Totenkopf* badges on Hell's Angels, caps. Wolfe's essay on surfing, the best in the book, doesn't square with the other essays on life-styles for just this reason, since it concerns a whole new aesthetic in which excellence is fundamental. Good surfers are poets, and mods are kewpie dolls: unless you are equipped with a cover-up prose style like Wolfe's you can't equate them. The many scenes making up the Wolfean Scene appear all of a piece only to people bereft of analytical powers – trendies, the New Lost.

The new *enjoying* is something Wolfe only *asserts* is happening. In fact it is only he and men like him who are doing the real enjoying, since only they are examining (as well as vicariously living) these new life-styles, and since it remains true that only the examined life is worth living. If Wolfe thinks that the apocalyptic future will have a 'happiness explosion' as its central problem, he's nuts. But really he's not that certain, and some doubts remain – he's not *completely* sure about Carol Doda, the girl with the silicone boobs. The superbly evocative essay on Edward T. Hall and Behavioural Sink is even more to the point. The essay on McLuhan hedges every possible bet – McLuhan is Wolfe's enemy's enemy, but can't possibly be his, or any other writer's, friend. The author's own drawings decorate the chapter headings: they are fairly conventional, as his writing is fairly unconventional. But exciting, there's no denying it.

(1969)

# 30

# A Whole Gang of Noise

Despite the relative civility with which *Against Interpretation* was greeted, Susan Sontag's reputation in this country has never really recovered from her first disastrous appearance with Jonathan Miller in an episode of *Monitor* which could have been called

'Captain Eclectic and Thinkwoman meet Public Ridicule.' The medium was the massacre: scarcely anybody came out of the programme with prestige intact and Miss Sontag was immediately incorporated into the British intelligentsia's typology of dreadful examples. Her appearances in print – a less damaging medium revealing neither her self-assurance rivalling Ethel Merman's nor her non-stop ponderosity which rendered even Miller unable to get a word in edgeways – have by now done something to correct this bad impression. In fact some of the home guard one might normally expect to be more careful when handling imported brain-power have started to overcorrect. 'She has all the qualities of an excellent critic,' avers Alvarez in an unwise statement which the publishers are now employing on the jacket of *Styles of Radical Will*: 'she is intelligent, perceptive, and impressively well informed.' Can't agree. She certainly possesses the qualities named, but conspicuously lacks the one quality every critic must have and an excellent critic must have in abundance: the capacity not to be carried away by a big idea.

Except for the two political essays in the book, one of them being the truly superlative 'Trip to Hanoi,' her work is customarily marked by the use of a half-argued, hugely magnetic central notion which attracts examples to its surface so quickly and in such quantity that its outlines are immediately obscured. Sainte-Beuve once said that Montaigne sounds like one continuous epigram but Miss Sontag, like Harold Rosenberg most of the time and Hugh Kenner all the time, sounds like one continuous aphorism. The opportunity to stop the flow and ponder is rarely offered. When it is, usually by an over-glib employment of a 'thus' or a 'nothing less,' the results yielded by a good hard think are seldom happy. Her long essay on pornography, for example, is an impressive against-interpretation job of getting facts in and prejudices out, but even in this field, where she seems to have read absolutely everything, the urge to generalize blocks the way of ordinary observation: you need only have read Restif de la Bretonne, let alone the modern pornographers, to realize that her statements about the use of speech in pornography are wide of the mark. Similarly in her essay on Godard it's the little things that bring on the big objections and the eventual wondering whether the thesis really is a thesis. She briefly notes that Godard's handling of torture scenes is pretty sketchy. Card-carrying Godard fans have long since realized that they must defend him at this point or lose all: *they* say that the master's imagination is so exquisite he can't sully it by trying to represent (or *redeem*, to employ the dusty vocabulary of Kracauer which Miss Sontag puts herself on record as admiring) reality in such things. But Miss Sontag doesn't feel bound to defend him since what she is postponing is not interpretation but judgement.

Wherein lies the fallacy and this lady's besetting intellectual vice – because judgement is not some higher brain function you turn on after a set period of omnivorous data-gathering, it's a process which should be continuously operative and in the critic *is* continuously operative. Thus (there, now I'm doing it) her contention that Godard needs to be regarded in the totality of his films is easily countered by the contention that you will gain no wisdom from a fool's utterance by cancelling the rest of your appointments and listening to him all day.

Miss Sontag attempts to break free of the historical burden and ready herself for the new but her attempt, fulsomely documented and exhaustingly fluent, doesn't alter the fact that the historical burden is only burdensome *historically*: aesthetically the giants of the past are our contemporaries and must be competed with as if they were still around – we've changed, but we haven't changed as much as we *haven't* changed, and Miss Sontag unconsciously concedes this point by being vague about when Modern Man actually got started – i.e., stopped being the old kind. There is great play here with Hegel as the last of the religious philosophers: it appears that his materialistic component got picked up and carried forward but his spiritual component got neglected, which only goes to show that Miss Sontag hasn't made much headway with Italian idealism. None of her broad arguments about modern trends and currents of thought is very trustworthy and there is a tendency to identify the unholy American mess with a crisis in western civilization, a notion which ought to be resisted. The best and only solid part of the book is 'Trip to Hanoi' but it should quickly be added that you only have to write one thing as good as that to earn a name. Here for once her prose has grace, her argument clarity and her whole literary personality a human presence.

(1969)

# 31

# Rough Beast

Irving Howe's *Decline of the New* is marked by serious internal contradictions, but it is not really flawed by them: the wounds are honourable. Irving Howe has stuck by his socialist principles over a long stretch of modern American history, a period in which he has seen most of his contemporaries among the 'family' of New York intellectuals make their separate accommodations with capitalism, with brutalized democracy and with success. He edited *Dissent* through hard, bad years; and for his own magazine or for any other magazine in which he published, he provided contributions which had then, and retain now, a distinctively solid ring of integrity. The oldest of the essays in this book (the one on Silone) dates from 1957 and was first collected in his book *Politics and the Novel* – once published in this country by the *New Left Review* and recommended for perusal in the days when the New Left still perused.

The new book (which also contains the bulk of an intermediate volume, *A World More Attractive*) continues the lost fight that the older book began: a fight for socialist principles in a country in which socialism could never be institutionalized, but which could conceivably be ameliorated by a dedicated analytical and polemical pursuit of those principles. It was a stable and rewarding position for a writer to adopt, provided he was a courageous writer, which Howe certainly was, and is. Just because it was hopeless in the field of immediate practicality didn't make it irrelevant in the long run and the critical spin-off produced such classics of evaluation as the essay (included here) on Dreiser. But there was a joker in the deck: the long run shortened. The wished-for radical awakening actually arrived – and in the eyes of Irving Howe it turned out to be a monster. The continuity of the new radicalism was not with the old Left, but with barbarism. Suddenly he was fighting on two fronts. It is the sort of situation in which intellectuals tend to panic. Howe didn't, and it's the fact that he didn't which gives the newer parts of this book their dignity, and retroactively bestows on the older parts an intense illumination. Irving Howe is a hard character and this is a *good* book in a way that a lot of flashier New York intellectual products are not. Most of what is in it is tested against everything the author ever stood for, and the author is the kind of man who, when talking to himself, can get a word in edgeways.

All that said, the contradictions must still be faced. They show up most vividly in the long (and from the documentary standpoint in-valuable) historico-critical disquisition called 'The New York Intellectuals'. The stellar names and all their constellations are mapped through recent history: Rahv, Phillips, Hook, Burnham, Corey, Macdonald, Kazin, Rosenberg, Trilling, Arendt, Greenberg, Goodman, Abel, Shapiro, Chiaromonte, McCarthy, Fiedler and many more. The theme is the turning-away from Stalinism, a process whose various results Howe describes in a series of brilliant summaries. The essay is an absolutely reliable document of the successive trends down to quite recent times: its triumph is to draw group portraits that are not cartoons, and its governing tone is one of approval for the complex states of mind these rejections led to – even though something had been lost, and the turning-away was from the fruitful kinds of commitment as well as the fruitless. A specimen conclusion:

Later in the Forties and Fifties, most of the New York intellectuals would abandon the effort to find a renewed basis for socialist politics – to their serious discredit, I believe. Some would vulgarise anti-Stalinism into a politics barely distinguishable from reaction. Yet for almost all New York intellectuals the radical years proved a decisive moment in their lives. And for a few, *the* decisive moment.

For Howe the lasting, and limiting contribution of the old guard is one of style – the 'brilliant' style. Howe can admire this brilliance without being persuaded by it: in more ways than one, he would not be capable of Mary McCarthy's powerfully silly essay on Orwell, and his own placidly sensible essay is here to prove it. He represents the continuance of a purer, more contemplative spirit, based on confidence in his complex historical position rather than on self-confidence. But when the new, apparently simplistic radicalism arrives, the complex historical position is injured in its dignity, and Howe's reaction to events, for such a long time subtle and forbearing, at last lapses into coarseness. He sees the new opposition as an indivisible monolith; he attributes to it a collective psyche; not only can it do nothing right, but nothing good can come of it. There's no suggestion that the new thing might develop complexities of its own. Howe's conclusions come pat in a language become glib:

For if the psychology of unobstructed need is taken as a sufficient guide to life, it all but eliminates any need for complexity – or rather, the need for complexity comes to be seen as a mode of false consciousness, an evasion of true feelings, a psychic bureaucraticism in which to trap the pure and strong. If good sex signifies good feeling; good feeling, good being; good being, good action; and good action, a healthy polity, then we have come the long way round, past the Reichian way or the Lawrentian way, to an Emersonian romanticism minus Emerson's complicatedness of vision. The world snaps back into a system of burgeoning potentialities, waiting for free spirits to attach themselves to the richness of natural object and symbol – except that now the orgasmic black-out is to replace the Oversoul as the current through which pure transcendent emergies flow.

Howe is right to regard those clerks as treasonable who have fallen for the ahistorical cultural assumptions of the new radicalism: what he is saying, which cannot be argued with, is that intellectuals ought to remain intellectuals. But the main force of passages like this is directed against the new radicalism as a political whole, and the contradiction is obvious: if he thought the 'polity' was healthy *before*, why did he fight it? And if he thought it was unhealthy, what kind of opposition to it did he expect to emerge?

The very fact that he is involved in this dilemma is proof of Howe's worth. The fact that he does not see it clearly is proof that there is a time in these things and nobody can stay alert for ever.

But Howe stayed alert a long time and the older essays in this impressive book go to show it.

(1971)

# 32

## He Didn't Stifle

Back in 1938, when Sartre was still pushing John Dos Passos as *le plus grand écrivain de notre temps*, he wrote a paragraph which doubtless had its truth then, but in the light of *The Best Times* seems exactly wrong today. *Fermez les yeux, essayez de vous rappeler votre propre vie, essayez de vous la rappeler ainsi : vous étoufferez. C'est cet étouffement sans secours que Dos Passos a voulu exprimer. Dans la société capitaliste les hommes n'ont pas de vies, ils n'ont que des destins : cela, il ne le dit nulle part, mais partout il le fait sentir ; il insiste discrètement, prudemment, jusqu'à nous donner un désir de briser nos destins. Nous voici des révoltés ; son but est atteint.* Considering what was to happen to Dos Passos's writing in the years to come, this passage is irony unmixed. For in his post-war writing from *Chosen Country* through to *Midcentury* Dos Passos has promoted as a major theme the idea that capitalist America is exactly the place where a man *can* live his life without having it distorted into destiny. *Chosen Country* is an acceptance novel and as anyone who has waded through it knows, it shows a monstrous falling-off in creativity from the triumphs of the *USA* trilogy, which was the work Sartre was mainly thinking of. To the superficial eye Dos Passos over his whole creative course from *Three Soldiers* until now has gone through one of those sideways feats of mental travel that one thinks of in connection with Steinbeck and Max Eastman and which seem always to end up in the offices of *Reader's Digest*. But if *The Best Times* has any intellectual value, it lies in the fact that Don Passos, in reminiscing at low pressure – and incidentally turning out some of his best writing for many years – is able to

show that his own cast of mind has never allowed for such an interpretation at any stage. Sartre got him wrong.

The radical view of Dos Passos is that he was a great political
writer, ideologically sound in the first instance, who eventually sold
out. The libertarian view is that he was a great political writer,
opposing all ideologies, who eventually cracked under the strain
and plumped for the ideology that guaranteed his personal freedom
to function – capitalism. But the only possible consistent view (and
this is the view that *The Best Times* unconsciously, and therefore
convincingly, supports) is that Dos Passos was never a political
writer at all. Considering his associations, through the Norton-
Harjes ambulance service and the subsequent revulsion towards
the sanctity of the allied cause, through the *New Masses*, the New
Playwrights' Theatre and the Sacco-Vanzetti defence, this view at
first looks paradoxical. But on close examination we see that Dos
Passos nowhere in any of these institutions and on any of these
issues took quite the line that was expected of him. When he made
his trip to Russia (and he made it before the terror had really got
going) his rejection of communism was not the intellectual kind
made by Edmund Wilson and Eastman, but the artistic kind,
like Cummings's and Gide's: it picked up danger signals on a totally
different set of antennae.

When we look back and recall the historical setting of *USA*
(which really is an historical novel, a fact often neglected) we find
that it is the Wobblies who hold his closest sympathy – and by
the time *USA* was being written the Wobblies were certainly not
the group that any real politician was likely to put his money on.
If Dos Passos has ever backed anyone he has backed losers, usually
when he already knew they were losers. So if he was ever a political
writer, he was one of a disengaged kind whose relationship to
politics cannot be seen in terms of preparing the future. And although Sartre did not have much difficulty deducing from *USA* a
total condemnation of capitalist America, he was plainly far from
being able to judge the significance of the fact that Dos Passos was
able to publish the book in America, and the significance of the
fierceness with which Dos Passos would cling to, and proclaim the
value of, this freedom. The preoccupation of *USA* is with the over-

whelming power of impersonal forces – Department of Justice investigators, censors, witch-hunters, strike-breaking army units. *USA* is really a set of parables which show men trying to retain their individuality before these forces. But the awkward fact, for those radicals who consider the early Dos Passos their champion, is that this preoccupation will do as well for the right as for the left: the individual resistance to central pressure is what the American right considers itself to be all about and the reason why it is able to document itself so well constitutionally. It is a fact that Dos Passos has ended up pretty far to the right. But I think it's a mistake to assume that he started very far on the left.

He comes out of Dreiser's school of naturalism, a kind of naturalism that needs material; and eventually he ran out of material. His early scope was wide and impersonal and took in a lot of stuff nobody else wanted to touch. The interest of his writing was dependent on this breadth of view: to Scott Fitzgerald, much the more gifted writer, Dos Passos in these years looked like a genius. He was a camera, but a man can be a camera for only so long. In time he became more personal, his novels were given a protagonist (Huey Long in *Number One*) and in *Chosen Country* the world was given the autobiographical novel that most writers turn out at the beginning of their careers: it was like a clumsy start in a kind of introspective narration he was never to be any good at, the past seemed as shallow as if the hero was eighteen, and there were unending references to Gibbon as night trains chugged through the bosom of the motherland. Like Hemingway's, Dos Passos's career was back to front, the masterpieces first, the duds last.

Hemingway's personality is one of the continuing threads in *The Best Times* and helps make for the immediate interest the book will hold even for those who have not read the early novels. Dos Passos is deeply cultivated, has been everywhere, done everything. He helped Goncharova paint the scenery for *Noces*. When tiny he met Mark Twain. Like Edmund Wilson he heard Cummings, the most solid claimant for the title of Talker of the Century, in full voice. He met the big fish and the little fish: Joyce, Fitzgerald, the Murphys, Pudovkin, Léger, von Sternberg, Dietrich, Blaise Cendrars, Eisenstein. He has had a good life and he is grateful for it, and although his work has declined with the years and made little of Sartre's temporal judgment, when all our battles are done the best of it will read well in eternity.

(1968)

# 33

## The New Lost

If you encounter a web-footed bird, blind in both eyes, minus its wings and with two broken legs, there are no prizes awarded for calling it a sitting duck. Although Colin Wilson's 'preliminary' volume of autobiography, *Voyage to a Beginning*, is only a history of his intellectual development, and contributes no new ideas to what might wildly be described as his position, enough argufying takes place in it for the attentive reader to confirm earlier estimates of his philosophical powers. Wilson can't think straight and that's that. It is scarcely relevant that most critics do not take Wilson seriously now: they are not very different from (in some cases they are the same men as) the critics who swallowed him hook, line and sinker back in the *Outsider* days. The key essays on that strange interlude are still Cyril Connolly's original recension of the book, which set the tone of clownish approbation, and Dwight Macdonald's essay which blew the whistle on the whole freaky scene. Aghast at the intellectual gullibility revealed by *The Outsider*'s reception, Macdonald made a preliminary description of an ailment which writers like Enright (on Durrell's *Alexandria Quartet*), Conquest (on Ezra Pound's 'learning' and 'technique') and pre-eminently Medawar (on Koestler and the Teilhard de Chardin phenomenon) were to worry about further: the absorptive credulity of a semi-intelligentsia educated 'far beyond their capacity to undertake analytical thought'. (That's Medawar, but Macdonald arrived at a formulation substantially similar: 'a sizable reading public whose cultural aspirations exceed its knowledge and sensibility.')

The problem posed by this semi-intelligentsia is by now acute.

Things aren't as bad in this country as they are in America, but they are bad enough. It is doubtful whether the general decline in the capacity to think straight for two consecutive minutes is caused, or even exacerbated, by egalitarian education, as the *Black Paper* would have us believe. More probably the rise of the semi-intelligentsia was made possible by the long retreat of British formal philosophy away from 'plain language': as philosophers like Quinton remind us, philosophy here and now has nothing much to do with wisdom. Wisdom, however, is something that the intelligentsia, from passive appreciators all the way up through the clerisy to the creators, likes to have handy. Unfortunately there has been no Great Man to agree with or fight. It has been a century of light heavies. Even when Moore typified the Bloomsbury-Oxbridge axis, his thought was by no means common currency among the whole intelligentsia. After Wittgenstein, plain language went the way of personal relationships. By the late thirties the field was left to the literary critics, the world-savers/commonsensers, and the shady purveyors of philosophy-fiction. An awkward situation then arose: the literary critics (type Leavis), who had most of the real ideas, disclaimed pretensions to philosophical rigour at the same time that the world-saving (type Russell) plain-language philosophers, who had most of the unreal ones, disclaimed pretensions to literary scrupulosity. As the first became incoherent the second became unreadable. The common-sensers (type Joad) dissipated themselves by expanding into the resulting vacuum. After the Nazis had presented him with certain facts, the post-war Briton with highly developed literary tastes – but with few clues on how the European philosophies of the previous century had circled back into history as virulent myths – could scarcely continue to slake his sublime thirst for coherent argument on the philosopher-fictionists (type Gurdjieff), who were probably head cases, or even on the French imports (type Camus-Sartre), who were working in a hard Left/soft Left dialectic of uncomfortably desperate practicality, all very foreign. Obviously anyone indigenous who could turn on the big sound, the biggest sound of all, the profound sound of *seriousness* (preferably not social), would hold the room. In walked Colin Wilson.

One adopts the language of whizz-bang farce because the situation was farcical and remains so. Before Wilson the profundity habit could be satisfied only on the sly: Ouspensky wrapped in a pullover and shoved in the sideboard like a half of spirits. After Wilson the habit could be brought out in the open: the right to a *weltanschauung* was extended to all, never to be withdrawn. All it had taken was the emergence of a writer with no literary sensibility whatsoever (those who knew he couldn't write called him a 'genius') for English to be discovered as rivalling French in its adaptability to monkey-talk. And you couldn't explain the sales of *The Outsider* merely in terms of a younger generation being handed an easy way to feel special: it was a large proportion of the educated in all generations who had bought the book. The detritus of all the modern educated generations had revealed itself as having formed a semi-intelligentsia, in the same way that the detritus of all social classes forms the mob. A new semi-intellectual mass with its own mass semi-intellectual tastes: not just a frighteningly augmented transatlantic recrudescence of Mencken's booboisie, but something on a higher mental plane, where the vendor–consumer relationship deals in spiritual instead of material goods. They were with us and their voices grew louder in the land: *les enfants de parodie*, the Sontag and bobtail of the intellect. The New Lost.

The young Colin Wilson was the prototype of the New Lost intellectual: not in what he had to say, but in not realizing that he had nothing to say. In mistaking excitement and stimulus for thought, in looking for connections without first establishing divisions, in getting out of Shaw and T. E. Lawrence what is common to both (or out of Sartre and Gurdjieff what is common to both) and imagining that what he had got out was anything more than a sort of abstract urgency, he translated names and local habitations back to airy nothing. As *Voyage to a Beginning* unintentionally reveals, while being omnivorous in his studies he had no conception of the objective nature of truth. He was a man of destiny, he suffered cruelly, he was persecuted by a succession of po-faced landladies, he slept in the open air, he suffered rebuffs, but he won through. (It must be admitted he showed an admirable fortitude during his early struggles.) It still hasn't occurred to him that the same identification of heroic personal odyssey and triumph of the intellectual Will applies to the author of *Mein Kampf*. The mass of men are weak and stupid, Wilson confides – in the same shrilly superior tones as Ayn Rand (another atavistic embodiment of the Will's triumph) and in the same duff prose. One asserts oneself or one goes to the wall: 'recognition' is a recognition of the vision powering one's unshakable determination. There is no conception of the idea being separate from the man. There is no plane on which a Wilson idea can be tested without Wilson himself taking it as a personal attack, and he is right: every thought in his head is a self-expression and nothing more. It follows that all those critics who have shredded his books are suspect, thought to be in league.

But when the fashion turned against Wilson it turned in the terms which he had helped establish – that is, without attention to issues. He had been in and he had gone out and in neither case was it anything much to do with true or false. The word had filtered around (it does not nowadays filter down) and his reputation ebbed away to the peripheral bed-sits of the barely employable not-quite-bright, where it lined itself up along brick-and-pine bookshelves in a row of paperbacks from progressively less prestigious publishers. It has all been hellishly unfair, and should never have happened – not with this dreadful inevitability anyway. The David Frosts deserve their success but something less revolting should happen to young writers, whose first books, once out, can hardly be lured back in. Nobody has ever examined the culpability of Victor Gollancz in this sort of boon-doggle: he was the first 'great' modern vendor of written spiritual goods and for every one of his famous finds it seems to me there were at least two helpless beginners he catapulted into oblivion by putting their first efforts irretrievably on public view.

On the evidence of *Voyage to a Beginning* Colin Wilson still has little idea of what has been happening to him. He has been looking for ways forward from the position taken in *The Outsider* but plainly the task has not been easy: after such knowledge, what forgiveness? He has written all kinds of things while somehow clinging to the notion that they are the one kind of thing, subsumed by genius. His style is prairie-flat, self-absorbed without at any time being self-aware. He is impervious to analysis in the same way that a jellyfish is bullet-proof, and scorns criticism in the same way that lemmings are not afraid of heights. He inaugurated an era.

(1969)

# 34

## The Fascist Intellectuals

As a study of fascism and the intellectuals, Alastair Hamilton's *The Appeal of Fascism* is far better than one had any right to expect from a man who was minus two years old when the last war started, and I commiserate with the author that the praise for his effort has so far not been markedly intelligent. There seems to be a general impression that a book of this type has been done before. It has not been done before. The four separate studies – of the relevant intellectuals in Italy, Germany, France and England – are done with tactful inwardness, sound judgment of character and dedicated scholarship. Alastair Hamilton has done well to avoid the apocalyptic tone: the cast of characters are men we can recognize as human, all too human, and the way things happen to them is a way we can recognize as not only historically inevitable, but likely at the time. Above all, Mr. Hamilton's sense of history's flow is an intelligent sense: he uses hindsight to illuminate events without pretending that such illumination was ever, to anyone, available then. All this I find admirable and would like to say straight away that *The Appeal of Fascism* is a book of considerable importance to the study of modern cultural history.

The situation in Italy is treated first. This section is the best researched, the best written, the best organised and for several reasons the most interesting intrinsically. Given the chaos in Italy from the end of the First World War up to 1922, and given Mussolini's will to power and his genuine ability (for short-term ends, at any rate) to wield it, there is no mystery about Fascism getting itself established. Nor is there much mystery about it keeping itself established. As Mr. Hamilton summarizes with deceptive plainness: 'Fascism survived partly because of the Duce's accomplishments on a national level, and partly because, after the dissolution of the opposition, there was simply nothing else.' Ideologically, Fascism ranged from Gentile's idealistic, rather touching and finally tragic humanism, through the shrill aggressiveness of D'Annunzio, Marinetti and Malaparte, down to Pirandello's naive longing and gratitude for a theatrically satisfying leadership. From some of the minor intellectuals there were outbreaks of thuggishness along the way, but the civilizing influences were strong enough to keep Nazi-style violence out of the picture until after Italy's surrender and Mussolini's sad rebirth as a German puppet. Practically, Mussolini kept relatively clean, from the disbandment of the Squadristi right up until his diplomatically motivated espousal of anti-semitism in 1936, which led to the passing of laws in 1938 but to no action until after the Italian surrender, when the appropriate persecutions and deportations became the hobby of the embattled Germans, irrational to the last.

If Mussolini had disallowed the assassination of Matteotti in the first place, and refrained from trying to please Hitler with race legislation in the last, there would have been comparatively little for the major intellectuals to recoil from, early or late. Most of them, anti-Fascist as well as pro, saw nothing damnable about the invasion of Abyssinia. Few of them looked back to the immediate post-war parliamentarianism with any nostalgia. The fact that Mussolini used violence to come to power ceased to be an issue once power was attained. Use your own extremists to knock out your opponents, then purge your own extremists: the technique is familiar now – it looked like responsibility then. It was the colossal stature of Croce which gave the non-Marxist opposition to Fascism a rationale. Mr. Hamilton is careful to point out that even Croce was willing to accept Mussolini in the early stages, rather than go back to the post-war chaos. It's the gravest failing of this section that Mr. Hamilton does not sufficiently explore Croce's intellectual reasons for going into opposition. The reasons were complex and the reader should not be left to guess.

Intellectuals were objects of intrigue within the Fascist movement; far more than manipulating events, they were themselves manipulated; with the exception of Gentile, Fascism's one genuinely tragic figure among the geriarchs, those involved in the regime's destiny were men whose character failings were compensated for by a whiff of power. Mussolini knew just how to flatter them. He had Pound's early *Cantos* on his desk when Pound came to visit: Mr. Hamilton forgets to remind us that this sublime moment, the confirmation of Pound's insight into the profoundly artistic nature of the Duce, was solemnly recorded later on in the *Cantos* themselves. It is inconceivable that Mussolini had actually ever read a line. Similarly he knew exactly what to give Pirandello – a medal. After the race laws nearly all the first-class men became disaffected. When the Republic of Salò started torturing people, even Soffici (ex-Futurist, long-term 'realist', permanent ingénu) realized that liberty counted. Finally Mussolini got his, in a scene of butchery which Pound (who had never been good at imagining the mass suffering taking place beyond the screen of his own rhetoric, but who could comprehend the fate of one man who had flattered him) immortalized in the opening lines of *The Pisan Cantos*. Gentile, whose idealism had been compromised all the way to fantasy, and who was too civilized to be unaware of the uses his distinction had been put to, was fortunately bumped off by the Communists.

The German section of the book is not as good as the Italian, perhaps because it is, intellectually, a necessarily less interesting scene. Mr. Hamilton traces Mann's early backing of German 'culture' against foreign 'civilization', of the 'artist' against the 'intellectual', but sensibly does not try to include Mann, or any other first-rate figure, in an intellectual movement ancestral to Nazism. He follows Arendt in placing the intellectual (the semi-intellectual) antecedents of National Socialism among the *völkisch* nationalists and the race scientists – the detritus of politics and the intellect. He follows Taylor (mainly his neglected *Course of German History*) in tracing Hitler's political base to the conflicts of Little v. Greater Germany: indeed, it is sometimes easier here to put Hamilton's book down and pick up Taylor's. Heidegger was no fool: he was just a fool about politics. Croce wrote to Vossler pointing out that Heidegger was Germany's Gentile, an acute remark. Benn, sickened like Céline by his early experiences as a doctor, just wanted to be a hero, like D'Annunzio and Marinetti: by 1933 he was out of favour and the dud Blunck was in. The party's hack minds – Krieck and Bäumler, Johst, Blunck and Binding – achieved a stature they could never have won ordinarily. Bronnen was influenced by Goebbels in the same way in which he was influenced earlier by Brecht: he was simply weak, and had to spend most of the thirties trying to prove that he was not a Jew because his father had not sired him, which implied that his father *was* a Jew, and put *him* on the hook. It was a farce. The faction fights were terrific, with Rosenberg trying to frame everybody Goebbels favoured. The regime obviously stank from an early date and no man of intelligence could be in two minds about it – only about what to do about it, which is a different thing.

The section on France is much more rewarding, the issues being so much less clear-cut. The material on the intellectuals is matched with difficulty to the shape of history – one is continually losing track of a character only to pick him up again at a later date – but it is hard to see how it could be any neater, considering the complexity of what went on. Maurras is traced back all the way to the Dreyfus case and Mr. Hamilton does not forget to point out how much admired Action Française was by Proust, Rodin, Gide and Apollinaire. The emphasis on will-power attracted the bright young men later on: Bernanos, Montherlant, Drieu La Rochelle and (surprise?) Malraux. The shadings and gradations in anti-semitism were marvellous, the character weaknesses almost engaging. Brasillach blamed the sympathy attracted by Jewish refugees for increasing the risk of war! There were lots of theories, but it took the Nazis to import the realities: torture sessions in Fresnes and box-cars rolling east. A tough way to bring down a fever.

The section on England (Eliot, Yeats, Campbell, Lewis, etc.) is well done but familiar. Except for Mosley, fascism never happened, only reactions to it, and most of those involved eventually settled down to an uneasy peace with the democracy they despised. If they got the chance, that is what nearly everyone involved did, in all four countries. The whole experience taught them about the limits of ideal artistic concepts of society and the danger of the irrational. Those it didn't teach can still teach us, by their fate. I could wish the book to be better proof-read and in places better written, but I could not wish it to be a more distinguished product of my generation or more relevant to the generation now coming up. This was the story, it still is the story, it will always be the story: clever men without imaginations, gambling with the liberties of the defenceless for a dream.

(1971)

## PART SIX

# From the Largest Island

# 35

## Tell England: or, In the Penal Colony
## (A Broadcast)

A funny thing happened to me on my way to the front door in a dressing-gown and a two-day stubble a couple of weeks ago. I got my very first piece of hate-mail telling me to go home. It came as a bit of a shock after spending ten years in this country: ten years is a hefty stretch of time and you've sort of decided by then that you *are* home. But this lady didn't think so. She said that there were altogether too many fast-talking Aussies clogging up the media and that I should do the decent thing, if I was capable of it, and immediately reduce their number by one. It turned out that I had failed her. She had gleaned from my appearances in the media that I was tough on all this noisy modernism and liked things classical and cool – a critical position she approved of. Why then, was I going on *Late Night Line-Up* and slyly suggesting that Adrian Mitchell's new musical might be a couple of degrees better than intolerable?

My reputation as a critic, she said, I could from now on consider to be in shreds, she said. Well, I could live with that. And then – go home, she said. I kicked aside some milk-bottles, sat down on the stairs, and processed this data through the scruffy nylon cogs of my early-morning skull. It was a bleak moment. Outside in the dawn – well, outside in the 11.30 a.m. to be precise – droves of tourist coaches were arriving in Cambridge, full of people who were taking a quick look around England before going back to where they belonged. Why hadn't I done that? If I'd done that, about nine and three-quarter years ago, I wouldn't have now been squatting there on the lino-covered stairs and holding in my hand the refeened, civilized, ever-so-upper-class version of 'Go home nigger'. I tottered to the front door and opened it. There was no cross burning on the lawn. I checked the letter-box in which the missive had arrived. Not a trace of human ordure. Had my wife received any threatening phone-calls? When would they promulgate the directive that all Australians would have to wear a cut-out kangaroo on their arm? Back upstairs, I crashed into my special writer's chair – it's got a strobe-light to keep me awake and a time-lock seat-belt that won't let me out at intervals of less than 1,000 words – and opened the newspaper.

Richard Neville pulls fifteen months in stir on obscenity rap: Judge speaks of deportation for Australian. Judge speaks of what for who? Deportation, boy. We're going to send you back to Botany Bay to start all over again. You can do the whole thing *da capo*, or as we say in the legal trade, you can take it from the top. Twelve thousand miles in irons and you step off the boat into a swamp. Off with the irons and on with the chains. Tame forest, plough land, earn freedom, start business, get rich – working flat out, you might just about get back to England again in a couple of hundred years. A condemned man, I ate a hearty breakfast: one glass of stomach powder, shaken violently without even trying. Outside, somewhere down there in London, Richard Neville was getting his hair cut off. Not much of mine left to do that to me, but who's to say they wouldn't think of something else? Make reflex clutch at crotch. Look into shaving mirror: not a pretty sight. Passport number 34557775 James, C. V. L.; political sub-category, Australian; class of citizenship, minus 13: caught red-handed tolerating Adrian Mitchell in the presence of Sheridan Morley and other pure-blood Brits. It was own-up time: time to keep that long-delayed appointment with my identity crisis.

Well, not really. Australians in my line of work don't often ask themselves what they're doing here because the answer's too obvious: as Captain Ahab shouted while lying strapped down by harpoon lines on the heaving flank of the submerging Moby Dick, 'I'm here because this is where the work is'. Unless he's a talent of truly enormous robustness, a writer is bound to head for the language centre – and for the English-speaking world the language centre is still England. The penalty for staying home is to accept provincial standards, and if you are tough-minded and refuse to listen to those, you have only your own standards to fall back on.

You'd have to be more than a pretty good writer to do that and still produce good work. As Peter Porter said in the *Times Literary Supplement* recently, there's nothing more debilitating than reading bad works of art produced by people whose general views of life you agree with. So you come away to where the stakes are high. Only the poor artists and a tiny few of the very, very good ones stay behind, finding their level because they *know* their level. None of this applies to the Americans, of course – although until recently it still applied to some of the *major* Americans, particularly those who felt the lack of historical depth in their national background and wanted to plug themselves back into European continuity.

European continuity was on my mind, too, when I arrived, but the nice thing about European continuity is that once you've got into it you can stop thinking about it. I went through *phases* of thinking about it, none very satisfactory. Just think, I thought one day while drinking my first pint of British bathwater in a famous hostelry in St. Martin's Lane, I am standing in Dylan Thomas's favourite pub. I got that mood in perspective when I found out there were fourteen other of Dylan's favourites between there and Great Portland Street. I spent four years being broke in London and I did a lot of walking, not all of it enforced. Greenwich, the Wren churches, all the nooks and crannies: with a copy of *The Waste Land* in my hand I traced out the whole geography of the poem in the streets around the Bank of England. I checked up whether St. Mary Woolnoth really does keep the hours with a dead sound on the final stroke of nine. The crowds flowed over London Bridge, so many. I made a promise to myself that I would learn the whole city but gradually I ceased to keep it. People like Sir John Betjeman do it so much better. Gradually I just took it for granted. And when I went up to Cambridge to do a second degree and part of a third, the initial passion for knowing all about that beautiful city soon waned. I never stopped looking but I stopped *learning* – why panic, why try? I was home, and home is the place you jog along in. By the second of my winters in London – that terrible winter of 1962 – I already knew that I would never leave England. Perhaps I'm kinky for snow.

When old Australian friends on a visit finally assimilate my assurances that I'm never going back to Australia to live, they invariably ask why I don't go home on a visit. Well, until a year ago I never had the cash for even a down-payment on the plane ticket: for some reason the aircraft on the Australia run are built out of platinum and use Arpège for fuel, and the passenger is asked to defray the cost of keeping these Byzantine beauty-parlours in the air. I could have gone by ship, of course, but only with my legs in irons and a deportation tag around my neck: I remember the trip over too well. I spent five weeks locked with a couple of rugby players in a phone-booth-sized salonette on deck Z of a Greek ship whose crew had to be replaced in Brisbane because a passenger shot an albatross. The propeller shaft was in the cabin with us and if one of us stood up to get dressed the other two had to go back to bed. On deck we all threw beer-cans into the empty swimming-pool or crowded to the rail to watch the ship being overtaken by a turtle. It was agony. But I suppose I could just about afford a round-trip by plane now: one of those semi-scheduled flights in a clapped-out old unpressurized C54 flown by a Polish Battle of Britain ace with an eye-patch – one of those wing-and-a-prayer efforts that have no trouble getting permission to take off but have to negotiate for hours before getting permission to land. So why not make the trip? you'll be asking, especially if you're the little lady who wrote that letter.

It's hard to say. When I try to let Australia flash into my mind – not an easy trick, but worth trying – I first of all get the picture of all-round *toxicity*: an overall hostility on the part of Mother Nature. There are a lot of things out there that bite you. I often wonder why Australia House doesn't keep a special glossy pamphlet about them, for handing to prospective immigrants whom they're eager to discourage, like those dark people they considerately turn down on the grounds that there's no point going out there if you're not in a position to benefit from the ultra-violet.

I can think of three extremely interesting kinds of spider. There's the trap-door spider, which lifts up a tiny coal-hole door with one mandible before ambling out to give you the kind of injection that cures you of everything. There's the funnel-web, whose nest is a kind of launching tunnel in the ground, like a missile silo, from which it emerges in a savage parabola and descends on its hapless prey – sometimes a capstan-lather operator from Wigan with a 'Come to Sunny Australia' brochure in his hand. Finally there is the red-back, bearing on its tiny dorsal area the crimson stripe of the Richtofen Circus: its favourite trick is to hide under the lavatory seat, from which vantage-point it delivers a bite that leaves you with the huge problem of where to put the tourniquet and only five minutes to think about it.

Above and beyond the spiders, so to speak, are the snakes. These come in several categories, in ascending order of consequence to health. First of all there are the harmless, i.e. dead. Next there are the lethal. Above these there are the totally devastating and right at the top there are the absolutely ridiculous, of which the pace-setter is called the taipan. The taipan can kill you, and your horse if you are riding one, in something under ten seconds. It is one of the few snakes in the world which will actually attack a man unprovoked. Crazed gangs of taipans have been known to steal cars and cruise up and down the Pacific Highway, looking for trouble.

And then there are the sharks: nature's Nazis, the irrational bent stormtroopers of the deep. Like most inhabitants of Sydney I spent three-quarters of my time out of my depth in the Pacific Ocean and I can honestly say that the little darlings were never out of my mind for a moment. The greatest loneliness I have ever known was hearing the shark bell ring when I was out body-surfing at the third line of breakers. The bell went off and everybody sprinted like mad to catch the next wave. I was the only one who missed it, I think: it doesn't matter if there were others, because when you do miss that wave, you're the only one. So there you are treading water – very quietly and yet very rapidly, so as to get as far out of the water as possible – and waiting for the secret police to knock. And somewhere down there it is, or usually, they are: jet-propelled bags of razor-blades with black crosses on their sides and the personalities of homicidal maniacs. There are sharks in Sydney Harbour that actually come out of the water and *get* people – nobody shakes Rocky's mob.

None of this is exaggerated, or anyway not much – taipans don't steal cars, they rent them – but of course it's not the whole picture. There's the sun and the wealth and all the other things the pamphlets tell you, and it really is a wonderful country to be young in. The trouble, as far as I'm concerned, is that it's also a wonderful country to *stay* young in. Intellectually, Australians tend to mature late, if at all: for example, the country as a whole still hasn't woken up to the fact that the arts are not commodities. This slowness to mature goes on affecting you long after you've come away: when I went up to Cambridge I was about seven years older than most of the freshmen but felt about two years younger, and it's only now that I feel I have caught up with the Englishmen of my generation. I've learned to relax a bit, and I don't just mean in the sense that I no longer feel required to roll up a newspaper and hold it poised while I lift up the lavatory seat to check for lurking spiders: I just lift up the seat and give it a casual glance. Nor is it a matter of having learned which fork to use – a problem I solve by eating everything with a bowie-knife. No, I mean that ten years of England have at last softened the harsh illusion Australia offers you that the whole world is there to be begun again: that fatal fancy that the world can be made over in your own image.

Australia seems set on repeating in little the American dream of infinite possibilities – which means in effect that it is condemning itself to unlimited banalities. It is not a good place to be interested in ideas for their own sake: people will always be asking you what *use* they are. For example, there is an illusion that the whole population knows what freedom is and nobody needs to write it down or even work it out – and yet there are freedoms of speech and freedoms of behaviour which are repressed in Australia in a way which suggests that not only the repressive agencies, but the ordinary people, have simply no idea of what freedom is. The assumption that everyone is heading in the one direction – onwards – leads to the rule of everyone over anyone. What England has given me is the realization of a greater complexity in the body politic, of a lot of separate liberties managing to accommodate to one another. Things can happen to make dents in this realization – the *Oz* verdict was just one of them – but by and large England is a very advanced country politically, far more advanced than an advanced country like Australia even fancies itself to be. Here you can turn your hand to almost anything legal and still feel part of the country's daily life. For any kind of artist this is a very desirable condition to be in: it keeps the ego trimmed to size and makes sure that not too much energy is wasted on setting the stage for posthumous fame. Australia continues to drive away most of its best artists because it does not want them for their art, it wants them for their lustre – it wants to keep the prestige and throw away the thing itself. Here it is easier to just get on with your work. Which, having said my piece, is what I now propose to do. I'm not going home, because I *am* home, in the country I was born to live in and doing the work that such powers as I have fit me to do. A delectable situation, although that letter-writing lady would probably not agree. Incidentally, dear, the green ink was the final touch.

(1971)

# 36

## A Poor Report on Violence

The BBC's report *Violence on Television* takes me back to Australia at about the time of the Korean War, when I was wearing short trousers – a certain sign of a non-combatant – and regularly attending the Saturday matinées at the Rockdale Odeon, a picture palace situated only a few miles from where Captain Cook landed but for whose décor he was plainly not responsible. For five shillings of the old-style money you could get a trolley bus there and back, a ticket to the upper deck (which looked like the *Titanic* going down – there were about a million kids climbing all over each other), two Hoadley's Violet Crumble Bars (fibreglass dipped in brake fluid), one Polly Waffle (gutta-percha dipped in brake fluid and sprinkled with iron filings), one packet of Fantails and a tutti-frutti in a tub. At the trifling cost of forgoing the trolley-bus rides and legging it for an hour each way you could top off this feast with a packet of Smith's crisps – crunched up small to last longer – and a box of Jaffas, red sugar-coated chocolate spheres of the size and tensile resilience of ball-bearings that would bounce on a pile carpet and when properly launched through the dark would ricochet off a juvenile cranium with the noise of a Mills bomb's returning base-plug. It took three or four days of steady comic-swapping to build up a bank of five bob, but it was worth the effort to be properly equipped for the orgy.

You got in there with all this food stashed all over you, the lights went down and it was on: one feature, four episodes from four different serials and sixteen cartoons. The features were of the oriental kind in which Mari Blanchard wore chiffon and George Macready played the Grand Vizier – nobody except the little kids paid them any heed and the Jaffas went past your head in lethal short bursts of Bren-fire. The serials were for laughs and nobody was fooled: we enjoyed the exigencies of their tiny budgets without ever realizing that Susan Sontag would one day show up and spoil it all. But in a whole afternoon of full mouths and worthless footage there was one thing that was adorable on its own terms – the *Tom and Jerry* cartoons. They stood out from the ruck a mile. They left the *Looney Tunes* and *Merry Melodies* for dead, and when that MGM logo went up on the screen there was a roar from the auditorium that stripped the calsomine off the plaster caryatids holding up the roof.

These were the great days of *Tom and Jerry*: the early crudities were far in the past, the later carelessness was far in the future, Quimby was firmly in charge of production and Hanna and Barbera were personally supervising the most dynamic animation the art form was ever to achieve: they controlled not just the extremes but the in-betweens, the clean-ups and even the inking in every sequence. The results were sensational. Tom took off after Jerry with a noise like an F100 cutting in its after-burner and he really *flew*: there was none of that awful slow lope with the speed faked by blurring the background. When Jerry opened the refrigerator door in Tom's face he hit it with an impact that looked as solid as it sounded. In the famous tennis match everything was funny because nothing was skimped. When Jerry hit the steel tennis ball it distorted his racket and headed down the court with a deeply satisfying 'boing', and when Tom held up his racket in front of a hugely confident smile the ball went through both racket and smile like an 88 mm shell, Tom cracking all over like a Ming dynasty glaze and falling to bits with tinkling perfection.

It was violence (waffles were coming in world-wide at that time and Jerry made one out of Tom's tail) but it wasn't *sheer* violence: other cartoons were just as violent, but they weren't as funny. Still, Tom and Jerry were violent all right, and I doted on them every week, as did all the other kids in my gang. But here's the rub. With our trolley-bus fare blued on sweets, we trekked home for miles along Rocky Point Road, our heat-resistant bare feet crushing the spongy bubbles in the asphalt. And at least once and often twice in every one of those weary voyages we were chased and usually duffed up by a pack of under-privileged ragamuffins who couldn't afford to go to the pictures and who were fifty times as violent as we were. These kids were brilliant autodidacts, whereas I, who studied the stuff formally every Saturday, failed miserably. I'd be bending over copping a Chinese burn and feebly wondering why people were like that. Twenty years later I'm still wondering.

The report falls into two parts: 'An analysis of the amount and nature of the portrayals of violence in British television programmes, November 1970 to May 1971' (research conducted by Irene S. Shaw) and 'Studies of the functions served for viewers by selected programmes containing violent sequences' (research conducted by David S. Newell). The two research workers have each grown an American-style middle initial but thankfully still fall short of the commensurate sociological self-confidence, and in the text it is engagingly admitted that not much has been discovered. B. P. Emmett, Head of BBC Audience Research, endorses their modesty in his foreword: talking about Part Two, he appears to be bending over backwards to avoid giving the impression that his team has got anywhere. 'Though the two projects are in a sense complementary, it must be emphasized that no direct and easy relationship was expected between the amount of violence portrayed in a programme and the "effects" on viewers of exposure to the programmes – certainly not in the sense of finding people "imitating" what they had seen. Nor was there any real expectation of finding a "cathartic" effect – that is, an apparent purging of aggressive feelings through identification with the violent behaviour portrayed. The long-term effects, if any, of viewing programmes containing violent action also lay outside the scope of these studies.'

If, after this, the lay reader asks what Part Two *did* hope to find, let him turn to the relevant tables and conclusions, where he will discover that there is not much connection between the number of violent incidents in a programme and the viewers' tendency to perceive it as violent. The researchers decided – correctly, if I understand the tables – that no connections could be made. If there is no connection, nothing can be made of it. But I think more could have been made of the lack of it. The viewers in Part Two were asked to judge the programmes according to all kinds of functions: Stupid/Intelligent, Happy/Sad Ending, etc. The monitors in Part One were asked to look at the programmes and count and classify the violent incidents. The inconclusive muddle of Part Two is quite harmless and might even do some good, since it can be drawn upon to stave off the attentions of careerist busybodies. But there is an empiricist complacency about Part One that looms dishearteningly behind its author's (i.e. Irene S. Shaw's) diffidence of intention. Certainly Mr. Emmett roundly overstates her case in his foreword when he suggests that her study 'provides *facts* (or as many as could be digested) about the violent content of the programmes transmitted and would thus seem to be a pre-requisite in the exploration of the hypotheses about moral develop-ment, about "desensitising" and about the symbolic messages transmitted'. I'm afraid that facts are exactly what Part One of the report does not provide, for all its wealth of tabulated data – not, at any rate, the kind of facts with which Mr. Emmett might con-ceivably arm himself in order to explore hypotheses about moral development and desensitizing. The monitors were asked to separate two things – the context and the incident *tout pur* – and then, when they had totted up the incidents, to look at the count beside the context. It turned out that the overwhelming proportion of violent incidents were justified in context. But twenty shows turned out to be more violent than the monitors felt was justified, and three of these were *Dastardly and Muttley*, *The Road Runner Show* and *Perils of Penelope Pitstop*!

Now the whole point of these feeble products of the Hollywood animation mills is to bash their characters about: they have violent incidents every ten seconds. But does anyone suppose that the monitors, while applying to these uninspired extravaganzas their sets of empirical criteria, were moved to disgust or to any emotion at all except boredom? Of course not. They were responding on everybody's behalf except their own – as people tend to do when they are asked to give objective judgments. Unless you have your pencil poised over your classified scale of violent incidents, these three cartoons seem like nothing except a rigmarole of bad drawings and silly voices. Science has lent them an interest they don't possess.

It seems to me that the methods espoused in Part One of this report must yield trivial results all along the line. The monitors have achieved unanimity in their coding only because the codes are entirely schematic and all questions of aesthetics have been left out, as though they cropped up at the periphery. The whole thing is organized like the Hays Code, in which if a man and a woman lay down on a bed the man had to keep one foot on the floor or it was intercourse. Context and incident are an *a priori* synthesis, not to be picked apart in so confident a way. All that has been discovered is the comparative amount of violence on television from channel to channel and from time to time: the amount of violence, that is, when violence is what you're looking for. But as Part Two demonstrates, this amount tends to retreat or even disappear when you are looking at the programme whole. The fallacy of the report lies in the supposition that Part One is hard facts while Part Two is tentative and sketchy. The reverse is nearer the truth, and Mr. Emmett should press for an expanded version of Part Two, so as to deduce a workable set of perceived violent situations which may replace the largely unworkable set concocted for Part One. None of this means that Part One is entirely useless as it stands: it's just that what use it has is so open to abuse. It's an encouragement to piecemeal thinking of the type gone in for by switchboard-jammers. For example, it's quite possible to think of a programme whose hero inflicts pain on his opponents without warning and is finally tortured and killed by the bad guys, thereby infringing several of the categories set up in Part One. The first scene is Christ cleansing the Temple, the last his crucifixion.

The representation of violence, like the representation of anything else, is not susceptible to materialist analysis: it's the spirit of the thing that matters, and the spirit of the thing can be estimated only by a critical sensibility. For example, the most violent thing I've seen on television in the last year has been Reginald Maudling's serenity. It seems to me that television is on the whole too alienated, too uninvolving a medium to condition adult behaviour: there isn't much on the box that's powerful enough to suspend our uninvolvement, let alone our disbelief. Children's behaviour is another matter, although judging from my own memories I'd say it's what happens in real life that counts. When footage of actual atrocities crops up on the News, it's a nice question whether people's ability to accept it is not more disturbing than other people's tendency to be revolted by it. In the fictional and documentary programmes it's mainly a matter of taste and manners: I don't know whether or not *Big Breadwinner Hog* was taken off because people complained at its being so violent, but I'm certain that it should have been taken off earlier for being so lousy. Bad artists think art is made out of effects. Good artists know better. It's up to the Programme Controllers to pick their personnel. Problems of judgment can't be passed to computers, although it's sometimes tactically handy to pretend they can.

(1972)


# 37

## Supplementary Viewpoints


It would be incestuous if the contributors to this column ('Viewpoint', in the *TLS*) were continually to join issue with one another, yet I can't refrain from calling Anthony Burgess out into the yard over his remarks on literary journalism. His views on the parasitic ephemerality of the craft coincide so neatly with Cyril Connolly's famous exhortations in *The Condemned Playground* that I don't see why we shouldn't apply to them that especially irritated suspicion we reserve for opinions too smoothly rehashed. It was Connolly's notion that literary journalism was one of the Enemies of Promise which got in the road of writing masterpieces. Since Connolly's journalistic flights plainly *were* his masterpieces, this argument had little substance when applied to his own case: nobody in his right mind would claim to discover more of Connolly's individuality in *The Rock Pool* than so vigorously exists in 'Told in Gath' or 'Where Engels Fears to Tread' or (getting closer to now) 'Bond Strikes Camp'. With Burgess we are in another part of the forest, he being the man who actually gets written the novels that other men only dream of writing – or, rather, that other regiments only dream of writing. Yet if Burgess's literary journalism was meant to be such an inherently inferior activity he might have done us the grace of being worse at it, so that we could have saved the money it cost to buy *Urgent Copy* and the time it took to enjoy it. I have that excellent collection of pieces in front of me now, almost falling to bits from being read in the bath. I turn it over and find on the back a dramatically lit photograph of Anthony Burgess. But where is the Government Health Warning? Where does it say: 'Listen sucker, the stuff inside was tossed off for the bread when by rights I should have been assembling another twenty-seven novels *e il modo ancor m'offende*'?

Creative people should be slow to put sharp weapons in the hands of their opponents; and their opponents – in the short term if not the long – are in the academy, not the metropolis. Taking the brunt of new creative work is one of the things literary journalism is all about. It can do this well or badly, but at least it is committed to getting it done, whereas the academy is committed to not doing it – not yet. The academy has other tasks. Unfortunately the academy's other tasks for a long time included the task of branding the London literary journalists as a subterranean mafia bent on draining the living culture of its precious bodily fluids. Ludicrous as this accusation was, it was levelled long enough and hard enough for some of it to rub off, and the opinion is by now widely disseminated that literary journalism is donkey-work and easily done.

To which the answer is: it is easy to do badly and hard to do well; and that even at its worst it is not so dispensable as the average of academic writing; and that at its best it is the full complement to the academy's best, the accuser of the academy's average, and the necessary scourge of the academy's worst. In the business of criticism the academy and the metropolis have a certain relationship to one another, and the line of this relationship is the backbone of a literary culture. On the one hand there are dons, and on the other hand literary journalists, who fail to see the necessity for this relationship, but that doesn't make it any the less vital. Even when a scrap develops, it is really a struggle for the same blanket by two people in bed together, so a truce is the only workable outcome.

Certainly a literary journalist's flexibility of response can decline rapidly into flim-flam if he fails to back it up with diligent study. Reviewing interferes drastically with one's reading, and a typical early situation for a literary journalist is to find himself snowed under with review copies which do nothing to advance his education and sap the energy required for those books he should feel obliged to absorb. Unless he can read books of his choice at a ratio of about three to one with the books he is asked to review, he is unlikely to get out of the fix and establish himself as anything more exalted than a competent hack. This is the automatic levelling mechanism of literary journalism and has as much to do with sheer energy as with intelligence. People lacking an inordinate capacity for print are not advised to join in.

Of the reviewers with the ability to go on educating themselves while working there will be a few who write exceptionally well. These are the élite, and they are no more a conspiracy than are the Continental circus of Formula I drivers – they are simply self-selecting. What happens to them next has a lot to do with the esteem, or lack of it, in which literary journalism is held. Fewer first-class literary journalists would do such a numbingly thorough job of relaxing into lucrative but undemanding weekly posts if there were more outlets in which to publish solid work. As it is, in each paper we get permanent names doing temporary work, instead of vice versa. Anthony Burgess is just one of the people who have encouraged the notion that only the longer article is worthy of preservation – this despite the fact that his own book is full of exemplary 1,000-word pieces. Economics and the temper of the times allowing, the best literary journalists should collect and publish all their pieces every couple of years. The short literary essay is one of the key forms in modern critical writing – think of Conrad Aiken, let alone the towering example of Edmund Wilson. As it is, to assemble a representative collection of the best twentieth-century literary journalism you must haunt second-hand bookshops until your sinuses clog up with dust, and be prepared to bear away hulking great anthologies for the sake of a single article. A necessary lesson in the variety of culture, although often enough you will stumble on a real prize – *Urgent Copy*, for example, which I got for ten bob in a Charing Cross Road basement.

\*     \*     \*

S. J. Perelman, I see from a bookshop catalogue, is currently offloading his collection of presentation copies from Ogden Nash. I don't see much sense in paying extra money for an inscription, but in this case I would break the rule if I had the loot. Perelmania gets people that way. In a Sydney bookshop – E. Hugh Fugace's, as Perelman might have dubbed it – I once bought *Listen to the Mocking-bird*, *A Child's Garden of Curses*, and *Westward Ha!* in a single batch. Revelling in the stuff, I suddenly realized it was going to be all right: a mixed style was legitimate, so long as you could muster the discipline. What I did not realize at the time is that it takes about ten years of flat-out sweat to muster the discipline. It is apparently a paradox, but on experience plain truth, that a mixed style cannot be evolved solely from studying mixed stylists – there must be a pure style for the mixed one to break free from, or else the freedom will mean nothing more than delinquency. Nevertheless I find it wearying that so great a proportion of the writing in British magazines and papers is done in a pure style. A humorous writer like Alan Coren might derive (brilliantly) from Perelman, but for most of the cisatlantic scriveners it's as if the Americans had never existed. For myself, I find it hard to take a journalism uninfluenced by men like Mencken, Nathan, Perelman, Liebling,

Gibbs (in his reviews), and Stone – mixed stylists all. We shouldn't have to wait for a man's opinions before grasping his attitude to life: the style should tell us instantly. Literary journalism should be as compact as possible while still being clear, as resonant as possible while still being unambiguous. This is to endorse, not contradict, John Wain's demolition of R. P. Blackmur's stylistic convolutions, in which he correctly pointed out that the propensity of English prose to say only one thing at a time was not its limitation but the final refinement of its subtlety.

*     *     *

Few literary experiences come as a total surprise: we get too much advance warning. When I finally hit the mother lode and can buy enough time to learn Russian, I expect to be overwhelmed by Pushkin but not surprised by him – the calibre of his critical champions tells me too well the order of the experience I am in for. Lately, however, I have had a genuine surprise – discovering the imagination of Trollope.

I had suspected his novels to be dressed-up ledgers, as if he were a proto-Galsworthy. It has been exciting to be faced with the Signora Madeline Neroni in *Barchester Towers*, a grotesque who proves her creator to be a master talent. Despite every scene-dodging lapse and constructional caprice, the Trollope novels I have so far read strike me as capital works. Somebody once called E. E. Cummings's poems speeches from an unwritten play. I suppose Trollope's books are scenes from an unwritten novel – certainly the reader doesn't often feel that the point is made or the story rounded out. But they get you in. They are jumping with the unexpected. I am buying up the old, out-of-print Oxford editions wherever I find them, thankful that I knew next to nothing about the man before I started to read him. In fact I only got on to him because of the guilt engendered by doing a radio interview with Paul Johnson about James Pope-Hennessy's recent critical biography. Feeling compelled to understand something of what I'd just been listening to – an unsettling proportion of which had been said by me – I read a copy of *The Warden* that had been lying around the house for years. The long road to learning is often the surest.

\* \* \*

In a letter written from Calcutta in December 1935, and preserved in George Otto Trevelyan's *Life of Macaulay*, Macaulay casually gives an account of his reading over the previous year. Fasten your seat belts, folks:

During the last thirteen months I have read Aeschylus twice; Sophocles twice; Euripides once; Pindar twice; Callimachus; Apollonius Rhodius; Quintus Calaber; Theocritus twice; Herodotus; Thucydides; almost all Xenophon's works; almost all Plato; Aristotle's *Politics*, and a good deal of his *Organon*, besides dipping elsewhere in him: the whole of Plutarch's *Lives*; about half of Lucian; two or three books of Athenaeus; Plautus twice; Terence twice; Lucretius twice; Catullus; Tibullus; Propertius; Livy; Velleius Paterculus; Sallust; Caesar; and, lastly, Cicero. I have, indeed, still a little of Cicero left; but I shall finish him in a few days. I am now deep in Aristophanes and Lucian.

Now that our jaw has dropped wide open, Trevelyan makes sure it stays that way by inserting a stout stick. His gloss runs thus:

That the enormous list of classical works recorded in the foregoing letter was not only read through, but read with care, is proved by the pencil marks, single, double, and treble, which meander down the margin of such passages as excited the admiration of the student; and by the remarks, literary, historical, and grammatical, with which the critic has interspersed every volume, and sometimes every page. In the case of a favourite writer, Macaulay frequently corrects the errors of the press, and even the punctuation, as minutely as if he were preparing a book for another edition. He read Plautus, Terence, and Aristophanes four times through at Calcutta; and Euripides thrice.

It is at moments like this that I begin to regret (well, to go on regretting) those youthful years squandered on memorizing the contents of *Flight* magazine – every copy disfigured by pencil marks, single, double, and treble, meandering down the margin of such passages as excited my admiration.

\* \* \*

People with high standards of junk are an ever-present threat. Whenever I join with a literatus in conversation about the trash we read in childhood, it invariably turns out that one of us devoured a better class of trash than the other. Speaking as the other, I can only announce a simmering envy for anyone who beefed up his reading skills on Rider Haggard, Rice Burroughs, Baroness Orczy and E. Phillips Oppenheim. Missing out on the stuff then, I missed out on it forever: there's no point in trying to catch up, and no sanction for it, since with the age of innocence far in the past it's no longer possible to ignore the fact that time put in on *She* is time subtracted from the permanent task of battling through the block-long sentences of *La Prisonnière*. Not to mention Thomas Mann: that I got through *Tod in Venedig* in German (earning the *Leserkreuz* with crossed eyes and nut clusters) can't go on forever serving as an excuse for not tackling *The Magic Mountain* in English. Another time, as Auden put it, has other lives to live. All one can do is take a crumb of comfort from having once read *King Solomon's Mines* – if that was the one about the cave full of spiders and the big white hunter who longed for a Gatling with which to clear a plain thronged with tinted warriors in five minutes. Pretty sure I read the actual book there, and not the *Classics Illustrated* sepia-coloured comic. Not, let it be said in passing, that the *Classics Illustrateds* were to be disparaged. Their comic-book version of the Bible was a better way of assimilating the key quotes than pasting deckle-edged texts in a Sunday School album: Christ's speech-balloons were rimmed in pink, like clouds at sunset, and did a lot to focus the wandering juvenile attention on their gnomic contents.

At home we had few books, but we did have a cupboard full of out-of-date magazines – the Australian edition of *Reader's Digest*, wartime copies of *Picture Post* and *Life*, and any amount of *Redbook*, *Colliers* and the *Saturday Evening Post*. I read them continually, as a supplement to my *Modern Marvels* encyclopedia. At about age ten I moved on to Biggles books, staying faithful to W. E. Johns for the two years I spent in an opportunity class – an institution dedicated to providing upper-bracket IQs with bigger sand-trays. It was in this class that I received my first blurred hint of other realms. There was a day when selected members of the class were asked to stand up and give a summary of any book they might recently have read. I gave a masterly précis of *Biggles Flies East*, complete with an extended-arm version of the epic aerial duel between Bigglesworth and Von Stalhein. It was tedious to find this performance upstaged by some clown who had been dipping into the early chapters of Joyce's *Ulysses*. Having a schoolmaster for a father, my rival – it seems obvious now – was being brought up in an altogether superior intellectual climate. The hint did not take: I had no means of assessing its implications. While my rival was doubtless moving on to the letters of Madame de Sévigné and the *Duino Elegies*, I made the huge jump from Biggles to the Saint, quickly becoming a world expert on the writings of Leslie Charteris.

As my teens wore on (the days consumed in a technical school where I read five mathematical subjects with small result) I added further detectives and freelance adventurers to the roster. I read the complete works of Erle Stanley Gardner (including the A. A. Fair novels) in about a month, a feat of voracious celerity exactly equivalent to winning a pie-eating contest. I read all of Sapper – the wartime short stories being perhaps my first fleeting taste of realism – but none of Saki, who rested untouched in that other world, the world of estimable achievement on which by a sad miracle my hungry eyes never impinged. Ellery Queen, entire: but never Raymond Chandler. The Nero Wolfe books, but never Father Brown. Like a loser truffle-hound coming up with nothing but rocks, I must have had an infallible nose for rubbish.

In the two or three years before becoming eligible (just eligible) for university, I got on to war books, reading every best-selling author from Richard Pape (remember *Boldness Be My Friend?*) to Chester Wilmot, on every subject from the *Tirpitz* to midget submarines. It was during this obsession that I stumbled on the first clear cases of quality in writing, diffident in ambition though they now seem: Pierre Clostermann and Paul Brickhill (especially in *The Great Escape*, although *The Dam Busters* was a more engrossing subject) clearly stood out. And from Russell Braddon's *The Naked Island* I got a terrific jolt, probably the most formative literary experience of my life: the early chapters of that book (still the most

evocative writing about modern Sydney, with the possible exception of T. A. G. Hungerford's *The Ridge and the River* and the
certain exception of the early chapters of *Kangaroo*) dealt with
experience I could actually test, and seemed to endow a known
reality with an extra significance. After that, more by accident than
planning – I enrolled in the Arts faculty because I liked to draw –
university happened. Happened overnight. I met a young poet on
the first day, listened bemusedly to his chatter, and was reading
*Four Quartets* on the second day.

The best you can claim for such a grossly inadequate educational
background is that it supplies a hefty impetus once you finally get
the message. Being used to reading a tremendous amount of slag
was at least a quantitative preparation for reading a tremendous
amount of literature, the sense of shame providing an additional
spur. That, at any rate, is the way I rationalize it. But there are
some lacks that must remain clear losses. I found it reasonably easy
to learn modern languages later on, but Latin was harder and
Greek impossible. For anything in Latin beyond the simpler
declarative sentences of Cornelius Nepos I need a parallel text. A
memory stocked with hundred of lines of Virgil, Horace, Propertius
and Catullus scarcely compensates for a deficiency like that: the
lines were all learnt parrot-fashion, and one is always conscious of
a shaky grasp on the poetry of any language when one cannot parse
an average sentence of its prose. As for Greek, it will have to wait for
a five-year stretch when there is nothing else to do. Reading Rider
Haggard instead of finishing Proust is a minor crime compared with
beginning Trollope instead of learning to read Homer, but the latter
is the crime I now find myself committing. One big compensation
for being in such mental turmoil is, however, impossible to deny –
literature will always be an adventure for anyone who came to it
late. One has the eagerness of gratitude, if not the confidence of
universal scholarship.

*        *        *

I suppose I was forced towards the above reflections by the fact
that life of late has been lots of action, little meditation and no study

whatsoever. I am in the kind of fret that the medieval literati dreaded like heresy – alienated from the spirit of contemplation. The state of mind breeds strange jealousies. Who, one wonders sourly, is the best educated man of recent times? Putting Curtius into times past, it would probably be a toss-up between Edgar Wind and Gianfranco Contini. But no; it has to be Contini, with his habit of revealing whole new ranges of erudition at a few seconds' warning – such as the time when he walked into his first-year Romance philology class at Florence University and greeted an Arab freshman in Arabic. What stuns you about Contini is that his learning never outstrips his judgment. His essays (collected in that treasure-house of the mind, *Varianti e altra linguistica*) on the stylistic differences between Dante and Petrarch are instantly convincing to the lay reader of those two poets, yet the learning on which they are based is simply and strictly unapproachable. And just by sitting down to write about the intellectual experience conferred by reading a scholar like Contini, I find the sense of frustration ebbing away. Humbling in one way, minds of this order are liberating in another. By being beyond our aspirations, they help turn our aspirations towards encompassable aims. It is not a thing which should be said too easily, but now that I have got it said I will feel better about spending another day working in front of the cameras. Donne was right about the urge to study being the most ungovernable of the passions. But there is still the rent.

\*    \*    \*

The loneliness of the long-distance reader is an exquisite one: the rewards for tackling and conquering the more impossible literary massifs are necessarily largely personal, since one is unlikely to encounter anyone else ready to evince a proper sense of inadequacy at not having attempted the task himself. In the four years since I finished Motley's *Rise of the Dutch Republic* I have been unable to meet (a) anyone who has read it, with whom to compare notes; and (b) anyone appropriately dissatisfied at not having read it. To compound the dissatisfaction, the only bit of the book I have succeeded in remembering is the bit about the little children crying in the streets – a line known even to people who think Motley is a theatrical costumier. Useless to pretend that reading Motley was anything other than a struggle. I read *War and Peace* in two days and a night, drawn forward like a thrown rider with his foot caught in a stirrup. The *Dutch Republic* was read by fixing a daily task (five pages of the Everyman edition) and convincing myself it was a ration. I hope to find Mommsen more compelling, as Prescott arguably was and Gibbon definitely was. The Mommsen has been on my shelves for years, a long-standing rebuke in five fat volumes. The Duc de Saint-Simon, thank God, hasn't yet got into the house: very good for one's French, I understand, but very long. Boswell's *Johnson* was a breeze – Caxton's *Golden Legend or Lives of the Saints* so far hasn't been. For the past few Saturday mornings a set of Grote's *Greece* has been lined up on David's bookstall in the Cambridge market, whining for me to give it a home. I might hold out for another month at most. The month after that, I'll be half-way through it – guilty because it isn't Livy.

\*      \*      \*

Boswell said a man should keep notes on his reading: it's the impulse, I suspect, at the heart of his journals. I've been keeping a journal of my own for about five years. By now it runs to eleven volumes, and contains all the detail of my working life – everything from fair copies of lyrics to types of aircraft flown in – while revealing nothing at all of my private life. It's a working journal, and therefore not in competition with Pepys, Evelyn, Greville or Gide. In fact it's not in competition with anything, except, possibly, old railway timetables and obsolete telephone directories: some Pottle of the future might find it a useful source for computing walking-distances between editorial offices in the area Great Portland Street/Soho/ Fleet Street/Printing House Square, but beyond that it's nothing more than a manifest of compulsive activity. The main function my journal serves is to repair the kind of mental lacuna by which one finds all the past easy to remember except the recent. For this deficiency a daily record comes in handy. There was a stage when my journal doubled as an elaborate commonplace book, and indeed

I still note down sentences and short passages from a thousand different sources: but I took warning from Leopardi's notebooks and ceased copying out long passages from books I already owned anyway. Leopardi, I suppose, read more than anybody else who has ever lived, Saintsbury not excluded. But the transcription damagingly extended his daily stint at the desk, until one day he tried to straighten up and found that his beloved literature had turned him into a hunchback.

(1972)